TINY LIGHTS FOR TRAVELLERS

TINY LIGHTS FOR TRAVELLERS

UNIVERSITY of **ALBERTA** PRESS

NAOMI K. LEWIS

Published by

The University of Alberta Press
Ring House 2
Edmonton, Alberta, Canada   T6G 2E1
www.uap.ualberta.ca

LIBRARY AND ARCHIVES CANADA
CATALOGUING IN PUBLICATION

Title: Tiny lights for travellers / Naomi K. Lewis.
Names: Lewis, Naomi K., 1976– author.
Series: Wayfarer (Edmonton, Alta.)
Description: Series statement: Wayfarer series
Identifiers: Canadiana (print) 20190053437 |
    Canadiana (ebook) 20190056843 |
    ISBN 9781772124484 (softcover) |
    ISBN 9781772124750 (EPUB) |
    ISBN 9781772124767 (Kindle) |
    ISBN 9781772124774 (PDF)
Subjects: LCSH: Lewis, Naomi K., 1976–
    Travel—Europe. | LCSH: Grandchildren of
    Holocaust survivors—Canada—Biography.
    | LCSH: Jews, Canadian—Biography.
    | LCSH: Jews—Identity. | LCSH: Identity
    (Psychology) | LCSH: Intergenerational
    relations. | LCSH: Judaism and secularism.
    | LCSH: Europe—Description and travel.
Classification: LCC FC106.J5 L48 2019 |
    DDC 305.892/40971—dc23

First edition, first printing, 2019.
First printed and bound in Canada by
Houghton Boston Printers, Saskatoon,
Saskatchewan.
Editing by Kimmy Beach.
Proofreading by Maya Fowler Sutherland.
Map by Wendy Johnson.

University of Alberta Press is committed to
protecting our natural environment. As part
of our efforts, this book is printed on Enviro
Paper: it contains 100% post-consumer recycled
fibres and is acid- and chlorine-free.

University of Alberta Press gratefully
acknowledges the support received for its
publishing program from the Government of
Canada, the Canada Council for the Arts, and
the Government of Alberta through the Alberta
Media Fund.

Canadä   Canada Council   Conseil des Arts
          for the Arts   du Canada

Alberta
Government

In memory of Josua van Embden

Despite himself, he has assumed the role of the wise son at the Passover seder, who enters so personally into shared Jewish experience that its history becomes his memoir.

—REBECCA GOLDSTEIN, *Betraying Spinoza*

And I wondered, with mounting anxiety, what I was to do here, what I was to think.

—ALAIN DE BOTTON, *The Art of Travel*

THE SKY WAS FULL OF HUMANS, and I was one of them. Way above the Atlantic Ocean, I exhaled, and had no choice but to refill my lungs with air expelled from inside the strangers crammed close around me. According to the digital map on the seat-back in front of me, we were about halfway there. My nose began to tingle, and that could only mean one thing: I would grow a cystic pimple, a massive throbbing lump, right there, a millimetre above my right nostril. At thirty-nine, I was travelling alone for the first time, and my reasons for crossing the ocean seemed, from this vantage, murky at best.

An attendant came by with his cart, and I asked for a coffee. Leaning my head back, I pressed the hot cardboard cup under my nose against the tingling spot, since heat often warded off cysts before they really got going. Oh, go away, painful nose-swelling, please go away. Soon I'd meet relatives I barely knew, and I'd face strangers for the rest of the month. Not to mention Matteo. Hotter than optimal, painful, really, and I didn't want to burn myself, had to get it just right. But, I thought, this is a particularly sensitive spot, that's why it hurts so much. Three minutes is usually good. How long has it been? Okay, three minutes starting now. I closed my eyes.

There were approximately half a million humans in the sky at any given moment, travelling at hundreds of miles an hour. That's a million socks and a million shoes, not counting all the shoes and socks packed in a million suitcases. Arms and legs, and human hair, each strand growing in its follicle. Bodies. Bodies of people who died on holiday and whose remains must be buried at home. Bunnies in cages, cats and dogs. Urine. Germs! *E. coli* and HIV. And tumours, and bedbugs.

Three minutes. Okay. I put the coffee cup down.

Lingerie and parkas, I thought. Jeans and lipsticks. Paper and ink. All just zooming through the sky, all day every day.

I touched the spot under my nose, and the skin didn't feel so good. When I made my way down the aisle to the toilet, and looked in the mirror, the end and underside of my nose appeared, sure enough, an angry red. Burnt. The rest of my face looked oily and yellowish in that special plane-bathroom glow that seems a perfect embodiment of the urine-and-disinfectant smell that accompanies it. Even my eyes and hair were tinged with sickliness. I folded the door in toward me, stepped out of the bathroom, and scanned the scene before me, a grid of indistinct blue chair backs and lolling heads. This was why I had never travelled alone before: lost already, on the plane. Breathing into my ribs to ease the stab of panic, I wandered the plane for at least ten minutes, peering into each row for my new yellow headphones before I spotted them in the middle of a chair, my white notebook tucked into the mesh pocket with the magazines and puke bag. My row-mates jostled to let me back in, and I sat for several minutes with the note-book gripped in both fists before opening it again. I felt like I did when I was twelve, when I'd kept my navy-blue diary tucked between my mattress and the wall, tucked it into my schoolbag each morning, checked for it throughout the day, reaching in to feel the comforting cloth cover against my palm.

Inside the white notebook, I'd tucked my retyped and printed-out pages of my grandfather's seventy-three-year-old journal.

In the year of our Lord nineteen hundred and forty-two, when brute barbaric violence and injustice reigned over the greater part of Europe, I was one of the hundreds—if not thousands—who by a secret escape fled the violence and injustice which directly threatened their lives. What follows here is a short chronicle of that pilgrimage to safer places.

Jos van Embden had written these words long before he became a husband, or a father, or my Opa. In July 1942, now exactly seventy-three years ago, he was thirty-three years old. A young man, tall and blue-eyed, his blond curls styled into a meticulous side-parted pompadour.

It is merely a matter-of-fact travelogue, from which few, if any, extraordinary or shocking facts will be omitted. Let it be noted by way of an excuse, that it is not my intention to compose something meant for publication. But now that I am here in the unoccupied part of France and have found—at least for now—a somewhat safe anchorage, I want to write these facts down for myself and possibly also for relatives and friends in this moment when all the peculiar-ities are still clear in my mind, so that later on when we live again under happier and more humane circumstances, the memories of all of this will not have faded completely.

Jos's account covered two weeks, during which he escaped from German-occupied Europe. He'd been fired from his job at Royal Dutch Shell, with the heartfelt regret of his employers. The new German government had passed laws barring him from working, from visiting movie theatres, from riding a bicycle, or riding in a car, or riding a tram, unless on the front platform. He was forbidden from leaning out of windows, or using balconies that faced the street, or wearing clothing that had not been embossed with a yellow star reading *Jood*. On July 15th, exactly seventy-three years before I sat in that plane, all Amsterdam telephone subscribers were required to declare their race, and anyone who admitted to being Jewish had their service cut off. Worse things were coming, there was no doubt. Opa's brother was going into hiding; his mother, already elderly, was sure no one could be bothered to track her down.

✳ A child wailed somewhere behind me, and I remembered, or thought I remembered, the agony of flying before I'd known how to yawn, the pain that built up inside my ears. I had flown across the Atlantic the other way when I was a toddler, not yet three. My parents' families, though they'd started out in England too, already lived in the US and Canada, and we were going too.

Once all on the same continent, my parents and my sister and I visited Oma and Opa every summer and every winter. Dad's family didn't celebrate Christmas, so Oma and Opa got us then by default. We made our annual sojourn in the car, first twelve hours from a DC suburb, and then just five hours once we moved again to Ottawa. Oma and Opa lived just past Toronto in the then-small town of Barrie, and they'd stand by the window waiting to see us driving up, then run outside to catch us in their cashmere-clad arms.

"Darling," said Opa, deep-voiced, hugging bodily, knees sharp angles through his corduroy trousers. He wasn't naturally inclined to cuddling, but let Chloe and me maul him, smiling, saying, "Oh, hello, hello, yes, yes. Hello."

"Girls! My girls!" I loved Oma the most, the most of anyone. Her cheeks so soft, always a whiff of perfume around short, smooth, greying hair. "Naomi," she said, the British pronunciation, all emphasis on the *a*, the *o* all but swallowed. She said my name as though she'd missed me unbearably, as though just as relieved to see me as I was to see her.

Oma hugged my parents, and Mum said, "Hi, Dad," kissing his cheeks Dutch-style, left, right, left, and Opa said, "Hello, Bernard," pleasantly enough, and shook Dad's hand, but I was inside by then, touching the walls, wrapping my arms around the stairs' wooden banister, hugging the house itself.

Those wintery days at my grandparents' Victorian-style brick house glowed with bone-toasting homey warmth, warmth like that of a plump breathing body, warmth practically solid enough to banish the trap-door feeling of everyday life. Snow fell gently on the nearby lake, gifts lay piled under the silver-tinsel tree in the living room, stockings hung waiting for Santa, who'd bring fruit and nuts and maybe a dreidel for my dad's sake, and the wood-burning stove heated the den for TV time after dinner. Inside the coziness, those days moved with a slowness that started out soothing but gradually became sedative, dragging like armfuls of thick wool blanket. The hours lay heavy between breakfast and lunch, and between lunch and teatime. Maybe a walk along the snowy lake-path before dinner, maybe a few turns down the slide in the park across the street, before back to sitting and sitting and all the grown-up blah blah blah. On Christmas Day, my aunt and uncle and cousins came over from their house in the nearby countryside, and the ten of us sat facing each other, someone droning on and on about the new high school curriculum or a transmission problem or worse. My sister and cousins and I slumped into the sofas, barely bothering to stay awake.

"Trivial Pursuit?" said my uncle. Hours would pass. Opa knew all sorts of answers. He was old! He knew all about history and litera-ture, though nothing about sports or entertainment; he teamed with my uncle, who knew all about those. Opa remembered what scientist discovered the cure for some disease in olden-day novels, and what general led his troops into some battle in some far-off country prac-tically a million years ago. I was officially on their team too, so sat on the floor by Opa's customary armchair, but I didn't even know what contin-ents the countries were on, never knew a single answer, and wanted to lie on the floor and moan, and wait for my aunt and uncle and cousins to leave, so I could read my new Roald Dahl and Judy Blume books.

"*The Little Prince*, by Antoine de Saint-Exupéry," Opa responded to one question. He went on to quote the book in French, and then English. "For the travellers the stars are guides. For others they are nothing but tiny lights." He pronounced his *th*s like *d*s.

I leaned listlessly against Opa's legs, removed one of his slippers, and tried to straighten his long crooked toes inside his black dress sock. He rested his giant hand on my head. "I do like children." Opa wore a navy dress shirt with a knitted silk tie, and a wool cardigan. "Especially with a nice Chianti." That was his favourite joke.

We sat at the dining table boy girl boy girl. Since Opa was Dutch and Oma British, they had fashioned a Dutch-British Christmas-dinner tradition. Each of us received the first letter of our name in chocolate (Dutch), and we ate tins of cheese-infused crackers (also Dutch). We pulled Christmas crackers that sparked with a puff of smoke, and wore the paper crowns inside (British). We ate a goose (British), marzipan (Dutch), and mincemeat pies, fruitcake soaked in rum, and flambéed plum pudding (all British).

"Delicious." Opa patted his flat stomach. The adults sipped cognac from tiny glasses. And then my aunt and her family drove off, and that was that as far as they were concerned; we'd see them in the summer. Another week would pass before Opa stabbed cloves into oranges and simmered the little citrus hedgehogs in red wine to sip while the Times-Square apple fell on TV.

Throughout that week, Mum and Oma reminisced about their years in the Netherlands and England and Indonesia, and did the *Guardian* crossword together. Opa opened envelopes at his desk, wrote columns of numbers in his tiny handwriting and tapped away at a calculator. Shovelled the driveway, boiled the kettle for tea. Dad holed up in his room working, typed at a computer he'd brought with him, paced as far as the phone cord allowed, footsteps circling, rising and falling and rising and rising.

Once I'd finished all my new books, my sister and I tried to play a game involving cards with pictures of different animals, but the instructions were all in Dutch, so we gave up and watched TV. Watched TV and watched TV. At six, when the good shows ended and every channel played news, I pulled one of the Victorian hardcover children's books from the shelf, books that were old even when Oma was little. I wandered the house still hypnotized by the TV's cartoon glow. Prodded the backs of cupboards and closets, felt along walls, and peered behind books for secret doorways. In a novel, a child in a rambling old house would only stay bored for a page or two, tops, before finding a portal into another world, or a passageway into hidden rooms of delicious horrors, or the diary of someone who'd lived and died and left secrets.

❄ My sister and I shared a bedroom at Oma and Opa's, where, over the years, we'd share all the confidences that we kept to ourselves, in our own little rooms at home, for the rest of the year. When we were seven and four, though, we didn't have much to tell, only wondered what life in Canada would bring, played with our Cabbage Patch Kids, with their pungent baby-powder-scented plastic heads on soft bodies, and discovered that if we crouched beside the big air vent by the closet, we could hear conversations going on in the rest of the house, our parents' and grandparents' voices reverberating down through the furnace and whooshing back up on the warmed air. I strained for something juicy, especially when Mum and Dad and Oma and Opa stayed up late drinking Dutch Gin and playing mah-jong, clinking little ivory tiles at the kitchen table. Mostly they made muffled jokes that didn't seem very funny. Oma and Opa laughed in tones reserved for adults only, Oma mischievous, Opa open-chested, but at what? Mum and Dad laughed, but held back, as though they weren't sure. When the voices became loud enough to decipher, that usually meant an argument had begun.

"They have no *right*," Oma said, and, "not the only people anything bad ever happened to," and "persecution complex."

Dad's voice, quiet and tight, didn't come through so well. Just, "my mother," and "my grandmother," and "you've met my grandmother," and "six million."

"The point," Oma said in a loud clear voice, "is that you can't take someone's country and then claim God gave you permission in some made-up stories." Mum and Opa seemed to be trying to smooth things over or change the subject, but Oma's voice went on: "...no such thing as race...a religion. It's a *religion*!"

Later, our parents argued in their own bedroom, and their voices were so loud Chloe and I barely needed the vent to hear.

Dad said, "We're supposed to wander the world forever, with no home, persecuted wherever we go?"

Mum's response was muffled, frustrated, baffled. Something about, "Just say you don't believe in that anyway. You've never been there. You're not a Zionist anyway, so I don't see—"

"Your mother's a racist!" yelled Dad.

"...doesn't believe in race."

"Can't you think for yourself? Why do you have to agree with everything she says?"

"...just shhh shhh shhh," said Mum. Oma and Opa were right across the hall from them.

"What are they talking about?" Chloe whispered.

I didn't know. The argument always seemed the same, the same words and phrases drifting up, *racist* and *dogmatic* and *Zionist* and *persecution complex*, and *Holocaust*, which my father and his whole family pronounced differently—"Holly-cost"—but the words just hovered, anguished in the dark, with no meaning attached to them.

The next day, Dad did not emerge from his office until dinnertime.

☀ "Are we Christian?" I asked on January second, in the car, that year when I was seven and we were on our way back from Oma and Opa's house to Ottawa, where we'd just moved from DC. We were still living in a hotel, waiting for our house to grow innards, and to start our new Canadian lives.

"No," said Mum. "We're not religious."

"We're Jewish," said Dad.

"Well, maybe you are," said Mum.

"What are we, though?" I asked. Chloe was asleep with her head on my lap.

"We agreed before you were born that you'd have to decide that for yourself," said Mum. "You know that your father's family is Jewish. And mine isn't religious."

"Opa is Jewish too," said Dad. "That means you're three-quarters Jewish."

"No, he isn't," said Mum. "You're confusing her."

Oma's parents had been Anglican, Mum explained, which was a British kind of Christianity invented by a king who wanted to get divorced. She talked about Henry the Eighth for some time. Oma had been baptized, and had attended church as a child, but had become an atheist as soon as she grew up. Opa's parents were Jewish in the sense that *their* parents were Jewish, but even they weren't really religious. Even though he considered himself secular, a Dutchman and nothing else, Opa had left the Netherlands during the Second World War because the Germans took over, and they were trying to kill all the Jews, and they thought he *was* Jewish."

"Which he was," Dad added. "If you're born Jewish, you're Jewish. It's a race as well as a religion."

"No it isn't," said Mum. "And in any case, Judaism is matrilineal, passed down from mother to children. According to the religion laws. Oma isn't Jewish, so I'm not Jewish. I'm not Jewish, so you girls aren't Jewish."

"That's an antiquated notion," said Dad. "You girls *are* Jewish. You have three Jewish grandparents, so you're of the Jewish race."

"There's no such thing as race," Mum said. "Race in that sense is a fascist notion."

"That's a very unusual and—*weird*—opinion that you grew up with, Trish. But everyone else *on Earth*, every normal person, believes Judaism is a race."

"*Bernard*—"

"Your parents say they don't believe in race." Dad's voice burst out of him as though Mum had lit an explosive waiting inside his chest. "But they're just racist, and you refuse to reconsider, to think for yourself—"

Chloe blinked awake and peered up at the front seats, giant brown eyes dismayed.

"It's *your* family that's racist," Mum said. "It's *your* mother who thinks in terms of race at all, who thinks I'm not good enough because I'm not Jewish."

"You *are* Jewish, if you'd just admit it, and my mother is sensitive because of what she's been through, everything she's lost. Just try, just try for once to put yourself in someone else's shoes, to imagine the grief, the *grief*, the *crushing*—"

"Why are you yelling?" said Mum. "*Please*."

"Opa left Holland?" I said, loudly.

Dad fell into a tense silence.

"Anyway," Mum said through her teeth, grimacing at Dad, who turned for a moment to give her his most scornful scowl. She turned to face me. "Opa had to escape, to flee, with Nazis at his heels. Since then, he hated all religion more than ever. Don't ask him. Don't bring it up. Do you understand? He doesn't like to talk about it."

"Why?"

"Because when he went back, after the war, his mother was gone. The Germans had killed her."

"Just like they killed most of my family, in Poland," Dad added.

Don't talk. Don't talk about it. My sister sat up, and Dad drove and drove, and Chloe and I took up our customary car chant: "When are we gonna be there?" Any answer—four hours, two hours, half an hour— reaffirmed that the answer was, in fact, never.

But we did get there, to this new frozen there, and a couple of months later moved out of the hotel and into our house, and years passed, the eighties, nineties, high school and university and jobs, a new millennium, Toronto and New Brunswick and Alberta, and Chloe and I became more Canadian than English or American, Canadian through and through, and I never found any secret doors or diaries, never met any of the time travellers I'd always kept an eye out for.

Opa began losing things around the house, even after they sold the home for a smaller one, and over ten slow years he lost his whole self to Alzheimer's. He died in a nursing home, and after a few more years, Oma had Alzheimer's, too. My old diaries, boxes of them, drowned in a basement flood. I wrote a novel about a family that could only move past its secrets by deciding to forget, to stop looking. Like my mother's family, the family in my novel was Jewish, but only nominally; the grandparents had left that tradition, and that trauma, behind in Europe. Their silence held inside it a formless dread. I married Lev, and he stepped on a glass, and his relatives lifted us in chairs and gave us Seder plates and haggadahs as gifts, and he had to explain to me what they were for. I stopped celebrating Christmas. Lev hung a mezuzah over the door, but then it fell apart, the tiny Torah verse inside unfurling, and I put the whole thing in a Ziploc bag and shoved it under the dishcloths, and eventually he left me and set out to find a real Jewish woman to marry. I still loved time travel stories, but in real life, I knew, the past leaves only vague shapes, faint fragrances, like a party that's wrecked the room and dispersed, the preciseness of each moment lost and gone forever.

☀ But then it happened, my longed-for discovery. A secret diary at the bottom of a box. A map. My parents were moving Oma into an assisted living facility, and packing her possessions they found a yellowed, type-written document—thirty foolscap pages in Dutch and thirty foolscap pages in English. Though Mum hadn't spoken Dutch since leaving the Netherlands at ten, she knew enough to recognize the English document as a careful translation. My father scanned the pages and emailed them to Chloe and me.

Dad had sent each page as a separate file, and I opened and printed them one by one, skin prickling with anticipation.

I read the whole diary in one sitting, quickly, then slowed down and read it again. I hadn't spoken with Opa, not really spoken, since

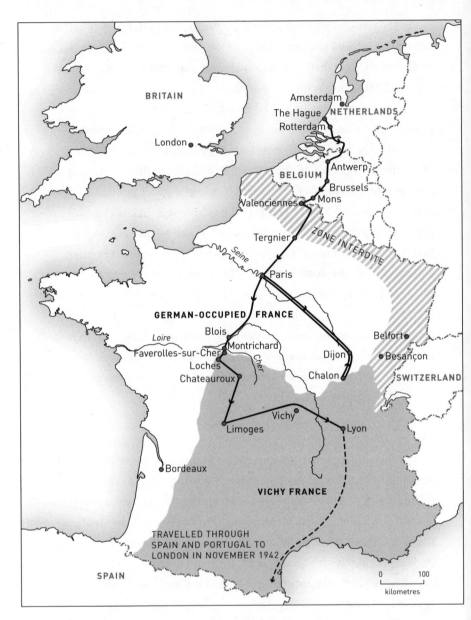

Based on Josua van Embden's hand-drawn map of his route from the Netherlands to southern France in July 1942.

my early twenties. He had died when I was twenty-six, but he had Alzheimer's for ten years before that. But as I read, I heard him in my head, his low slow voice, his Dutch accent. The meticulous way he described details, how he savoured meals, his sardonic amusement at the behaviour of people less rational. The way he expressed himself in the journal, the careful formality, the phrases and the hints of humour, it was all so clear, so *him*. Only on the third reading did I get used to hearing his voice from beyond the grave, and properly take in the events he described. Bored most days, sitting on trains, and waiting, waiting for something to happen, for the coast to clear. No huge revelations, no big secrets spelled out, but here were the events I'd heard about all my life second or third hand. He had hidden in office buildings and had used a fake name, and had used his connections, moving from place to place, seeking a chink in the border. He had crossed a river in the middle of the night.

I wanted to *do* something, but didn't know what, so I transcribed the entire document over several weekends. I wished I could ask Oma about the journal, whether she'd known about it, why and when Opa had translated it into English, but at eighty-eight she was losing herself to the same illness that killed Opa, and couldn't be consulted. Mum told me she'd tried, and Oma pursed her lips, squinted, shook her head, then said she remembered the journal well, that she'd translated it into English herself. "But who knows," Mum said, and I knew what she meant. Oma's mind had begun to rearrange every story around herself, as the protagonist. She could not have borne the version in which this document sat at the bottom of a box throughout her entire marriage, without her knowledge.

"What do you think we should do?" I asked my mother.

"I just—I don't—I. There's something creepy about it. About the way we're talking about it. Isn't there?" Opa wouldn't have wanted his account archived, certainly not in a Holocaust museum. All her life, Mum had known, this was the box you didn't open. And now I wanted to wave its contents in the air like a flag. I'd already retyped Opa's words, digitizing and reproducing them, and emailed them to everyone in the family, and printed them again, making multiple copies. Talking openly about the war, Opa's escape, his mother's gas-chamber death, even his Jewishness itself, felt to Mum like betrayal.

I wondered if she was right.

The night after I read Opa's journal for the first time, I dreamed of my grandparents' old house, the den, that front room where my sister and I spent long hours each winter, and summer too, in damp bathing suits, hypnotized by the TV. In my dream, I pulled books from the built-in bookshelves, pulled down Oma and Opa's massive atlas to find, behind it, a gaping hole in the wall. *Finally*, I thought, leaning in. Finally I'd find the reason, the answer, whole and perfect. Instead I saw dusty dim darkness, a gap between drywall and insulation, full of indeterminate shapes. But the shapes grew clearer and more sinister, and I realized I was looking at humans, dead humans buried in the walls, bony limbs emerging scrawny and twisted. I jolted back and into a room no longer sunny and cozy, but dark, without warmth. My shoulders tingled—someone staring—and Opa stood behind me.

"No," I said. "No, no—" but he had already grown fuzzy around the edges. Stooped, expressionless, he faded to see-through, and within seconds degraded to Opa-shaped mist, dark and immaterial as a shadow. I woke up sorry, so sorry for looking where I shouldn't have looked—that urge to say *I'm sorry I'm sorry I'm sorry*, as though remorse, if intense enough, could undo the un-undoable damage you've done.

※ I wanted to ask Oma what she thought, what she thought about everything, about Lev leaving me, but her memory had retreated and retreated, and she had forgotten I ever married in the first place. She had forgotten the whole ordeal, how she hadn't approved of the wedding and hadn't approved of Lev himself. I would have liked, now, for Oma to tell me all the ways my ex failed to measure up. Oma had always spoiled me in every way, but she never liked any boy or man I dated, the ones she met. She criticized each specifically and viciously: "unambitious," "terribly wimpy," "selfish little twerp." Before I married, she called Lev a conservative who wasn't as smart as he thought he was. She said he wanted a wife who'd stay at home with a bunch of babies and give up her career. I just figured she hated that I was marrying a Jew, though she'd done the same, and my mother had done the same, too. Oma did hate that I was marrying a Jew; she thought I was marrying a Jew in an attempt to cross some threshold, to become properly Jewish myself and thereby to assuage some longing that wouldn't leave me alone, which I was. But also, she was right about Lev, and about all those men I'd tried to love. She saw their flaws. She saw their flaws exclusively and magnified by a thousand.

I would have liked to tell Oma that I couldn't bear the thought of moving, was working two jobs, preoccupied with earning enough to stay in the condo Lev and I had bought together. I didn't want to move, couldn't bear the thought of it. I didn't want to go anywhere, ever, no moving, no travelling, didn't even want to go to work, really, just wanted to lie on my bed and hold onto the sheets with both fists; no one could make me leave. No. My life was trying to change, was trying to fly apart again, and I wouldn't let it, husband or no husband. I wouldn't, couldn't get up and go out and find my next home.

And by spring, I wondered what Oma would think of the fierce longing that had come over me to get as far from Calgary and the condo as I could, to take Opa's journal and his map, and to follow it.

☀ "You should do it," my friend Yael had said, when I told her about my idea to follow Opa's route out of Holland, taking the same trip on the same dates. We were talking on Skype, and it was late for me in Calgary, mid-morning for her in Singapore.

"I have been feeling like I should do something different. Get out of here for a while," I said.

"No kidding. You've had the kind of year that gives people break-downs. Maybe," she added, "you could see this trip as an ending to that year. A kind of reset."

It had been slightly over a year since Lev left me. In the aftermath, following a manic kind of compulsion, I'd run headlong into a reckless dating streak. Meanwhile, I'd worked multiple jobs at once to keep the condo, which also meant I'd dropped the ball on the short story collection I'd meant to write.

"It sounds like a significant thing to do—following my grandfather's footsteps—but I don't think he would have liked it. He would have thought it was stupid. And I don't know what I could possibly find, or get out of it. It's not going to be the thing that finally explains me to myself, you know?"

"Yes," she agreed. "Canadians really need to stop going back somewhere to find their roots." Yael emphasized for irony the *back* and the *roots*. I told myself I wasn't looking for anything as misguided as roots; I'd made that mistake when I married Lev, as though his sense of tradition could bloom in me and through me, connecting me to a network of people and meaning from which I'd been cruelly severed. I'd tried, but nothing had grown in me, nothing had taken hold. If I was looking for anything now, I had no idea what it was.

"You should do it," she repeated. "For your Opa. You loved him, and this would be a way of going back and facing what he couldn't face himself."

"But he really wouldn't have wanted me to. He didn't even mean me to find the journal."

"Well, he didn't throw it out. He kept it for seventy years. Why would a person do that, if they really didn't want their story to be known? And anyway, you said you always wanted to find a secret diary, and follow the map inside. You have to. And look, it doesn't have to mean anything, or facilitate any epiphanies. It doesn't have to be anything more than it is."

"I should," I said. "I really should go." But I couldn't imagine actually doing it.

I loved Opa, yes. I'd had one of those years, it was true, and I was about to turn forty, and I could actually afford a two-week trip, thanks to money I'd inherited from Opa himself. I'd longed, throughout my childhood, to find a diary, a map. Just like I'd longed to fall through a wardrobe into a wintery wood, or drive a car back in time. But I'd loved those stories as stories. What I hated, oh, hated, then and now, was travelling. I had moved often enough, but could only appreciate each place by living there, by staying, by not travelling. A new place was a site of torment for me, at least until I saw a familiar face, which I watched from that moment on. I followed that face as a lantern bobbing through roiling black wilderness. I did this gently, walking beside, not behind, hoping my travel companion wouldn't notice I had no idea where we were, or where we were going, or how we got here, or how we might get back to where we began, wherever that may be. I didn't get lost—I started lost and remained lost, and I don't mean a bad sense of direction.

I had only recently learned about developmental topographical disorientation, identified by a researcher called Giuseppe Iaria, at the University of Calgary of all places. People with DTD couldn't form cognitive maps, were always lost, despite having no brain damage or neurological condition to explain it.

When I'd called to interview Iaria, I told him how I'd often missed classes in high school because I couldn't find them, even after three or four years at the same school, and told him that I still took exactly the same route every time I went for a walk or run, because otherwise I'd spend the whole time in a panic, nothing familiar, afraid I'd never find my way home. As a child, back in the DC suburb, I once hesitated on my own street, unable to identify my house, and then took a guess and walked into the wrong one. As an adult, I didn't drive, because I couldn't trust myself to navigate the lanes on a highway, let alone the streets of a city, and I watched from the passenger seat in complete bafflement every time a driver friend performed the feats required to get in or out of a parking lot.

Iaria said yes: it sounded possible that I had DTD, though he couldn't diagnose me over the phone. If I did have DTD, he said, it wasn't as severe as for some people, who couldn't even find the bathrooms in their own long-time homes. People with DTD, Iaria explained, have no brain damage or malformation, but the brain's hippocampus and pre-frontal cortex fail to work together to form cognitive maps. Unlike brain damaged patients, DTD sufferers are lost from childhood on, even in places that should be familiar. Without cognitive maps, navigation depends entirely on memorizing landmarks and sequences, and we can only hold so much turn-right-at-the-lamppost, turn-left-at-the-blue-house in our heads. We can't see the big picture. We're lost.

After we spoke, I took the tests on Iaria's website, and failed the cognitive-map-formation section spectacularly. Like anyone with an embarrassing lifelong deficiency named and normalized, I was elated. That night, Yael's morning, I messaged her, told her the big news about my cognitive disability, and waited for her to congratulate me. I *loved* the idea that I might have DTD, even loved its poetic name, developmental topographical disorientation, and its other, less precise designators, which also include people rendered lost by brain damage—geographic agnosia, topographic agnosia, and place blindness. Yes, oh, yes. Place blindness. Spun in circles and then thrust forward.

"I have DTD," I reminded Yael. "I'll get lost."

"Well, you should still go," Yael said. "I promise you won't get lost. You'll have GPS on your phone, and if you do get lost, just take a taxi back to your hotel."

I booked the ticket to Amsterdam.

❋ Now, I slept the half-sleep of the plane passenger, neck braced in my doughnut pillow. My dreams were full of maps covered in lines that wouldn't stay still, and with my grandparents, and with Yael, and with Chloe, and with Matteo, with whom I'd exchanged love-texts nightly since our tryst at a writing retreat in the spring, and with Lev, to whom I was still technically married. I wasn't sure what they were all talking about, but I could tell they were making fun of me.

I woke with no moisture in my mouth and a wrenching pain in my neck, despite the pillow. The tip of my nose throbbed. On the seat-back screen, the little digital plane hovered almost over land again. Europe. It must have been tomorrow.

ON THURSDAY, JULY 16TH, 1942, Opa wrote, his "best and most trustworthy friend" introduced him to "a reliable relation" who arranged for him to be smuggled two days later out of the Netherlands and into Belgium. Since Jos had acquaintances in Brussels, he agreed to the plan. From there, he would set out for unoccupied territory—probably Switzerland. Seventy-three years later, on Thursday, July 16th, 2015, my plane landed in Amsterdam.

☀ I hadn't checked any baggage in Calgary, only brought my giant pine-green canvas backpack—giant for a backpack, but small enough to count as carry-on. In the late July morning, I lugged the bag off the plane, extracted its straps from their zippered compartment— already, I regretted the backpack. I'd read online to avoid suitcases if you're walking, especially on cobblestones; a pack is the way to go. But the green monstrosity doubled my size so that I feared turning and knocking down any child or elderly person in my vicinity. Leaning forward to avoid tipping over backwards, I felt like a five-year-old heading to the first day of school.

Arrows led me to Schiphol's shopping area, where I spotted one of the tiny pharmacies crammed with makeup and lotions that cost a fortune in Canada, and bought a tube of the lightest coloured cover-up to match my lightest coloured face. More arrows led me to the bathroom, where I brushed my teeth, then covered the burnt spot under my nose. Matteo was coming to meet me in less than a week in Brussels. He was in Italy for the month, staying with relatives, so we'd planned to meet. I pictured Matteo's own perfect skin. Only two nights together, only one full day. Please, not a day with a giant burnt nose pimple. Anyway, the makeup hid the burn well, and with an even complexion I could face the labyrinth before me. I headed for Arrivals.

Surely, Opa hadn't thought of his complexion as he prepared to flee everything he knew; I was already failing to take my pilgrimage seriously enough. But then, Opa did have skin like mine, pale and oily, and maybe it too bubbled with boils when exposed to the unfamiliar.

Whenever I'd flown before, someone had waited for me at the other end. That someone had often been Yael, her face, sharp cheekbones, bright green eyes, awaiting me at the Arrivals gate, so I could follow those cheekbones and eyes, and we would end up at somewhere specific. No one waited for me at the Schiphol Arrivals gate, and no one waited for me outside. My cousin Josette waited, but far away in the city, in some flat, in some building, on some street, along some canal. Josette was not my first cousin, but Opa's niece; her father, Sam, had been Opa's older brother. I had never met Sam, who, like Opa, died in his nineties. I'd contacted Josette and sent her Opa's journal. I explained that I was going to follow his escape route, and asked if we could spend some time together, talk about her memories of the war years. She invited me to spend the day and provided panic-inducing directions from the airport to her home, which involved taking a train into the city, then a tram, and then another tram.

I found my way down into the train station and tried in vain to make sense of the signs before asking a small American-looking man with a suitcase which train went into the city. An hour later, outside Centraal Station, I wandered in a daze around the bus and tram stops, then flagged a taxi. Once in the car, I relaxed. The driver knew the address, knew this place, knew it for a living. And he spoke English perfectly, with the same accent as Opa's. Hyper with gratitude, I answered his questions: "I'm visiting my relatives." I wanted to tell him everything;

he was my guide, had saved me. "I live in Canada, but my grandfather was from here, and my mother partly grew up here."

"Your relatives?" he said. "You're Dutch?"

"I'm part Dutch," I agreed. I belonged here!

Though I wasn't exactly *visiting* my relatives; I was staying in a hotel.

This was Amsterdam, grey sky, long streets, tall brick buildings all pressed together. Canals, canals, canals.

Once the taxi dropped me off, though, I realized the address I was looking for, the address I'd written in my notebook—number 10—did not exist. On my phone, I looked up my email exchange with Josette. Number 100. Not number 10. GPSed it. With my backpack strapped onto my body, I turned in the correct direction: yes, the correct direction; the little blue arrow on my phone inched toward number 100. I walked, and walked. At least Josette wouldn't see me arrive by taxi; she'd assume I'd taken the two trams, a feat about as available to me as flapping my arms and flying.

I'd left Canada in the late afternoon, and now it was almost noon here the next day, the air chilly and humid, with an unfamiliar heavy salt smell. The smell of Amsterdam. This is the air Opa grew up breathing, I told myself. And my mother, too. Finally, I found a building with doors outside numbered 94, then 96, 98, 102. No 100. Lugged my top-heavy self along the pavement and back. Up some stairs and down. I trundled a bit further, and turned around. No 100. Finally, a door opened.

"Naomi?" said the grey-haired woman around my mother's age, who looked a bit like my mother.

"Josette!" I said.

We kissed, one two three, and I was grateful I'd brushed my teeth at the airport.

"You must be tired," she offered, as I unloaded my bag inside the doorway, by the shoes and jackets.

"I will be, but I'm too wound up to sleep right now. May I use your bathroom, though?"

"Bathroom," she laughed.

"Yes. The—washroom?"

"We find this funny," she said. "The bathroom. The washroom."

"What do you call it?"

"The toilet. North Americans don't like to say *toilet*." Oma and Opa always did say that North Americans were prudes. Sex obsessed and vulgar, but also prudes.

"The toilet," I said.

I washed my hands and face in the bathroom. Beside the toilet itself, Josette and her husband Paul had printed and pasted a quotation by Leonard Cohen, the one about the crack and the light, and, beside the sink, one by Albert Einstein. The Einstein quotation was in Dutch, so I couldn't read it. On a shelf running along the top of all four walls stood hundreds of tiny shampoos, conditioners, and lotions, from hotels all over the world.

Josette made tea, and laid cookies and chocolates and marzipan, the very same cookies and chocolates and marzipan that Opa favoured, on a plate.

Sitting in the armchair across from me, she said she was sure she'd met me and Chloe once, as children. "I remember two little girls—one boisterous, one very quiet. Which were you?"

"The quiet one."

"Aha. Are you sure you don't want to sleep?" she offered again, and when I said I didn't, she launched right in.

"I'm sorry I didn't know your grandfather very well," she said, sitting across from me in the book- and CD-lined living room. He'd escaped during the war, she said, while her own father, Sam, hid. It was good that Opa left the country, Josette said—her father had stayed because he had a wife and children. Also, she added, Opa could pass, didn't look particularly Jewish, with his blond curls and blue eyes. "My father had dark eyes, and his nose was more Jewish." Like their mother's.

"What I remember, what I've been remembering, waiting for you to come here, is the day in August 1945 when I was playing outside the house with my sister Hermien, and a car drove up. An official-looking military car, and a soldier got out, and knocked on the door. We were very small and I was the smallest, and we were so scared, thinking it's about our father, our father's been caught and will be taken away. But that was a Dutch soldier come to liberate Delft. It was your father. I mean, grandfather. Jos. Germany had capitulated, and he was sent ahead into Delft, where we lived then. We saw a lot of him for a while. There was a fair after the liberation, and he took us. That was a proud experience—all the neighbourhood came to see the liberator."

"My mother was born around then," I said.

"Ah. Yes, but—Jos's wife was still back in England. Then she came over with the baby. That was your grandmother, and the baby was your mother. At first, we called Jos's wife Auntie Betty, and later she asked everyone to call her Mary."

"Her name's Mary Elizabeth. She always told us she was called Betty when she was young but hated it—she said Betty's a cow's name."

"She was beautiful, and I liked her very much. I remember I was jealous of that baby though. Your mother! That baby got all the attention."

We talked about her father, Opa's brother, who divorced his non-Jewish wife in the early forties, obtained a fake passport without the yellow star that identified Jews—"he did a lot of things to have another name, to have another identity"—and stayed in his own house, posing as "the lover of my mother." He stayed home all the time, not even leaving to shop or take a stroll, and his three little daughters, Josette the youngest, called him by his Gentile name, never slipped up. He was Uncle Jap.

"Did you know he was your father?" I asked.

"I knew it very well, but I knew that I never could tell it. It was a danger that neighbours would betray us, say, there's a Jew living there."

"Did he think of himself as Jewish?"

"No. He never did. Not even as a child." Josette explained that Sam and Opa's father was not religious, but their mother was. I was sure my mother had said it was the other way round. Their mother, Josette said, wanted Sam, her eldest son, to have a bar mitzvah when he turned thirteen. "And while he was doing that in the synagogue," Josette said, "he knew his father was walking through town and was not liking it. My father often told his story. He was sitting with all those men, with their—he called it blankets—and he had to say things, and he had a kind of panic, and he ran away. He ran out of the synagogue, and he didn't do it."

"Oh—wow. He ran away? And then did their parents want my Opa to have a bar mitzvah, too?"

"No, they didn't even ask it of Jos."

I told Josette that Oma had always insisted Judaism was a choice, a religion, and not a race. A fairly unusual, and unusually adamant, position, which I guessed she'd picked up from Opa himself.

Her father felt the same way, agreed Josette. "He had this feeling that it's up to him whether he was a Jew or not; it's a religion. After the war, he decided it was up to him. It was very unusual."

Josette showed me the photo of her parents' second wedding, after the war, with the three little girls standing round them.

"You know," she told me, "for a long time many Dutch people were interested in this history. There was much study of what happened, and everybody was interested in the Jews. But now it has become more complicated, because of what's happening in the world."

"What's happening in the world? You mean—?"

She nodded. "The Middle East. It's more complicated. It's harder to say those people are good, and those people are bad."

"Do you consider yourself Jewish?" I asked.

"No," said Josette. "Not at all."

We sat in silence for what felt like a long time, until I said, "I think I am tired. I can barely keep my eyes open."

She'd already put out blankets on the sofa, and I curled up, thinking about Opa, and about the brother and mother he left behind in the Netherlands. The sister-in-law and the nieces, Josette and her sisters.

In principle, there were two possibilities: to hide in one's own country or go into exile elsewhere. I have rejected the former possibility as one was completely in the dark how many months or even years it would be necessary to remain in hiding. The risk of discovery would necessarily increase over the course of time and nobody could tell, moreover, what the danger would be for the people prepared to shelter a fugitive inside their own country.

Opa rejected the possibility of hiding, but his brother did hide. So did their mother.

I drifted off, thinking about my plan. Was I really going to do this: tracing Opa's footsteps, travelling by train, as he did, to the same towns on the same dates? I'd have to travel alone for two weeks, lost. But I had my GPS. I was an adult.

✳ I woke a couple of hours later, clammy and disoriented, to a familiar-sounding song about a border, and surrender, and guns—"The Partisan," by Leonard Cohen. My cousin had cranked the stereo to wake me Canadian-style.

✳ After I showered, we took a tram—finally, the tram—and Josette pointed out the flower market, blocks and blocks of flower stalls, "very famous," and ended up back near Centraal Station, which she pointed out, and which I pretended to recognize.

"There is a special store I want to visit," she told me, leading me past cafés and restaurants, all with young men outside, lounging at small tables, smoking. I'd seen on Google Earth how this part of the city was laid out, with its series of nested canals, but without Josette I may as well have been in a maze.

"In here," she indicated. A health-food store. She bought tea while I perused herbs and vitamins and bought a clay facial mask that I hoped might help with the nose pimple and prevent more of the same.

"Are you spending tomorrow with Dick?" she asked as we set out again, along the canal and across a bridge.

"Well. No. That didn't work out."

While I was planning my trip, I'd received an email from Dick, an old friend of Josette and her sisters, he said, who lived in Voorburg, the town outside Amsterdam where Opa had lived with his mother in the early 1940s. Josette had told Dick about my travel plans, he explained, and he'd be happy to spend a day with me, to show me the house and another building Sam, who was an architect, had designed. Dick would also show me the memorial in a nearby park, the construction of which he had helped organize, commemorating Voorburg Jews who died in the Holocaust. One of the names on the memorial, he told me, was my great-grandmother's. Isabella Jacobs van Embden, 1880–1943, died in Sobibór.

In his next email, he sent a link to an extensive family tree—my family—explaining the relationships between Opa and his closest relatives, asked if I'd like to read a short story he'd written, and signed off, *Somehow I think you are a nice person. I hope I am right. Love, Dick.*

Two days later, he asked why I was taking so long to write back.

In his next message, he suggested I bring a bikini, so we could bike to a secluded beach to sunbathe and swim, and perhaps spend a few hours at a spa. I asked about his connection to my family, and whether he was an historian. He responded that he didn't know my family at all, and used to be a lawyer. He told me he'd written some limericks incorporating my name, but then decided not to send them, as they were too "spicy." He asked if I had plans for my other day in Amsterdam. I googled his name, and found a fairly old photo of a lawyer who appeared about seven feet tall. I pictured the day he'd planned (in a car, him explaining and explaining, on bicycles, at the beach in bathing suits, no one else around, at a spa—*naked?*).

I cancelled the meeting with Dick. I told him he'd clearly done important work regarding the plight of Dutch Jews, but that he'd made me uncomfortable with his "love"s, and his "xx"s, and his spa-beach-bikini talk.

He wrote back, retorting to each sentence of my email in turn.

I have done no important work at all regarding any plight of Dutch Jews, he informed me. *I don't know about the existence of such a plight.* He said I knew nothing about the war, knew nothing that I needed in order to write about this period, and would never know, not without his help. He certainly would not, he stressed, deign to help me now.

I am afraid that hearing/reading the word "Love" you think of sex, he continued. *Well, I don't. It is evident that you don't know that the simple word "Love" is used for many different things.* Moreover, he informed me that during my trip I'd meet many men who'd make me feel more uncomfortable than he had. His wife, who'd spent time in America, agreed.

"So I cancelled our meeting," I told Josette.

Josette said that, yes, Dick was irritating, and didn't understand other people's boundaries, which was why she'd avoided him for the last fifty years. Irritating but, she assured me, harmless. She seemed a little amused, a little dismayed.

"You were trying to teach him a lesson," she said. "But he's too old for that." I got it: he was one of those people everyone puts up with, because he's always been that way, he's guileless, really, and then some outsider comes along and doesn't know.

"He said he'd written 'spicy' poems with my name in them, and wanted to take me to some secluded beach. He said to pack a bikini—"

"I see. Yes. Here." Josette stopped. "This is where your grandfather and my father grew up as boys." The subject of Dick had apparently been closed. And we faced a black door on a white facade, a narrow building with—I counted—five storeys. A chandelier hung in the fourth-storey window. All those stairs! All those floors! That's where Opa lived as a boy? Did he have a whole narrow floor to himself?

Little Sam and little Jos, a century ago, must have worn down the soles of their shoes on this pavement, their shoes that they outgrew and kept wearing too long—at least, that was always Oma's explanation for Opa's oddly bent toes. And their mother, Isabella, holding their hands tight beside the canal, which still features no railings, just a sharp drop down to brownish water. Isabella with her shopping bags, her husband Hijman heading to work. Three minutes from Centraal Station, five minutes from the red-light district (Josette pointed: that way, and that way). Opa, just Jos then, ran for that black door, and opened it, and was home.

Waiting at another tram stop, Josette told me she'd read Opa's journal again, and so had her husband Paul. She tried for an English word to describe the quality they'd noticed in Opa's voice. "Quite— educated," she said. "But that's not quite what I mean."

"Highbrow?" I prompted. "Formal? Stiff? Superior?"

"No, not that. Not quite that."

"Classy?"

"Yes, that's about it. Classy. Something like that. But not—quite."

"He was sort of stoic," I said. "I mean, unemotional. Not cold, but."

"Yes," said Josette. "My father was like that too."

"Is that typically Dutch?"

Aritha, my Dutch friend in Calgary had read the Dutch version of Opa's journal, and tried to convey to me whatever quality had been lost in translation. "He's so Dutch, he's just so *Dutch*," she said. But she couldn't explain exactly. Of course she couldn't. She saw something in Opa that would remain invisible to me. Mannerisms and turns of phrase, turns of thought, that seemed so Opa to me, but so *Dutch* to her.

But Josette hesitated for a moment, said, "No." That quality, the stoicism that Opa and Sam shared, was a them-quality, not a Dutch one. Learned from their parents? Josette never knew either of her grandparents, couldn't say. Like Opa, Sam never spoke of them.

"Maybe Opa was a bit snobby," I said, as Josette and I boarded the tram back to her flat. "I mean, sometimes people thought—I don't know if you think—that my Oma, at least, was a bit snobby."

"Ha!" Josette doubled over to laugh, losing her cool for the first time since we'd met.

"Oh," I said. "So, yes?"

"Oh," said Josette. "Oh. I don't know if I should tell you this, but Mary, your grandmother, she left the Netherlands with her daughters and moved back to England."

"When my mother was ten."

"Yes, and she said—did she ever tell you why?"

"Because Opa had become so troubled, so haunted by his mother's death, that she couldn't live with him."

"Ah," Josette said. "Yes. Well. She told my mother she left the Netherlands because she didn't want her girls to marry Dutch men. That's what she called your mother and Karin. The girls."

"That's what she called my sister and me too! But, really? I never heard her say anything bad about Dutch men." Only Irish men. And Jewish men. And Catholic men, and men from Manchester, and men who wore shorts, and men who smoked, and men who wanted many children, and men who wouldn't hold babies, and men with beards, and men who voted conservative. "But," I added, "I can imagine her saying that."

"No one was ever good enough for the girls."

Oma had told me that when my mother was ten and her sister eight, Oma left Opa in Holland and moved back to London. A woman in her early thirties, alone with two daughters. Oma told me she worked as an assistant to a tea buyer that year, accompanying him to vast Victorian ballrooms in grand estates, where he slurped subtle tinctures from tiny silver spoons. "But my boss took rather a liking to me, I'm afraid," she said. "And that came to a sticky end." After a year, Opa convinced Royal Dutch Shell to transfer him to their London office, and showed up on Oma's doorstep, as she put it. Whenever she told this story, I pictured Oma opening her door to find him standing there, small suitcase at his feet, hat in hand.

"Darling," he would have said. "Mary. I am here on your doorstep. Please let me in."

She let him stay in the guest room, and he gradually seduced his way back into her room, into being her husband again.

"Your door is so hidden," I told Josette, after failing to recognize her home.

"*Is* it?"

※ During dinner in the garden behind Josette's flat, she told her husband, Paul, "We were talking about Mary and Jos." She passed me a plate of beef, potatoes, and huge flat green beans with a deep earthy flavour—just *snijbonen*, according to Josette. "Paul," she told me, "very much enjoyed flirting with Mary."

"Mmm," Paul agreed. His moustache turned up at the sides, like a smile on top of his smile.

"She was very beautiful," said Josette. "And such a flirt. Paul loved it."

"I didn't mind," he agreed. Paul was exactly the type of man, charming and calm, with a deep, kindly laugh, who would have set Oma to full-on seduction mode. So would Matteo, whom I'd see in a few days, in Brussels. Yes, Oma would have called Matteo "awfully dishy," and told him stories about her wild youth, during the war, which included loading a soldier, and then his severed foot, into an ambulance, and also included meeting a handsome young Dutchman, who would be my Opa, for weekend trysts. When they parted, Oma would have put her hand on Matteo's arm and indicated for him to bend down so she could kiss his cheeks. She might even have informed him, "You have my stamp of approval," just as she told my brother-in-law, Andrew, before he married my sister. Finally, I had a lover worthy of Oma's flirtation, but she was too old and sick, would certainly never meet him, however things worked out.

"By the way," Josette said, "did you write a novel in which Mary drives an ambulance during the war? She told my sister Hermien that you wrote that book, and Hermien searched and searched for it."

"Oma said that? Really? No. I didn't. I never wrote anything like that. It's not a bad idea. But, no."

"Hermien looked online for it, in bookstores. She was certain Mary said so..."

"I think—" Oh, Oma. "I think, when Oma was getting sick, for a while she had trouble distinguishing between things she wished happened and things that actually happened. She thought I found other members of the family more interesting than I found her, because I wrote a novel about Jewish family, kind of, partly during the war. She wanted me to find *her* story interesting enough to write about."

"Aha." Josette said this word the same way Opa used to. Brief and decisive, as if she'd seen something complicated, understood it, and accepted it. *Aha.*

"I hear you had a bit of a confrontation with Dick," Paul said, amusement twitching his kind smile.

"He wouldn't tell me anything," I defended myself. "I didn't understand. Is he Jewish? He's not, is he? Is he an historian? Why does he know so much about our family? He wouldn't answer any of my questions."

Josette nodded. "In fact, when he was very little, a little boy, in forty-two or three, his father hid a Jewish family in their house. He was caught, and they were killed. His father, too."

This mildly introduced information stunned me, and I blinked, blushed. I'd been dumping on this guy, who as a tiny child lost his father, murdered for hiding Jews in their house.

"But why didn't he tell me that?" I said, finally. "Why didn't anyone? I mean, if I'd known—" But if I'd known, what? I still wouldn't have gone to a secluded beach with him.

"He never told me, either. Someone else did." Josette said Dick never defined himself by those events. Dick would not want me to think those events relevant in any way to anything. *I don't know about the existence of such a plight.*

☀ Josette told me how to the take the tram to my hotel after dinner, but, afraid I'd take the wrong one, I walked instead, giant backpack strapped on tight. According to my GPS, it wasn't far, and involved walking straight down one street most of the way. After ten minutes, I stopped abruptly, sure I had set out the wrong way, turned somehow onto the wrong street—or somehow, impossibly but only too possibly, already passed my hotel? No: my GPS assured me. Keep going and I'd end up where I was meant to be.

Before long, I noticed two billboards advertising a sale at a store called Hema, and realized I'd seen several identical billboards throughout the day. A sale on what, though, I wasn't sure.

When Lev and I were married, I did not own a smart phone. On my flip phone, I called Lev when I was lost. I'd tell him what I could see, landmarks, the names on the street signs, and he'd tell me where I was, which way to turn. He did not always do this happily. He didn't know I had DTD; he thought I wasn't paying enough attention, was lost in my head, which was plausible. He wouldn't have been the first to tell me, "You're the stupidest smart person I ever met," which I'd always taken as a compliment: at least those people thought I was smart in a way. Now I had no one to call. I had my phone itself.

Up until a few years earlier, even when Oma's memory had started to fade, I'd still called her when I need comforting. I didn't say, comfort me, just, "Hi, Oma."

And her "Darling! Naomi!" already made me feel better.

"Am I calling too late?" I asked.

"Oh, no. I'm always up late these days. I have terrible trouble falling to sleep. I get in bed but then I can't sleep, so I turn on the television. There's this one channel," Oma told me. "It's all couples, or well, sometimes more than two people. In bed, or not necessarily in bed, but—"

"Having sex?"

"Oh my goodness, yes."

"You mean pornography?"

"Well, yes. I suppose so. In any case, sometimes if I can't sleep, I put that on. Most of the things those people do never even occurred to me. I can't believe it. After half an hour of that, I'm just exhausted, and I fall straight to sleep."

"Oma!"

"Yes, darling."

I laughed.

"Opa was always interested, of course," she assured me. "Well into his eighties, he'd join me in my bed before we slept."

"That's good!"

Oma and Opa had always slept in separate twin beds, with a small dresser in between. That, they said, was the civilized way. Each morning, he brought a rolling table from the kitchen—steel pot in its cozy, two mugs, milk in a porcelain creamer—and they drank tea in bed, news on the radio. When I was little, I'd wake early at my grandparents' house, run to their bedroom, and get in bed with Oma for a morning snuggle. I'd squeeze her as tight as I could and fall asleep again as she attempted gently and in vain to loosen my grip a little. I wasn't allowed to cuddle Opa; he wasn't into that kind of thing. On those mornings, though, he brought up three mugs.

"Do you regret that you never thought of doing those things, from the TV?" I said, mostly so Oma could have the pleasure of shocking me again, but also because I really wanted to know. I felt bad for her for missing out.

"Hm," she considered. "Some definitely not. Some do seem rather nice. But it's too late now."

"It's not necessarily too late."

"Oh, dear! Oh my goodness. Maybe if I could find a nice boy toy. But an old man? No, thank you very much."

Oh, Oma.

I wondered how many people Oma had told that her granddaughter wrote a novel about her, an ambulance driver during the war. Such a fine line between what existed and what didn't, what existed and what ought to exist. Some plaque in the brain and it was easy to lose track.

After my first book, my novel, was published, Oma read it, and told me she loved it. "But I hope you won't write any more about—" She squeezed my hand, sipped her tea.

I knew she hoped I'd expunged my interest in the Holocaust, and in the Jews who'd fled, and the ones who'd died, and the children and grandchildren of the ones who'd fled.

"I think you're terribly interested in all this," she went on. "Because you like feeling part of an exclusive club. A special group. But it's exclusive because it leaves people out, darling. Don't you see?"

"But. Listen. I have this history in my family, so of course it affects me, of course I think about it. It's part of my history."

"It's not your history, darling," Oma said. "You weren't raised with all that superstitious nonsense. And you're not Jewish. Whether you like it or not. You're a goy. Like me."

"But I'm not even talking about being religious." I slipped into the familiar unwinnable argument. "The Holocaust affected our family— Opa, and my dad's family—because they were Jewish, whether they wanted to be Jewish or not." I decided against trying to tell her, as I had before, that race was socially constructed, if not essential or genetic.

"Oh, that word!" Oma went on. "Holocaust! As if it were the only genocide, the only bad thing that ever happened to anyone—the Holocaust—"

"So it doesn't matter, because other equally bad things happen?—"

"No. It matters. But why don't we stop thinking about the past and think about things happening now, which are just as bad, and that we might be able to do something about? And you weren't there. I was there. And the war was nothing like what you've learned in school. You just don't know, and you—you can't."

Oma and I held eye contact, sighed.

"Oh, Oma." I took a bite of ginger cookie rather than toss out more words for her to bat back at me. She was right that I couldn't know. And anyway, I was working on my second book, a short story collection, and it didn't have any Jews in it, not explicitly, at all.

"In any case," she said. "You wrote your novel. Now you don't have to think about all that anymore. That will be nice, won't it?"

☀ Eyes fixed on my phone, with its map and its blue dot, I found my hotel, where every room was cubical. I had chosen the least expensive option, so my cube, with its concrete floor, walls, and ceiling, had no windows, and was lit with dim bluish fluorescents, like a nightclub. The bed sat in a raised cube inside the cube, built right into its frame, which made it difficult to lift the mattress and check for bedbugs, and hopefully difficult for any such bugs to take up residence. Still, I eased up the lowest sheet and peered underneath, poked and peeked into the corners for telltale black spots—bedbug excrement; that is, human blood.

Human blood comprises the bedbug's entire diet. I learned this fact when I was sixteen, and briefly had a nineteen-year-old boyfriend who worked for Greenpeace and lived in a boarding house. He told me about the time he'd spent in India, finding himself, or looking for himself, anyway, and how he'd watched bedbugs crawl nonchalantly across the floor of his small room, in plain daylight. "I thought, if it weren't for me, those bedbugs wouldn't exist," he said. "Those bedbugs were made of me." I never asked why he'd left school, or what part of India he'd lived in, or how he paid for his plane ticket, or how he'd come to live in a boarding house at nineteen, or why he'd never mentioned his mother. He had travelled alone to a place as different as another planet, a place with bedbugs, which were as gruesome and foreign as aliens. I believed the Greenpeace guy halfway magical— a grown-up man.

I lay on the uncontaminated bed. Was my cube inside a cube of smaller cubes? Was my windowless room in the middle of the hotel? How big was the building, anyway? How far in might I be? Too worked up to think clearly or sleep soundly, I dozed, and woke with no way to guess the time, noon or midnight, thanks to jet lag plus no windows.

I checked my phone: only about an hour had passed. Still barely after-noon. The bathroom—toilet—in my cube had no door; all its facilities occupied a raised platform, and when I peed, I had no choice but to watch myself in a giant full-length mirror. I sat up straighter.

What have a lot of flat-footed peasants wandering through the desert to do with me? Josette remembered Opa saying. He was talking about Moses, and the exodus from Egypt.

When Josette first described Sam's efforts to shed his Jewish iden-tity before going into hiding, I thought of the approximately twenty thousand other Dutch Jews who went into hiding too, about half of whom would survive the war. The other half, including Sam and Opa's mother, including the Jewish family in Dick's childhood home, and including Anne Frank and her sister and mother, were not so lucky. But Sam did not want to be counted among those numbers, just as Opa's journal did not mention, not even once, that he himself was Jewish. Opa had to leave the Netherlands, he wrote, "because of a situation that suddenly became a lot worse in the first half of July."

By July 16th, as Opa prepared to flee, it had become illegal for Dutch Jews to travel by car or bicycle. While Opa spent the day making plans, two trains left Amsterdam, each loaded with seven hundred Jews who believed they'd been called up for work camps in Germany. In Paris, the German occupiers were in the midst of arresting 13,152 Jews—a raid that came to be known as the "Grande Raffle." Most were crowded into the stadium Vélodrome d'Hiver, where they lived for several days without water, food, or toilets; the rest were kept in similar conditions in internment camps. Finally, all of them, including four thousand children, were herded into rail cattle cars, transported to Auschwitz, and murdered.

Oma felt I'd betrayed Opa by writing a novel that included a Dutch Jew who'd hidden in a neighbour's house, and then, worse, by marrying a Jewish man in a Jewish ceremony, and if she'd known that I was following Opa's journal she'd have felt that I was betraying him again, that I wouldn't let this thing go. Why wouldn't I let it go?

I imagined Opa in my cube, sitting on the plush purple cubical stool with his huge hands resting on his knees, shaking his head at me as I wrote in my white notebook. *Silly girl*, he'd say. *What has any of this to do with you?*

FRIDAY, I WAS BACK ON BEETHOVENSTRAAT BY MID-MORNING, dressed in a blue linen dress. I'd brought my wedding ring, the slim white gold band I'd removed from my finger the day Lev left. A useful object; I could wear it while travelling, to ward off men—though, did men actually look for wedding rings before harassing lone women travellers? In any case, I couldn't bring myself to wear the thing after all, so carried it in the right breast pocket of my jean jacket, in case of emergencies. With no Dick to go and meet, I had decided against visiting Voorburg without a guide. Instead, I would wander Amsterdam's centre, with the luxury of getting completely lost and then using GPS to find my way back. The route was starting to look a little familiar; I vaguely recognized a coffee shop, a store, the Hema billboard, another Hema store, this one not far from my hotel. In front of it, a tall, slim woman with long straight hair, a woman dressed like a model, sauntered past pulling a tiny red hard-shelled suitcase by its long chrome handle. A few blocks later, an equally well-dressed man, in a suit, pulled the same suitcase, only black.

☀ I arrived at the big intersection where the canals began, and before crossing with the flow of pedestrians checked both ways, congratulating myself on adjusting so quickly to the traffic coming at me on the wrong side of the road. But reality lurched. I wasn't so sure. Which side were the cars on? Which direction were they coming from? I floundered, as disoriented as if floating in the dark, with no idea which way was up. *Jamais vu*, the French call this feeling, the opposite of *déjà vu*—instead of the uncanny feeling that everything is familiar, the uncanny feeling that nothing is familiar, not even sense data itself, as though one were a sentient robot just switched on for the first time.

My heart and lungs went into overdrive. I clenched my right hand into a fist, my writing hand, and glanced down at my feet. My shoes for this trip covered my toes but showed just enough to reveal white and slightly less white; I was born with no pigmentation on the top half of my left foot, and had relied on that blanched skin all my life, to orient. Right hand, left foot. But it still took me a minute. The cars were on the right side of the street, not the left, as I'd believed all day yesterday. Was I sure? Did I misperceive my environment so profoundly, and remain locked in that misperception for twenty-four hours? Shit. Of course, *of course*, only Britain and (former) British colonies drive on the left.

That was why I hated travelling. *That* feeling.

Why couldn't I occupy the world as those model-looking women did, with their flowing hair, pulling their tiny bright suitcases as if to say, I just arrived from elsewhere, and I already belong here, and this sidewalk belongs to me?

I thought of going to the Anne Frank House, but I'd been there before, and didn't feel a need to go again. Twenty years earlier, when Chloe and I visited Amsterdam with our giant backpacks, we toured that once secret, now famous place. A museum, the building was marked with signs, and with the crowd of waiting tourists sprawled down and around the corner, awaiting their turns inside. The house was smaller and more ordinary than I'd pictured; to my surprise, it was just a house, a nice house on a canal, in a pretty neighbourhood. Inside, I pictured the empty rooms Gestapo-dishevelled, close-up of the diary on the floor, fade to today. *Back to the Future* style: the house where Anne Frank lived and wrote is now the Anne Frank House, empty rooms cordoned off, tour guides pointing out in English, French, Dutch, and Japanese, where the occupants slept and ate. But the empty space of the Secret Annex was just that, empty, like any home with its furniture removed. I stood on the bare floor and focused on the fact, the indisputable fact, that Anne Frank was here. *Here.* This is where she wrote, this is where she whispered with her parents, her sisters, and the van Pels family (called the van Daans in the published diary), and fell in love. *Here.* On this wooden floor. More than anything, the house made me think of my childhood home in Maryland the day we moved out, cleared of furniture—home already not home anymore.

Instead of going back to that house to line up, that house so well preserved that nothing could have changed in two decades, I bought a caprese sandwich, which I ate sitting at the edge of a canal. I leaned against what looked like some kind of phone box, until I saw a stream of liquid ease past me on the pavement and into the canal. Then I realized the box was a urinal, where men could step inside and just aim their stream at the wall. Later, I'd write to Matteo about my day, would describe sitting by the canal with my sandwich, but I wouldn't mention the urine.

Downtown, I wandered in and out of stores, watched people, locals, tourists. One of the stores was Hema. I peered in the window at piles of suitcases, all colours and sizes. On sale. The mystery sale: suitcases. I could buy a new suitcase. I could, and abandon the green backpack. Should I? I'd owned that backpack for twenty years. My mother bought it for me when I was nineteen, and bought my sister, then sixteen, a matching purple one. I'd carried untold loads of laundry to laundromats in my green backpack, camped with it crammed to the bottom of multiple tents, by my feet. I moved to Toronto, New Brunswick, Edmonton, and Calgary with my green backpack, while Chloe moved to Toronto and London and Vancouver and Norway with her purple one. What if I left it behind and regretted it?

At a stationery store, I bought an umbrella, a little red one. "We have wallets," the cashier noted, when she saw my red-and-black number, splitting at the seams so that change slipped out and credit cards poked through, their corners boring growing holes. I left the store prepared for rain, and with a bright green wallet with separate compartments for euros, dollars, and receipts. A vivid frog green, not pine like the backpack. In a candy store, I bought a bag of salt liquorice for my mother; she used to talk about eating that stuff as a child, how it turned her hands black, and I pictured her as a little kid, sitting by a canal, licking liquorice and salt from her fingers. I tried one of the candies, eager to love it. After a couple of seconds, I spit it into a nearby trash can.

With the help of GPS, I continued to Centraal Station, and back to Opa and Sam's boyhood home, where Josette had taken me. I stood once again with my back to the canal, facing the black door against its white facade. I stood and stared at the building, waiting for it to tell me something, to tell me what I was supposed to feel.

In Centraal, I bought a ticket for the next day, to Brussels, wandered through to the station's other side, and sat by the water, as though waiting for a ferry, just to sit somewhere Opa must have sat a million times when he was young. I headed back the way I'd come, through the city's centre, checking my GPS, toward Zuid. Zuid meant south. I might well have been heading south. All along the sidewalks, dirty-haired twenty-year-old boys with Velcro-strapped sandals clogged the side-walks, each swollen to twice his size by the giant backpack strapped to his body. Their obtrusive middle-of-the-sidewalk lumbering made me want to set my own green bag on fire. The whole point of being an adult, as Yael would say, was not to own a bag like that. Meanwhile, Chloe had abandoned her purple version a couple of years earlier for a hard-shelled lime suitcase that matched her husband's black one. They travelled together for exhibitions, residencies, and conferences with those suitcases. The suitcase made her feel more adult, Chloe said— though she was younger, my sister had always seemed to identify and banish markers of childhood and adolescence before I did.

I was hungry, or at least thought I should eat, since a caprese sand-wich was surely not enough nourishment for a whole day. If I had a companion on this trip, he or she would surely have chosen some restaurant with a reputation among tourists and known how to get there. Such an endeavour felt beyond me. I spotted a place on the corner of a grassy area, busy-looking, with an English version of the menu posted outside. I'd passed it twice the day before and once that morning, so it looked vaguely familiar, and hence inviting. Inside, a hostess shuffled me to a tiny table shoved against a pillar, then mostly ignored me. Throughout my meal, whenever I looked up from my book or my salad or my lasagna, I could see the waiters frantic to please a giant table of at least ten aging thick-biceped men. These men, closer to fifteen or twenty or them, I realized, occupied the middle of the room, on the other side of my pillar. Toward the end of my main course, I realized the two closest to me were speaking in English, each with a different vaguely Germanic accent.

"You think the good-looking ones don't have VD, but they do," the beefy neckless man told the thinner, bearded guy across from him.

"I don't know what you mean," the bearded man said, lowering his voice.

The beefy guy said loudly, "VD. Venereal disease."

"I know *that*." Even quieter than before.

"Whores. You think the good-looking ones don't have VD, you know? But they do. Right?"

"I don't," the bearded man said. "I do not. Know."

I ate one more bite of the lasagna. The lasagna was not amazing, and wasn't cheap, either. If I had a travelling companion, I would not be eating a mediocre expensive meal, but something delicious, something highly rated online.

I caught the waitress's eye. She nodded. Brought my bill.

"Well," said the beefy man. "Must get back to the wife."

The first time I travelled to Europe, at nineteen, I had no credit card, only cash, and only a few hundred dollars in the bank. At least I wasn't that clueless anymore, that helpless. I placed my Visa beside the bill, which didn't look so bad to me, because it was in euros.

Tomorrow, I planned to buy a new suitcase, first thing. At that smaller Hema on Beethovenstraat, the one near my hotel. One: get up. Two: Go to Hema and buy a suitcase. Three: Head back to the hotel, unpack, repack. What would I do with the pine-green bag? I'd ask whoever was working when I checked out of the hotel. But what if they said there was nowhere to dispose of it, and that they didn't want it, and they made me take it, and I had to carry that *and* pull the new suitcase? Well, that probably wouldn't happen. Right? Then: I'd take the train from Zuid to Centraal, and Centraal to Brussels.

The decent bearded man, alone now, smiled at me. He was apologizing, so I nodded back. Anyway, we understood each other: his friend, or colleague or whatever, was a pig; he knew it and I knew it. But then he fixed his eyes on my upper thigh, said, "I like what I see, but what does the rest look like?"

Oh. *Not* apologizing.

"A compass, isn't it?" he added.

Oh, my tattoo. Where my shorts hitched up when I sat.

"Right. Yeah."

The compass tattoo was only a little over a year old, just like my marital status (separated/divorced). I got the tattoo a few days after my marriage split up, though I'd made the appointment a month earlier, to cover the tattoo from my eighteenth birthday, the painfully silly Little Miss Sunshine, which I had considered ironic at the time. In the days after Lev moved out, I'd wondered whether to cancel the appointment. Somehow, everything seemed off the table; every plan I'd made, I'd made in another life, according to a different set of rules. But I did go, and lay for three hours, intermittently gritting my teeth and making conversation with the woman bent over me. The pain of the needles buffeting my skin freed the rest of me to chat with the artist as though my life hadn't just fallen apart. Suspended, those days, floating on the cusp of a future I hadn't had a chance to picture. I hadn't been eating much, and that contributed to the floaty feeling as well.

"I like it," said the bearded man.

"Thanks," I shrugged, and looked away. He gave up on me, signalled for his bill.

✳ Back in my cube, I rehearsed my plan for the morning, set my alarm. I couldn't figure out how to turn down the frigid air conditioning, and had only brought shorts and a tee-shirt for sleeping, so I wrapped up tight in blankets and opened my laptop to reread the first pages of Opa's journal.

> But now that I am here in the unoccupied part of France and have found—at least for now—a somewhat safe anchorage, I want to write these facts down for myself and possibly also for relatives and friends in this moment when all the peculiarities are still clear in my mind, so that later on when we live again under happier and more humane circumstances, the memories of all of this will not have faded completely.

Why did he decide to tell no one about the journal—after the effort of writing it, and then the trouble of translating the whole thing into English and preserving both copies in that box, along with his marriage license, passports, and military documents? Had he ever thought about the journal? Had he ever been thinking about it when we all sat in the living room and he was gazing off, mind somewhere else? Had Oma read it; was it true that she helped with the translation? Had they discussed it, planned to give the journal to Mum and Auntie Karin, but then forgotten, as both of them succumbed in turn to Alzheimer's?

In any case, Opa did not record his route so that his granddaughter could follow it seventy-three years later.

What an imposition I was, following him, what a drag on his coat-tails—could he sense it, my grip on his arm? But tomorrow, I'd begin. I was terrified. What was I doing here, why was I doing this, travelling alone, this activity most unsuited to me, most guaranteed to close the world off to me, to reveal nothing? Every trip I'd ever taken, I'd followed someone, or felt pulled along behind them. This time, I followed Opa, but I couldn't walk beside him, pretending to know the plan.

Giuseppe Iaria, the expert on developmental topographical disorientation, told David Suzuki, on *The Nature of Things*, that "getting lost, if you really want to enjoy it, is not to be confined to space and time, so if I define getting lost this way, it can be a very pleasant experience."

But surely one must feel oriented as a rule, to welcome disorientation as a freeing exception. I couldn't sleep, kept imagining my cube as a space capsule, suspended, with nothing but non-orientable darkness outside, like in *Alien*, as Ripley and her crew awaken in their hibernation tanks. "Swallowed up," as Blaise Pascal wrote in his *Pensées*, "in the infinite immensity of spaces of which I know nothing and which know nothing of me." Stop picturing the vacuum of space, I thought. Relax. I'm in Amsterdam; my grandfather grew up here, my Oma and my mother lived here, and Anne Frank, and my favourite philosopher, Baruch Spinoza, too. Outside the front door of this building lies a long walkway, and if I turn right and follow the path for a few minutes, a courtyard will open up beside me, full of coffee shops and bars, and from there I'll see the massive grey entrance to Zuid Station, full of signs with arrows. If I exit the hotel's front door and turn left, the pathway leads to a bridge, and then a dusty, chaotic traffic-heavy area, and then Beethovenstraat, which has Hema on it, with my future suitcase inside. And then I will travel to Brussels.

On the night of Friday, July 17th, 1942, Opa lay in his own bed, in the same house as his mother, the Voorburg house his architect-brother had designed, for the last time. He had organized his affairs, and made his plans for the next few days. Could he have slept at all that night? He was not the type for danger, for discomfort, for being a fugitive. He was a Dutchman, fleeing his own country, leaving his elderly mother behind, with no clear idea where he'd end up—in Switzerland, or in

Asia or America, or in a concentration camp—or for how long. But what else could he do?

And then the time for talking was over—it was time to act.

ON THE MORNING OF SATURDAY, JULY 18TH, 2015, Hema opened at 9:00. I stood from the patio table where I'd been drinking coffee and reading a memoir, crossed the street, and inside the store discovered that they had completely sold out of suitcases. Now what?

With the help of my phone, I found a street market: Albert Cuypmarkt. My GPS suggested a few different routes, and I chose the one down Beethovenstraat, back toward Josette and Paul's, toward the city centre. How boring of me, walking the same route again and again, not even trying to find a new one! I'm so boring, I thought. I'd always travelled with people who loved heading into new territory every day, as though treading the same ground more than once were a waste of time, with so much area to conquer. And me disoriented from the moment I left my hotel to the moment I returned, with no respite except the bed, which I loathed to leave and longed for all day.

But travelling alone, I could walk down the same street again and again if I liked—which I did—could see the same street until the store-fronts, the objects, along its length gained focus, density, existed more and more, and stayed put, promising to be there when I came back the other way. Just like when I moved to a new home, and gradually learned to navigate the streets outside my door. I remembered when I was eight, the spring we moved into the Ottawa house. I was riding my blue bicycle (named Trolley after the neighbourhood trolley on *Mr. Rogers' Neighborhood*) back and forth in front of the driveway while Dad did whatever he was doing in the back yard, which wasn't really yard yet so much as a patch of dried out mud, a smaller version of the to-be park across the street.

"You know," Dad called from the non-yard, as I rode past him for the tenth time that minute, "you could ride around the block." He explained what a city block was, that we lived on the corner of one. I pretended I could picture it. "You just keep going without crossing the street," he explained, "you'll turn four corners and end up back here."

"Are you sure?

"Absolutely sure."

"Promise?"

"Promise."

Okay. I set out.

The first stretch passed only the back of our house, the front of a garage, and the front of another house. Then I turned a corner. Brick house, brick house, brick house. Panic crept up my spine, but I kept going. Reached another corner. Turned. Now I was so far from home, I felt sure I'd never find my way back. Home might as well have moved to another planet, or slipped from existence. But Dad had promised. And a promise is a *promise*. Just keep going. Past the backs of two houses, then another corner, and turn again. Was it possible that I was heading back, instead of further away? I sped up, really terrified now, truly lost. Houses on one side, fence on the other, with tennis courts behind it. I rode so fast my feet threatened to slip off their pedals, but I couldn't help it. Go go go. Turn the corner. And there's a house and there's a driveway, and a man, it's Dad! Just, hi, honey, no big deal. In our driveway! Our house!

And, in the months that followed, and the years, I left my house in ever-widening circles, gradually pushing out the boundaries of home. First, left and right. Left my blanched foot, right the hand I write with. I learned one route to my school, which meant out the back door, turn right, keep going till the pizza shop, turn right, keep going till the school appears. I learned what happened if I departed from the front door: turn left, walk till Bank Street appears, turn right, keep going till the school appears. During my three-and-a-half years at that school, I tried new routes home, experimented more and more with the grid that I eventually understood held my house and the school on diagonal corners. I even walked my sister to school and back, and we both seemed to think I was the one who knew the way. One route featured the corner store run by the Italian family, where we could buy Swedish berries, two cents each. Another led us past the 7-Eleven, its parking lot full of aggressive floppy-haired skater-boys, all teenaged and flirting with fearless thirteen-year-old girls.

Sometimes, by the time I was ten and Chloe was seven, she walked with her best friend, and I joined with my friends Jane and Jeannine along a more complex diagonal route. About two-thirds of the way, Jeannine chased Jane and dragged her into a thicket between two houses. Always the same thicket, which belied Jane's half-hearted attempts to run away and then wrench herself free. "Help, help," yelled Jane from under the branches. Then, in her normal voice, "Naomi, now you save me." Then in her fake-scared voice again, "Help, help!" Abandoning Jane to Jeannine, I continued toward home feeling excluded. Jane was always getting people to chase her and drag her into tight spaces. I thought, if only I were prettier. If I had smooth, silky hair and a button nose. If I were beautiful. And. Or. If only I were smarter. Why couldn't I at least see how everything fit together and know all the words? Why did I have to be born a non-genius? Or at least if I could be cooler. How did people find out which bands to like, and which shoes to want? How did they get the idea to be the way they were, those kids slurping down Coke Slurpees outside the 7-Eleven? I passed the house with the girl with the curly, curly hair and red Converse sneakers who played in her yard alone, exuding an air of such absorption and calm confidence she seemed on the other side of some unfathomable threshold, proximate but of another world, as magical to me as a trapeze artist swinging overhead from one toe.

At home, Mum sat at the dining room table, bent over a book of logic puzzles with a pad of graph paper beside her and a pencil in her hand.

"Jane and Jeannine went in a bush," I said, peering over her shoulder. She wrote *x* as a backwards *c* and a regular *c* smushed together. "I found a quarter this morning," I said. "I bought twelve Swedish berries and got a penny back and it was an American penny. I got nine out of ten in spelling. I got *pursue* wrong. I got *excite* right. I got *recognize* right."

"Hm," said my mother, without looking up. She made a column of marks with her pencil: *if x, if y, if y and x, then...*

"I spelled *excite* right," I said again. "I can't remember where the provinces go," I added. "Or the oceans."

"Hmm," said my mother, still writing. *Then x > y and z < xy and...* "Well the Atlantic's in the east, isn't it? And the Pacific's out west."

"And Warren said I have a hook nose like a witch. Mum, do you think I could get my hair smooth instead of just—this—look at it!"

She bent lower, frowning in concentration.

"Mum!" I felt a kind of hysteria building inside me.

"*What?*"

"I'm stupid!"

"What are you *talking* about?" She finished her next line of symbols before looking up at me, face tight.

☀ But Saturday morning in Amsterdam I found a market online, and walked to it. Had I ever in my life, in a foreign city, simply solved a problem by finding the right place to go, by myself, and then gone there?

I loved markets, everything about them, the colours and fabrics, the cooking smells, sausages and waffles, food that could be prepared with minimal equipment, in a truck. And people bent over tables of merchandise, moving slowly, watchfully, and the murmur of commerce, but not just commerce, also of greeting, chatting, sitting, drinking coffee. Albert Cuypmarkt consisted of blocks and blocks of wares, and if I'd had time I'd have lingered and picked things over, not to buy but just because I loved markets, but instead I marched along like come on, come on. Yes, sure enough, a luggage store, with a canopy so that the display could spill outside into the road. Rows of suitcases, tiny, small, medium, immovably enormous. Cheap canvas sacks on wheels, backpacks of all shades and fabrics, colours, and prices. I limited my search to carry-on sized hard-shelled suitcases, considered a pink number with a glittery rainbow embossed on one side—wouldn't that be fun? I could practically hear Yael's voice in my head: *no; you're an adult*. But it's fun. No, think about it. What if you have to travel for work, or? I ran my hand over a white one, just plain white, but it would get dirty. As usual I bought the first item that had caught my eye, a little sky-blue suitcase, not the kind I'd seen the fancy people pulling, but nonetheless hard-shelled and carry-on sized, and only fifty euros.

I wheeled my new empty case all the way back to my hotel, where, back in my cube, I took everything out of the old green backpack.

On his July 18th, Opa packed carefully:

My equipment: an ordinary indistinguishable suit, a heavy leather motoring-coat to protect me against any kind of weather, a small suitcase with toiletries, a reserve set of underwear, and a spare pair of shoes as I am wearing my ski-boots with a double set of socks for the journey. And finally, divided over all my pockets: two hundred cigarettes as a special means of exchange, and as an emergency ration of food: smoked bacon, rich cheese, and ten bars of chocolate, all old stock of pre-war quality, high-value nutrition in small portions.

I'd planned at first to bring only as many items as Opa had, in order to understand his experience better. This, I had not managed. I refolded my blue linen dress, grey skirt, jeans, seven pairs of underwear, pink lace bra and black sports bra, two pairs of socks, five tee-shirts, one black tank top, jean jacket. Toiletries, including sunscreen, facial scrub, coconut-scented moisturizer, face powder to prevent shine, leave-in conditioner for curly hair, toothbrush, floss and toothpaste, tampons and pads, deodorant, condoms, Advil, migraine pills, Band-Aids, tweezers, nail clippers, and the three medications I took each morning to quell my chronic conditions, asthma, anxiety, and fertility: a flavourless mist to calm over-reactive lungs, a tiny ovular pill to inhibit quick-on-the-uptake neurons; a slightly bigger, rounder pill to quiet plaintive genes, to shush my coding's cry for a stab at immortality, or thwart it. My wedding ring was still in my jacket's right breast pocket. I repacked everything, in tidy piles, in the new suitcase.

In my small light grey backpack, which I'd originally stuffed inside the big green one but could now carry on my back: laptop, white notebook and stainless-steel fountain pen, phone, wallet (with extra turquoise, grey, and black ink cartridges inside), passport. I wore the grey tee-shirt with an octopus printed on it, and the darker high-waisted grey shorts that Chloe had traded me for a pair of my shorts. Another pair of underpants of course, plus the pink bra, and black shoes, a cross between hiking shoes and sandals, with closed toes and sturdy soles but no need for socks.

I would buy snacks. Granola bars, cheese, apples.

"I bought a new suitcase," I explained to the hipster concierge downstairs as I checked out. "And I want to get rid of this bag. Can I leave it here? Maybe another guest will want it?"

"Sure!" the guy agreed. "I'm sure someone will take it." A whole country of people who spoke in my grandfather's accent, which used to be his alone.

"I travelled with that one ages ago. When I was nineteen," I said, as he placed the green bag on a white table behind him. "I needed something different." It stood out against the white, lonely and frayed.

"Yes," he said. "That is the bag of a nineteen-year-old. This," he pointed at my new blue suitcase, "is the luggage of a young woman." Ha. He thought I was young. I'd hung onto that green bag for twenty years. I felt a tug, as though I'd left something important inside it, though I'd checked at least five times.

Outside, I turned right, and wheeled my little blue suitcase down the path, across the courtyard, and into Zuid Station. Organized, compact, and dignified, I found my platform with no problems, then bought a coffee for while I waited, sitting on my bag. Though I had always hated travel, the parts when I was lost, I did like waiting. I liked waiting for trains, planes, and buses, with the promise of few hours' journey ahead of me, time to write, and maybe just a good long sit-and-stare. Stare at the train tracks, the tiled floor, the people, especially the people. But I also loved the ports and stations themselves, didn't even mind airport line-ups or security, didn't even mind being singled out and patted down, though easy to say, since that rarely happened. I was invisible; I didn't have to worry about my features or skin tone singling me out. And Opa hadn't either, because he was blond and blue-eyed and his features classically Dutch, unlike his brother Sam's. Some of the Dutch Jews who fled in the forties dyed their hair and changed their noses, lips, and other features, sometimes with makeup, sometimes even with surgery. Did Opa worry, setting out, about whether his blue eyes and blond hair would be enough to disguise him? Was his Jewish ancestry visible in his features, after all? Certainly, he had the schnoz. Would he have been able to style his hair while he travelled, combed back and up the way he liked it, or did it frizz out like a mad scientist's? I ran my hand over my own curls, which I'd smoothed down with product.

The train just stopped in The Hague. On Saturday, July 18th, 1942, Opa boarded the train in this station. I mean, Jos. He wasn't Opa then, didn't have a wife or children, let alone grandchildren. As planned, his colleague met him at the station. Jos didn't specify in his journal, but the colleague must have worked with him at Royal Dutch Shell before the company was required to fire all its Jewish employees. Jos's colleague accompanied him to the south of the country, where the colleague had family who did business in Belgium and could change guilders for Belgian Francs. And his brother, Sam, surprised him too, took the train with them to Rotterdam—"A kindness," Jos wrote, "which I particularly appreciate, and which helps me to get over the depression of the farewell at home, where I had to leave my mother behind quite alone."

I stayed on the train instead of disembarking somewhere near the border as Jos did. He picked up his bicycle, which he'd sent ahead the day before, and met up with a smuggler named Sjefke, who was in his late teens. Sjefke would help him cycle across the border on a side-road, and then take the bicycle itself as payment. Jos waited alone through the morning at the smuggler's home—"an unbelievably dirty hole," while Sjefke and his connections did some snooping, gathering information about the border guards' schedule that day and figuring out the safest time and place to cross.

I endeavour to make the best of long hours ahead. It is my first experience of this journey, and it will be followed by many other similar ones: an important part of the trip consists of waiting, endless hanging around, and doing nothing at all, which seems the most nerve-wracking part of the journey, not the hours when one is active, courting real danger.

His hosts insisted he eat before leaving—a meal that Jos found distasteful: "a big iron-pot with spuds." Then it was time to go.

In the dangerous zone, we will operate in single file—first Sjefke, then, a hundred metres behind him, a man in a cap. Again a hundred metres behind him: myself. Provided I orient myself to the cap, and in the event that he waves—sign of danger—return immediately at full speed the way I came—it seems that my guides consider that I'll be reasonably safe.

For the time being, my guides cycle together and I follow them from a short distance like a lackey, out of the village and along the road to the border. We go on like this for the next two or three kilo-metres. I can't claim that I feel very confident—there is about the same kind of nervous tension you have before an exam for which you do not feel confident of the material, and here as there, once you're in the sweaty exam room: there is no way back.

My guides exit right over a narrow path, now at the distance previously arranged. So I slow up a bit and follow the cap. We go through heather and low bushes. After less than a quarter of an hour the danger signal comes. So I turn around, and when I look back over my shoulder and see that the cap is coming back too, I race away. After backtracking for about a kilometre, my rear guard, on whom I've kept watch by looking behind, gives me a sign that I can stop. There are now only the two of us, as Sjefke, who has apparently seen a German patrol, and has probably been observed by them too, has continued on his way so as to avoid suspicion. As border dwellers, these boys have the right to move freely in a narrow strip on both sides of the border.

We now follow another little road, and we make progress again, through thick and thin, because the heavy rains of recent times have flooded these little paths badly, and I am thankful to wear my leather coat, heavy boots, and waterproof leggings.

Near a little wood which provides some cover, I receive new instructions. My friend and refuge will cross the next stretch of open heather to see if everything beyond is safe. When I see him turn right near the pine wood which forms a barrier on one side, I can also proceed. So said—so done. When everything is apparently safe, I follow the appointed path, turn right near the pine wood, and a moment later come to a fork in the road. Now what? I look along one path which goes through cultivated fields. I see somebody with a bicycle talking to a farmer: no cap! The other road leads to a group of farms: no cap! Never before in my life have I been so fond of a cheap little light-coloured cap. I decide to wait, because to follow what might be the wrong road could be fatal. Thank God: after five minutes my friend appears again near the farms, and I rush towards him like a fly to a syrup pot. We meander for a little while through bushes and cultivated land, then my guide stops and gives me the sign to join him. He tells me we are in Belgium and that we have passed the dangerous zone. Suddenly I am aware that I am sweating like an otter and that my tongue sticks to my palate. But—under that cap I see a fire-red head from which drops of perspiration roll down, and when that face confesses that it is in urgent need of a beer, I realize with a certain satisfaction that I was not the only one who had been anxious.

A noise behind us on the road makes us jump: look there's Sjefke trundling along! It appears that he was the capless cyclist whom I had just seen just talking to the farmer. I cannot actually understand the explanation that follows, but it doesn't matter anymore. On we go, first along smuggling paths, then along roads. My friends ride together again—and I follow fifty metres behind them. A German military motorcycle with a sidecar comes roaring around the corner and startles me half to death. Otherwise: no further emotions.

We arrive in a village, and suddenly my guides slip into a small passage between two houses—visit to our first Flemish pub, which they call a staminee. Apart from being thirsty it appears that there is another more serious reason for this visit. On a crossroad a bit further into the village there is a check-post with three gendarmes who would probably stop me because of my suitcase, which I have behind me on my bicycle, and once these chaps start checking they will certainly also ask me for my identity card. The message is that I'd better watch out.

For the time being we drink beer and chat with the daughter of the family, apparently well-known to my friends. Sjefke tries to get out of the rest of his job. A rain shower, which broke out but minutes ago, serves as pretext for him to suggest that I should stay here until about six o'clock and then continue by bus, but I don't take his bait. After a little while when it's dry again we leave the house by the back, on the advice of the daughter, through a passage between a couple of estates, then along little paths through cultivated land and past farms.

Ten minutes later we are back on the main road on the other side of the village with the safe cover of a couple of hundred metres, including a bend, between our expedition and the gendarmes.

Half an hour later we reach our destination in the pouring rain and choose one of three pubs guarding the tram stop and wait for its arrival. A group of German soldiers who apparently have to take the same tram come and keep us company. Consequently, our conversation dries up remarkably quickly, and when the tram appears shortly after half past three, I say goodbye to my new friends as inconspicuously as possible.

A bit tired from all the emotions, but apart from that as fit as a fiddle, I travel on to Antwerp and eat a sandwich which I carried with me from home—the conductor winks when he sees me feasting, and I wink back: life isn't so bad after all.

☀ My own train stopped again in Antwerp; I was in Belgium. If I were a different kind of writer—a different kind of person—a man, maybe—I would have arranged to bicycle into Brussels, like Jos did. Of course it occurred to me that in Jos's, position, in his time, I would have been doomed. Fleeing over borders? Trying to appear inconspicuous, walking foreign cities without appearing foreign? It would have been impossible.

Like Jos, I travelled on to Brussels. He stayed with a friend of a friend; all he had was an address and a name, and he didn't record how he found the place. As my train pulled into the city's central station, I pulled out my phone to calculate my walk to the hotel. But my phone's screen was black. The battery had died—no GPS. I followed signs out the station's main exit and set out in what I believed must be the direction of my hotel, only to realize five minutes later I was at an intersection that shouldn't be there. Did I set out from the train station in the wrong direction? I retraced my steps to the station (a straight line; I didn't turn any corners: then I would be hopelessly lost) and set out again, in a different direction. No luck. I retraced my steps to the train station and found a taxi.

"You're Italian, right?" the driver asked me in French.

"Canadienne..."

"Ah," he switched to English. "That's why you look like Celine Dion."

"Nooo," I laughed.

"Oh, yes! So much! I love Celine Dion!"

I laughed again.

Of course, I didn't look the slightest bit like Celine Dion. I looked Jewish, which looked a little like Italian. For the rest of the day, I wondered why I didn't say, I'm Jewish, and knew the answer: whenever I said, "I'm Jewish," I felt two things: fear and guilt. Fear that the person I'm talking to would turn on me, if only with a subtle drop in friendliness and that familiar, "Oh," and the penetrating glance meaning, *you look almost like a regular white person, but wait, no, no, I can see it*. But I also felt guilty, guilty for lying, heard Oma's voice in my head: "You're not Jewish, darling. You're a shiksa, I'm afraid. A goy, just like me."

My hotel room in Brussels was big and bright, with a long row of windows and a giant bed with a pristine white cover that I untucked from the mattress corners before lifting the mattress to check the box spring. In the early 2000s, bedbugs made a comeback in North America and Europe. Before long, the bloodthirsty apple-seed-sized demons were found in American libraries and Canadian clothing stores, in European apartment buildings, and especially, in hotels all over the world. I studied hundreds of images of the flat reddish monsters online, in diagram and photo form, and memorized their life cycle. As I read, my skin tingled. I checked my bed every evening, trying to look when Lev was showering so he wouldn't catch me, but I often woke in the night with a start, to bolt out of bed and search for the creature I'd just felt crawl over my leg. Walking down the street, I'd ducked into doorways to roll up my jeans and examine my calves, sure I'd just felt a bug that had accompanied me in the seams of my clothes.

My rabid internet searches eventually led me to an article, and then another, on "delusions of parasitosis," which is exactly what it sounds like, that is, a "monosymptomatic hypochondrial psychosis" whereby sufferers believe, incorrectly, that they are infested with parasites. Then I read about the "matchbox sign," otherwise known as the "specimen sign." People with delusions of parasitosis are known to collect little bits of lint and hair, skin fragments, and other household micro-debris, and to keep them in a box, as proof. I read that paragraph, and from one moment to the next, I stopped believing I had bedbugs, like waking from a dream. The little Tupperware on my dresser was no longer full of bedbug sheddings, but of sofa lint and sock fuzz and my own hair, and the two tiny marks on my belly were not bedbug bites, but scratches from my own fingernails. That crawling sensation on my skin (called "formication," after the Latin *formica* for ants) was not evidence of bedbugs, but evidence that I had been thinking much too much about bedbugs.

But checking for bedbugs in hotel rooms was rational, and this one didn't have any.

I plugged in my phone. But I needed to eat and recharging the phone would take too long—I would have to go out without it. Find supper somewhere close. Somewhere that involved walking in one straight line.

The guy at the reception desk gave me directions to a restaurant less than five minutes away—just turn right and keep going and you can't miss it—but six minutes later, no restaurant. Somehow, I was lost. I stepped into a clothing store for a few minutes, then stepped out, and nothing looked familiar. When learning about developmental topographical disorientation, I'd read somewhere, that without cognitive maps, we effectively fail to achieve "object permanence"—like babies, we only really believe in the world we can see and touch, and when we leave a room, we can't be sure it still exists. At least, we can't be sure where or when it exists, and whether we'll ever see it again. But the hotel did still exist, it had to, and I retraced my steps, hoping that I was indeed retracing my steps. Six minutes later, I stood at the hotel reception desk again, asking for a repeat of the directions.

Outside, I realized I'd headed left instead of right. The whole time I'd known so certainly I was heading right, I'd been heading left.

After finding the restaurant, a cafeteria-style vegetarian situation where I ate soup and salad, I retraced my steps again, and safely in my room, opened several windows wide before lying in the middle of the big white bed, under the crisp sheets and puffy comforter, still not tired, but much more at ease. On my laptop, I booked a few hotels for the next part of my trip, in France. I had a suitcase now, and an umbrella. My phone's battery had edged up toward charged. I wondered if Opa ever washed his clothes during his trip. How did he smell by the end of it?

Jos—alone, cut off from everyone he knew, with two hundred cigarettes to his name and genocidal occupiers at the next table—was so stoical, but me, I was afraid, even when there was little to fear. Mostly afraid of getting lost. But also, afraid I'd sit on a public toilet and contract herpes. Afraid I'd get diarrhea when far from any toilet. Afraid I'd lose my wallet and passport to a pickpocket. Well, any of those things could happen. Maybe not the first one. (It could happen, but I read online, I'd have to sit down within moments of the herpes-infected urinator vacating the area, and I'd have to sit in a puddle of still-warm pee.)

The first time I travelled this part of the world by train, at nineteen, with my sister and our canvas backpacks, we began in England, where we stayed at the home of our parents' friends. We took the subway from the airport and exited at the correct station, taken up by the flow of humans, humans, so many humans, all running to their connecting trains. Our parents' friends lived in a large house with many rooms, each with a closed door that had to be opened with a key. They figured my sister and I could sleep in the same bed, and so did everyone we stayed with those three weeks. By the end of our three weeks of constant togetherness, we flew back to Ottawa and then didn't speak to or see each other for about a month.

That first night in London, I couldn't sleep. I felt like—how would I ever get back to Canada? It just seemed too unlikely that my body, now in London, could somehow reappear over there, over the ocean. My live body, back in Canada again, at the specific location of my home (that is, the house I lived in with five roommates)? No. I was just too far away. My sister seemed asleep, the house dark and silent, and I tiptoed down to the kitchen, where I phoned my on-again, off-again boyfriend in Ottawa, who was always reminding me that he wasn't my boyfriend, using our hosts' phone.

"Are you phoning from Europe?" he said.

"Yes, well, England. I can't talk long. I'm just calling to say goodbye."

"Goodbye?"

"I'm going to die before I make it back to Canada."

"Um. Okay."

"So I wanted to say goodbye, and thanks for everything, just in case."

"Okay, well. I really don't think you're going to die. Why do you think you're going to die?"

"I just have a feeling, a really strong feeling."

"Hm. Okay. Well, thanks for thinking of me," he said. "But I really don't think you're going to die."

"Fine," I said. "But just in case."

Years later, I considered apologizing to our hosts, but the apology seemed even crazier than the two-minute phone call itself, which they may or may not have noticed on their phone bill (but probably did).

I didn't need to feel lost right now, though. All I had to do was follow my grandfather's directions, like Dorothy, following the yellow brick road.

I needed to focus on my trip, on Opa. Jos. I examined his hand-drawn map and thought of Yael's imitation of me scrutinizing a map: "Oh, look. Lines." The shapes on the page just failed to mean anything to me, had no discernible relation to the world, or to me in it. In Grade 9, I once fled a geography test, retreated to the nurse's office, which had a bed. I knew what my teacher thought about the sudden onslaught of illness as she lay the test on my desk. And yes, I was faking to get out of the test. Sort of. Also, when I looked at the map of the continents, which I was meant to fill in with the names of countries, all those shapes and lines, blobs and borders, I swayed in my seat, dizzy and nauseated, and all the blood drained out of my arms and legs so they barely felt part of me, prickled cold and alien, too long, flopping against my desk and the chair.

I took one last look at Opa's journal.

—a couple of hours later I can lie in a comfortable bed and think back contentedly about my first travel day, but those thoughts don't last long.

I tucked myself into bed.

Soon I'd see someone I knew, thank goodness, someone I adored, actually, someone I thought about almost constantly. I thought about the nights we spent talking, in May, at the writing retreat where we got to know each other. I thought about the bourbon we drank, how I'd asked him, "What do you think it means to be an adult?" and he said, "I don't find the idea of being an adult very interesting." He told me one night that he hated love, and had no interest in dating anyone, so I made myself stop staring at his hands and his lips that way, and then one evening he held my hand and kissed me, and came to my room and let me kiss and kiss him back.

Matteo had green eyes, and he loved ice cream, but only very good ice cream, and he wrote poems about a lonely guy who wanted but didn't want love, that made everyone laugh and cry. Matteo didn't like crowds, and he spoke Italian, and he preferred solitude to dating, in general, and he'd once had a Norwegian girlfriend, of whom I was now irrationally jealous. And Matteo ate rice cakes every day for breakfast, with peanut butter, and he had long eyelashes, and did he really hate love? He would come from Italy on Monday, to stay with me for two nights, and we'd share the puffy white bed. Since May, he'd visited me once in Calgary. Now he was spending much of the summer with his Italian side of the family, near Rome. Both in Europe, an opportunity to meet up. I was supposed to be thinking about Opa, and the Holocaust, but I was thinking about this guy, and the way he'd leaned his head back and pretended to eat the pollen floating down from the trees, and the things he'd whispered in the dark. I couldn't wait to see Matteo, to talk and talk with him again, and to get naked with him again. That's not what I was supposed to be thinking about. How was I supposed to feel? Where was my sense of gravitas? I didn't know the word "gravitas" until a reviewer accused my novel, *Cricket in a Fist*, of too much of it, or of trying too hard for it. I had to look the word up. He thought my book too heavy, with no relief. Funny. I thought the book was funny.

But sometimes I told stories I found funny, and no one laughed, it was true. Yael hadn't laughed when I told her about the endless arguments at Oma and Opa's house, always about the same thing: were Chloe and I Jewish or not? Oma sitting at the kitchen table in Barrie, chopping fresh tomatoes for soup, which we would eat for lunch, fresh and flavourful with gobs of thick cream, did her best to win us over. Did we know that Jewish women had to shave their heads when they married? Did we know that Jewish women had to sleep alone when they had their periods, because they were considered dirty? Did we know that Jewish people were obsessed with their own victimhood?

Later on those afternoons, I lay by the pool holding a book. I remembered Chloe, on a towel across the pool, paused in her drawing to stare into the water, her eyes huge and brown and full of thoughts, a mustard-yellow pencil crayon in her hand. My sister had black-brown hair and a deep tan. It was hard to believe we were from the same part of the planet. Just like Opa and his brother Sam: one freckly pale and one olive complected. My mother sat in the deckchair beside me in a skimpy black and red bikini. She had long hair still, brown with scattered strands of grey; she didn't really like long hair, but had told me that she felt pressured to keep it that way. Hair dye, though, she refused. That summer, she was rereading her favourite book, Douglas R. Hofstadter's *Gödel, Escher, Bach*, along with Nagel and Newman's *Gödel's Proof*. The massive volume and its slim companion both lay open on the hot concrete, and she paused to scribble symbols on a pad of graph paper.

"Mum," I said.

She kept writing. The Hofstadter was open to Escher's Möbius strip, a print of a wooden model sliced through vertically, with a parade of ants traversing it in an endless circle. My mother had made Möbius strips at the kitchen table in Maryland, shown Chloe and me how to make our own and then draw a vertical circle in pencil, away away away from its starting point until suddenly we both found ourselves back where we'd started, and we'd drawn on both sides of the looped paper without lifting the pencil. How? Because, she explained, these strips of paper have only one side. Each transformed by a twist and a piece of tape into a two-dimensional object.

With my eyes, I followed Escher's ants along the Möbius strip, around and around, over and under, trapped forever, because they believed themselves in one world but had found themselves in another—because they believed in a dimension that did not exist. I squinted up at the perfect blue sky.

"Mum," I said. "Mum."

At home, I'd decorated the walls and ceilings of my bedroom with glow-in-dark stars, so that at night, when I couldn't see the space posters taped to my walls, I could imagine myself floating in space, and lying by the pool, eyes tearing from staring too long at the brightness, I thought again that if I get could get far away enough and look back, I'd finally understand how everything was laid out.

"*Mum.*"

"Mmmm."

"Mum?"

"*Yes?*"

"If you could go into space, but you could never come back, would you do it?"

She stopped writing. Looked up at the sky. "Yes."

My mother was supposed to say. "What do you mean? Would you?" And then I could say, "Yes." And then she could say, "But so many people would miss you so much! You have so much to accomplish in your lifetime *here*." And then she'd ask questions and I'd answer them, until I understood why I felt like a bug pinned to a board, and understood how to unpin myself. But *yes* was all she said, and once again I had no response, only this new piece of information about my mother, that however badly I wanted to want to escape, she *actually* wanted to.

The pool's blue water glittered, looked so fresh and clean, but wasn't, because that morning Opa had scooped out a drowned squirrel in a net on the end of a long pole, and we had to wait for the germs to die. Now, on the other side of the black iron fence, Opa pushed his lawn mower, a Tilley hat covering his dense still-blond curls and protecting his face. He'd already had some skin-cancer spots burned off. He had a big nose like mine, too, but he looked fine, looked good, handsome, a man. He was old and getting older, over eighty, had retired long before I was born, that's how old he was. Once he'd run away from Nazis; once he'd seduced a beautiful young military ambulance driver who turned out to be Betty, who turned out to be Mary, who'd someday be Oma, and once Mary had left him, because he was impossible, because he banned conversation during dinner, and slammed his fist on the table if anyone disobeyed, all because of what happened during the war. Because of what happened to his mother. Once he'd won Oma back. Once he'd earned a lot of money in Holland and Indonesia and England, calculating the economics of oil and petrol production and refinement, and now he had a good pension, now he was a nice old man with a lawn mower. I loved him so much.

But what happened to his mother, *exactly*? And why did Oma leave, and how did he win her back? Whenever I asked Mum these questions, she'd answered in a foreboding tone, through clenched teeth, as though her jaw had clamped down to keep the words from getting out.

But wait. What about—

But I only got a bit at a time. *We don't talk about that.*

But wait. But wait—

At the table in Maryland, in that kitchen with the orange and brown paisley wallpaper and lime green fridge, Mum had handed Chloe and me scissors and told us to cut along the lines we'd drawn, to snip our

Möbius strips down the middle. "What do you think you'll find?" she asked.

"Two loops." But we stretched them out and found no separation; each of us held a longer, slimmer, twistier version of the same.

FOR SUNDAY, JULY 19TH, 1942, Jos wrote a half-page entry recounting his meeting with a business acquaintance in Brussels to make plans for his trip into France. The acquaintance would help him change guilders for French francs, but Jos would have to wait until Tuesday to pick up the cash. The 21st, he'd forgotten, was Belgian Independence Day, and so everything would be closed on Monday, making for a long weekend. "On the whole," he concluded, "I have spent this day in measured rest; besides, it is horrible weather, with incessant rain from early morning till late in the evening, which prevents touristic excursions."

That same day, Himmler gave the order to complete the Final Solution in the General Government. The Germans confiscated bicycles in Rotterdam and The Hague. Anne Frank wrote nothing in her diary that day. For the whole two weeks of Jos's journey, Anne Frank wrote nothing. She and her family had just gone into hiding on July 6th, and as she settled into her new life, she found that nothing really happened, nothing worth writing down.

☀ Brussels was rainy on Sunday, July 19th, 2015, too, but I decided to go out anyway, following my GPS under my new red umbrella after I ate a croissant with scrambled eggs and cheese and fruit in the hotel's little dining area. I chose Place du Jeu de Balle for its flea market and its appealing name, pictured little Victorian children standing in a circle, tossing a ball, bustling market stalls in the square behind them. The picture in my head came from one of the antique children's books in Oma and Opa's old den. The route took me back through the neighbourhood I'd found the night before when I was lost. With its narrow, winding streets, this part of the city seemed built entirely of stone, all hard grey, cobbled and mortared.

On my way, I passed a poster advertising a Jewish History Museum. Should I have gone that way instead? Of course I should, but I didn't want to abandon my plan. Lev would have insisted, would have followed that arrow without question, because in a foreign city a Jewish museum is home, if not quite as much a home as a synagogue. That's what Mimi, my paternal grandmother, would have advised if I told her I felt at a loss, away from everything familiar: find a synagogue. Move to another city, travel to another country, find your people, and words you know, words about you and for you. But I never learned that language, didn't quite believe its speakers spoke to or about me, never learned to feel at home in those homes, though I tried.

Another place Mimi had always felt at home was in a clothing store. Me, too. I browsed through a store filled with ruffled colourful dresses and bought a green not-too-wild one, along with a pink shrug, a big pink fabric flower sewn into its shoulder. That's it: no more clothes on this trip. I didn't have the space in my suitcase and didn't want more to carry; I'd heard the subway stations in Paris had no escalators.

And then the flea market—a hundred or more stalls sprawled out on a cobblestoned square, though many of the stalls weren't stalls, but piles. Piles of sweaters, piles of blankets, piles of fur coats. Piles of jewelry. Plenty of antique or antique-like furniture stood not quite in piles, but in clumps. A musty smell of damp wool rose from a pile of hats, and I leaned closer, toward a fold of purple felt. Couldn't bring myself to touch it. Bedbugs. The sheer mass of stuff, damp rained-on mounded stuff, overwhelmed me, seemed to go on forever, and my hair and my jean jacket and the pile of hats oozed humidity, fibres musty and thickened in the drizzle. A downpour seemed imminent, so

I crossed the square and stepped inside the sprawling red-brick church on the square's far side.

I sat in a pew near the front, the altar, and rain fell hard on the roof. Rabbi Gerry had told us in the conversion class I took with Lev that Orthodox Jews were forbidden from entering churches at all. "But Rabbi," I now imagined myself waving my hand in the air. "Rabbi, what if you were out in the rain and saw a church, and it was empty, just an empty church, and you were very cold and tired—could you go in *then*?"

My family was baffled when I told them I was taking that class, that it meant a lot to Lev and his parents. I was converting to Judaism? Converting from what? "Do they know about your relatives who died in the camps?" Dad said. He added, "You're Jewish enough for Hitler." Was I turning *religious*? my mother wanted to know. But my in-laws weren't sniffing for the stench of death, and not for piety, either. I may have had three Jewish grandparents, but my mother's mother wasn't Jewish, so I wasn't either. Israel wouldn't grant me citizenship, my mother-in-law noted, and if Israel said I was not a Jew, that was good enough, or bad enough, for her. Even more than that, though, my in-laws wanted someone who'd gone to Jewish summer camps and knew the campfire songs as well as the blessings for bread and wine. Growing up, I didn't know about Jewish summer camp, though I would have begged not to go, as I begged not to go anyplace jam-packed with kids and bugs, both of which seemed out for my blood. But as an adult, I realized that's where and when Yael and Lev each learned their home was among Jews. Yael and Lev learned belonging at the campfire, pubescent, singing and praying, eating kosher hot dogs and getting felt up to the call of loons across an Ontario lake—that's where the feeling of belonging wrapped around each of them like a Hudson's Bay blanket.

My grandmother Mimi had encouraged me, in my twenties, to find a nice Jewish boy to marry. I said, "But a nice Jewish boy wouldn't consider me a nice Jewish girl."

"What do you mean?" she said.

Maybe my father hadn't told Mimi that my sister and I celebrated Christmas, and didn't know when the Jewish holidays fell, and didn't know any Hebrew blessings, not even the Sh'ma.

Dad told this joke once, when we were at Oma and Opa's house for Christmas. A Jewish man, Moishe Tennenbaum, wants to join a restricted club, so he practices talking and walking and dressing like a gentile, and shows up, and they ask him, "What's your name?" Moishe says, "Martin Taylor." They ask him, "and what's your ethnic background?" He responds, "I'm a goy."

I didn't get that joke. "What's a goy?" I asked, and Oma had to explain, "Someone who's not a Jew. But no one would say, I'm a goy. Only Jewish people use that word. It's not a very nice word. It means a non-Jew but means it as an insult. Because," she went on, "Jews believe themselves the chosen people, chosen by God, and better than everyone else."

"No," said Dad. "It's not like that. It's just a—a—word. A synonym for 'gentile.'"

"No it isn't, Bernard," said Oma. "It's derogatory. And so is 'gentile,' for that matter."

"'Gentile,'" said Dad. "Is definitely not derogatory. I never understood either of those words as insulting in any way."

"It's not insulting?" I said.

"It *is*, darling," said Oma.

Dad frowned so hard I couldn't look at his face without feeling my own bones wrench down frown-ward.

"Tricia is a goy," Oma went on. "Judaism is matrilineal. Passed down through the mother," she looked from Dad to Chloe and me. "I'm not Jewish, so Trish isn't Jewish, so you girls aren't Jewish." She turned back to my father. "Sorry to tell you this, Bernie, but you married a shiksa. Just like Jos did."

"Darling," said Opa. "All right."

"You know she *is* a shiksa, darling," Oma told him. Oma and Opa always called each other *darling* to express disapproval. That was the closest they came to arguing in front of us.

"What's a shiksa?" Chloe asked, and I avoided Dad's face, which was now frowning so hard it had started to shake.

Oma said, "Shiksa is a derogatory word for a non-Jewish woman who's married a Jewish man. If you girls marry Jewish men, you'll be shiksas, too. And Hitler is long dead. I daresay he's not calling anyone much of anything these days."

Dad's voice was at the edge of yelling now. "No you *won't* be—you girls won't be—you—you'll be perfect Jewish wives if you marry Jewish men, which I hope you do."

"*What?*" said Mum. "What are you—"

"Enough of this nonsense," said Opa, slightly louder than usual.

Dad went on, "Mary, you don't know—you don't—you just don't know what you're—" He caught my eye and shifted his tone to lighter. "I just don't know where you get these unusual ideas, Oma. These eccentric ideas of yours." The high, fake laugh at the end the sentence made my shoulders clench.

Many years later, I started reading more and more about the Holocaust, and then about Judaism. Research for my master's thesis, my first novel. By thirty, I had finished my degree, and almost finished my last draft for the publisher, when I bought and read *How to Run a Traditional Jewish Household*, by Blu Greenberg. Just to make sure I hadn't messed up the Jewish traditions in my novel's mostly non-traditional household. As I read about Orthodox life, the blessings for bread and wine, the ritual immersion in the mikvah after menstruation, the gift of Shabbat, I pictured myself running a traditional Jewish household, with every task and blessing and culinary process laid out, a rulebook. According to Greenberg, "Judaism takes the physical realities of life and imposes on them a set of rules or rituals. By doing so, it transforms this reality or that basic necessity of life into something beyond itself." Judaism, she writes, finds holiness in "the experience of waking up alive each morning, or eating to nourish the body, or having sex with one's mate"; it finds holiness in "establishing clear demarcation between work and rest or investing everyday speech with a measure of sanctity."

My first book, the one about a Jewish family, was finished and with the designer by the time I placed a profile on the dating site J-Date. I'd first heard about this service from Oma of all people, when she explained, with great disdain and amusement, that the owner of her local bookstore met her husband on a website called "Jew Date." Shoshana, Oma said, went on Jew Date because she was racist. "Looking for a someone Jewish, darling, that's racism; that's what racism *is*. A goy's not enough for her, is he? That's what racism *is*."

Turned out, it wasn't called Jew Date. One evening I was home, clicking around, and, trying not to imagine Oma's disdain, I posted a profile, scrolled through the men's profiles. Just to see. Holiness? Sanctity? Imagine if I could cross that threshold. If I were to run a traditional Jewish household, who might I run it with? There weren't many eligible Jewish bachelors in my age category; I lived in Alberta. Within half an hour, I received a message from an earnest-looking guy with black curly hair and glasses. In his profile photo, he lifted a loaf of challah like a trophy, face set and serious. Oh, no, I thought. He's mistaken me for a real Jew! In a panic, I deleted my profile. A week later, I went for brunch with some new friends, and they introduced me to a serious-faced man. Hungover, I took a few minutes to realize this serious-faced man was the challah guy from J-Date; luckily, he didn't seem to recognize me. He and I, it seemed, had a lot of mutual friends, and we all ate many more brunches together. He was smart and ambitious, decent and nice. He was Lev.

Lev did not mistake me for a real Jew, but he thought I had the potential to become one. After we'd been dating for a while, he even took me to services at a temple, which, he explained, was what Reform Jews called synagogues. Rabbi Gerry, a skinny man in his fifties, led the service. There was a bar mitzvah that day, and a bat mitzvah; a thirteen-year-old boy, and then a thirteen-year-old girl, read their Torah portions, both in clear, proud voices. After the service, we stood in the foyer, and Rabbi Gerry recognized us as newcomers, and came up to chat.

"I'm not exactly Jewish," I felt obliged to explain, before the rabbi heard my Hebrew first name and looked at my face and mistook me for someone who belonged there. Or, even worse, maybe he'd already recognized me as an imposter. "My father's Jewish and my mother's father was Jewish, though," I said.

"She wants to learn more about it," said Lev, who felt no need to explain or justify his own identity.

"As far the Reform movement is concerned," Rabbi Gerry told me, "you're Jewish. If you have a Jewish parent, you're Jewish." He leaned in as he spoke, and since he stood at around my height, we looked directly into each other's faces. His body language told me he was on my side. Lev put his hand on my back. Together, they were ushering me in.

"I *am*?"

"Absolutely."

"But—I wasn't raised in a Jewish household—"

"I wasn't either," he said. "Not really. You can have your own Jewish household now. And those ideas are outdated, the matrilineal line. This is what Reform Judaism is all about—updating outmoded ideas, while preserving the core of the religion. As far as I'm concerned, you're Jewish. You're welcome in our congregation. And if you want to learn more, I offer a course. Once a week for a year." He told Lev, "You'd come together. It's a conversion class, but you could take it just to learn."

"*Could* I convert?" I asked. "If I wanted to? Even though you already consider me Jewish? Just to—sort of—feel like there was no longer any ambiguity?"

"Yes," said the rabbi. "At the end of the course, if you still wanted to convert, I would convert you. Absolutely."

"And would I be unquestionably Jewish, then? I mean, no one could say I wasn't?"

"Well, no," he said. "Orthodox Jews still wouldn't consider you Jewish—not unless you were converted by an Orthodox rabbi. The government of Israel still wouldn't consider you Jewish. Unfortunately, some institutions still have some catching up to do."

"Okay," I nodded. "I'll think about this. Thank you, Rabbi."

"You're welcome, Naomi," he said. "I'm so glad you're thinking about coming back to us."

Coming *back*. To *us*.

I was no longer an atheist, I told my friends. I was now officially agnostic. Agnostic! Oma and Mum would just collapse if they knew, they would freak, Opa would turn over in his grave—his ashes would turn over under that tree—I mean, *agnostic*! I was going to take a conversion class, a couple of hours a week for a whole year. "From a Reform rabbi," I explained. "Lev grew up in the Conservative tradition, which is more liberal than Orthodox, and Reform is even more liberal than that. In fact," I went on, having learned these distinctions only recently myself, "Reform rabbis consider me a Jew already, since my father is Jewish, so the conversion will just be for me, symbolic, to *feel* more Jewish, you know? And for Lev and his family, to see that I'm *committed* to being more Jewish."

I told my friends, with an unfamiliar elation, that I was going to learn Hebrew and stop eating pork. Or at least learn the blessings for bread and wine, and stop working on Saturdays. I was going to do these things; I hadn't started yet.

"Don't you realize that Eastern European Jews are related?" Oma asked. "Your children will be inbred."

She told me that according to Jewish tradition, a groom's parents drag him into the room of his wedding to that canopy-nonsense, while he does his best to run away.

I repeated all this to my then-future husband, and he denied that we were related, and also denied that tradition dictated any such drag-in. He would know—he'd attended a private Jewish elementary school, not to mention a dozen or more Jewish weddings. Lev liked to tell a story about a speech he gave in Grade 7, in which he talked about the "Cathoholics" who populated Haiti. He had never met a Catholic (never mind a Haitian), and did not know what one was. I was grateful in contrast for my own public school experience, with classmates from all kinds of backgrounds. But I was mesmerized by the fact of Lev's early theological education, the ancientness, the solemnity.

"What did you learn at your Jewish school about God?" I asked, when we were already engaged.

He pursed his lips sardonically, sang, "HaShem is here, HaShem is there, HaShem is truly everywhere..."

But what about the profound intellectual discussions I'd pictured? Had they discussed Maimonides? Had they talked about Spinoza, and whether he was really an atheist, which he denied? Had they wrestled with why, if God is just, bad things happen to good people?

"No," he said. "HaShem is truly everywhere. That's about it."

"What does HaShem mean?" I asked.

He looked a bit shocked, and explained that HaShem was Hebrew, literally, for The Name, and often stands in for any actual name of God, since uttering the name itself is a serious matter.

"You know how religious Jews are always saying, *Baruch HaShem?*" he said.

"Sure." (I didn't, but I did know that *Baruch*, as well as being Spinoza's first name, meant "blessed," so put two and two together.)

But HaShem is truly everywhere? That's what they learned at Jewish private school? That can't have been quite *it*. Not quite, no. They also learned the Sh'ma. Judaism, they learned, begins with and rests on that prayer: *Sh'ma Yisrael, Adonai Eloheinu, Adonai Eḥad.* Hear O Israel, the Lord is our God, the Lord is One.

I learned the Sh'ma in the conversion class with Rabbi Gerry. He told us converts-in-training to chant it again and again until it became our own. I chanted it so much I found myself absent-mindedly singing in the shower, singing in Hebrew about God while I lathered my hair— but I didn't chant the Sh'ma enough, I guess, because it didn't quite become my own. At services, I still felt like a visitor to a well-practiced game, grateful but mostly alarmed when someone took pity on me and tossed me the ball.

I had a bad attitude in the conversion class. For the first time in my life I was that student waving her hand in the air, holding things up with my but-but-buts. Though I was always arguing with Oma and Mum's blanket dismissal of all religion and religion-affiliated behaviours—accusing them of throwing the baby out with the bathwater—now I couldn't stop arguing with the rabbi, sometimes using Oma's words. But Rabbi, can you explain the principle behind reforming a religion? If the religion is so fundamentally flawed, then why hold onto it? And at what point have you changed it so much that it's not the same religion anyway? Or not a religion at all? I wanted to debate him, but mostly because I wanted to lose. I wanted Rabbi Gerry to convince me.

"What about a Jew who doesn't want to be a Jew anymore?" I asked one week. "What about a lapsed Jew?"

"That doesn't happen," said Rabbi Gerry. Jews, he explained, just don't do that. It's not about faith, like Christianity. You don't ask yourself whether you believe, and whether, therefore, you're a Jew.

"But my grandfather did."

"Your grandfather did what?"

"Said he didn't believe in it, so wasn't a Jew."

"I don't know what to say," said Rabbi Gerry. "I've never heard of anything like that." He paused. "Let's get back to the months of the Jewish calendar. The leap month, Adar 1—"

"But, Rabbi," I said. "What I really want to know is, for Jews, for you, is there a God? And, if there is, I mean, since there is—what is it?" I struggled a little for my next breath, embarrassed. I'd asked the way a child would, the way I had as a child. But how else to begin? Lev groaned a little beside me; I was always asking him the same question, and he didn't look any happier than the rabbi about trying to answer it.

Rabbi Gerry shook his head. "No," he said. "Too heavy. Too heavy. I can't answer that. Let's go over the calendar one more time—"

But now much of the class was nodding. Yeah, they said. We want an answer to *that*.

"I can't—I can't really—well." The rabbi paused. Keeping a Jewish household, Rabbi Gerry said finally, is important primarily because children need structure. It's unhealthy to grow up without rites and rituals to organize your life. Both the progress of life and the meaning of it. "Judaism's not about faith," he added. "Faith is a Christian notion."

"Then you're saying it's important for us to be observant Jews because it's psychologically healthy for our children?" I knew I was that student, the one who won't shut up. I couldn't believe I was that student.

Rabbi Gerry paused. "Yes."

Wait—then he saw no reason for an adult to become observant, an adult without children, without any intention to have children? Is there nothing in it for the adult herself?

Before I could ask, Adah, the lawyer who grew up Orthodox in Teaneck, New Jersey, spoke up. "But," she said. "When you pray, do you believe someone hears you?" She was marrying a pretty-faced construction worker named Jordan, who sat beside her, silent, with his baseball cap pulled low. Reform Judaism was a compromise for them, somewhere between zero and eight million.

Rabbi Gerry blinked up at the ceiling. "No," he admitted, finally.

A murmur ran through the class. Someone gasped.

"*No?*" said Adah.

"No. But. That's not the point. Let me rephrase. Someone hears me. I hear me. My children hear me. I hear them."

"But not God?" Adah, with her blonde curls and solid arms, was a good lawyer. I could see that from her posture. Her voice rose, her spine straightened. "I really can't accept that you're saying this," she said. "You're mocking the religion I grew up with."

"I'm not mocking—"

"You are. You stand there mocking Orthodox Jews every week, but I don't say anything. You talk about them—my family by the way—like they're idiots. But I don't say anything, because this class isn't for me. Why are we here, Rabbi? What's Jordy supposed to think? You're telling him he's joining a religion where you pray constantly to a non-existent God? I don't want Jordy to think that's what Judaism is. That's not the

Judaism I know. Wait, Rabbi, I'm not done. I understand that this is *Reform* Judaism, but you're taking the reforming too far."

What was Jordy supposed to think? What was I supposed to think? I didn't take a class from a rabbi to have my atheism reinforced. I wanted my atheism coaxed out of me, by someone who embodied wisdom too potent to resist.

✴ Sitting in that Catholic church in Brussels, I was thinking about Rabbi Gerry and the conversion class, but what I was really thinking about was Matteo, coming to see me the next day. I had a lot of feelings about Matteo, or one feeling, but a lot of it. But I didn't have many stories about Matteo yet. My stories about Matteo were mostly Matteo and me telling each other stories, and talking about writing, and hiking up Tunnel Mountain, and making out.

"What was it like being married?" Matteo had asked me, during one of our late-night talks in Banff.

"I don't know, we were together for years, so it was like lots of different things—"

"—yes, of course, but—"

"I don't know, I felt safe, sort of. Sort of anchored." I had felt safe enough to write a short story collection about heartbreak, to look back smugly at a time when I longed for intimacy and rarely touched another person. "But also—"

But also, I'd sometimes tell friends that Lev would meet someone more suitable and leave me. And I half believed myself as I said it. I felt anchored, but provisionally anchored. Earlier on the very day we split, I stopped at a coffee shop and ran into a friend who told me about a man who was in the midst of a divorce and had declared his love for her. She agreed to meet him for lunch on a patio, but his wife followed him there. She rode up on her bike and yelled at them from the sidewalk, "He's lying to you! You don't know him!" I told my friend, "Oh, I remember how hard it is, being single, trying to connect, and trusting the wrong people." I explained that marriage isn't easy either, but you compromise, and you keep working at it, and the point is, you're committed. Well, not that guy she met for lunch. But me. I said that and meant it when Lev had already decided to leave me.

Lev liked to tell me, to tell whole dinner parties, that he loved me because I was *so funny*. He'd tell this story about our first date, how he asked if I'd already eaten, and I said, "Yes, but I can throw up." Lev said, "I knew then that she was something special—I'd never met a woman who'd say something like that!" Oh no, I thought. Don't love me because I'm funny. You should love my soul, and my soul isn't funny. My soul is a deep dark pit. Or maybe my soul *is* funny. Maybe my soul is funny, and my anxiety is a deep dark pit. But why would anyone love a deep dark pit? Anyway—I don't believe in souls.

Lev loved dinner parties, and his eyes glazed over while I told him about my work, and sometimes he even picked up his phone to check Twitter while I was still talking, and sometimes my eyes glazed over while he talked about his work, and sometimes he blew his nose right on his hand, without using a tissue, and when he washed vegetables, he didn't really wash them at all, just splashed them with water. How much pesticide did I ingest throughout the eight years we were together? Also, I too often chose the company of others, the company of people who liked to talk and talk about books and stories and what it's like to be a person. I'd think of the first wife in Anne Michaels' novel *Fugitive Pieces*, the flighty first wife with her puns and friends, her red hair and flirty persona. I *was* that first wife. She wore a beret. I would never wear a beret. But otherwise. I pictured future-Lev telling people, at a dinner party, my first wife was funny, I'll give her that, but. Even then I imagined him finding a second wife like the one Anne Michaels had conjured up, clearly so much better, so much more wholesome and Jewish and sturdy and real. When I read *Fugitive Pieces*, all my sympathy lay with the maligned first wife.

The suddenness of our split shocked me, but I was not surprised. For a couple of weeks, things hadn't been right. Things hadn't been right for longer than that, but for a couple weeks, things had been different. For instance, I told Lev about a pair of shoes I might buy for the summer, and wanted to show him. His eyes widened in a kind of panic. "Just buy whatever shoes you want," he said. He didn't care what shoes near-future-me would wear. That future me was someone he'd never know. And we went to separate events at the same bar, mine a poetry reading, his a gathering of urban cycling enthusiasts, and when I went over to say hi, he didn't introduce me to the bicycle people, just muttered, "Don't you want to sit with your own friends?" Later, he told me he might apply for a job in Toronto, not in a what-do-you-think-about-moving-to-Toronto way, but in an I'm-making-plans-without-you way. I felt crazy accusing him, even as I said it, accusing him of this impossible thing, this absurd, impossible thing, of picturing his future without me.

Our marriage had to end. Separating was the right thing, but the suddenness shocked me. I curled like a fetus on my sofa for three weeks, and when mutual friends told me my ex wasn't fetal at all, but already seeking a mother for the children I hadn't wanted, I thought I'd die, and I couldn't cry or even breathe.

But the three weeks passed, and pretty soon Yael said, "You seem okay. You seem so okay, I'm waiting for you to lose your mind and kill someone." I *was* okay, far too okay, and I knew it. Relieved, even, as though I'd been waiting in anguish for the guillotine to fall on my neck, and now it had, and up I'd sprung to skip away, much lighter without my head. So light and headless I couldn't sleep, and didn't want to eat, and grasped at every outstretched hand, taking everything anyone offered and more, saying sorry sorry I don't have anything to give back and laughing and jumping away and clutching at someone else.

I found I could relax in hot yoga classes; and once relaxed, often dozed off on the floor. Which was fine. I didn't mind lying flat asleep in the middle of a dim sweaty room with slick-skinned flex-muscled people all around me.

"Wherever you are is perfect," said the yoga teacher. "Just be where you are. Present. Authentic." And something about the universe, and blah blah blah. Roll my eyes as I might, I did know the words in yoga—though I didn't know the words in synagogue, or in church—with the same kind of superficiality as most temple- and church-goers. I blinked awake again, from a dream that I was lying there naked, and hoped I hadn't been snoring. Everyone else bum in air, downward dog. I pulled myself up into a triangle. Present. Be present. This has got to be the stupidest, most vapid advice, the most absurd of absurd adages. Animals live in the present, the moment—the tiniest moment for the tiniest brain. A goldfish swimming round and round in its bowl, surprised by the brand-new landscape at each turn. When we're at the beginning and the end, with no past, no future, we might live "fully in the moment," but otherwise we live in our memories, bending and mending them and adding to them and rubbing bits out, and we live in the imaginary past before our memories begin, and in all the possible futures our minds fabricate. There's even a word for this mental time travel—chronesthesia.

One of the signs of damage by Alzheimer's disease to the brain's temporal lobe, according to the Alzheimer Society of Canada: "living in the present moment."

I didn't believe for a second that exercising in a sauna was clearing toxins from my body, let alone my soul, but it felt good. And when that crap about the universe came up, I just closed my eyes and thought about something else. About Oma packing her suitcase and putting on her coat. Sitting on her bed in the retirement home, waiting for her ride back home, to the condo she'd forgotten she'd sold. I pictured the work piled on my desk in my office at the magazine, and pictured my divorce lawyer with her tissue boxes and giant breasts and giant fees. I imagined sex, all the sex I could have now, with whomever I wanted, though who was I kidding, I was old, almost forty, with cellulite on my thighs, and also, how many men did I really want, with most of them so unhygienic, and so stupid, or sexist and mean, don't forget mean, and don't forget STDs, they're called STIs now, or just bad in bed or—

"Just. Breathe. Just. Be," said the yoga instructor.

The grad student I dated a few months after my husband moved out liked to talk about the present, all into Zen koans and beat poets instead of pomo philosophers like the grad students I knew when I was a grad student. When the grad student recited his insights and Zen-inspired parables, I widened my eyes as if thinking hard. I did think about what he said. Part of me thought, maybe he's right and I'm an idiot, and part of me thought, he's got a framed photograph of Friedrich Nietzsche on his wall. That's like framing a photo of Courtney Love, which the bass player in my terrible punk band did, in the nineties, when I was seventeen and the bass player twenty-three. Part of me thought, I'm so judgemental, and our band wasn't that bad, we were having fun, and anyway that bassist is now a rich Manhattan executive, so that's where framing your posters gets you, and part of me thought, what kind of man frames a photo of Friedrich Nietzsche, and not only that, but explains to me, that's the philosopher Friedrich Nietzsche, and part of me thought, just don't think about it.

I wasn't thinking, because my head had been sliced off.

The grad student, giant, like a boy magnified, reminded me of someone I'd have dated in high school, with dime-bags in the pockets of his huge hoodies, dime-bags he opened and offered to share, as though I weren't thirty-eight and married and wearing a business suit. I needed to delay my brain's regrowth, which could only bring thoughts of my husband living on the other side of the river. Before long, the student was mean to me in a giant-little-boy kind of way, and I broke it off with him and cried, and it felt clean and pure, I mean clean and plainly sad, to cry over such a stark and simple meanness instead of choking on the big gooey gob of a mess my husband and I had made.

"Spread your toes," said the yoga instructor. "Engage your glutes. Pull your thighs toward each other. Level your hips. Reach out forward and back, and *engage* those fingers. Listen to what your body's telling you today."

Organized exercise, with a tinge of religion. Oma rolled her eyes at women who exercised for the sake of exercise instead of to get somewhere, or for fun. Especially joggers. "Silly girl," she'd say, when one jogged by. That's what she said about women who married the wrong men, too, or who slept around and got pregnant or herpes, or who thought white chocolate was actually chocolate, or who got religion. Oma came to my wedding, and though she was already losing herself, she knew enough to call me silly, worse than silly if anything could be. She hated it, hated it, the semi-religious ceremony, the singing in Hebrew, the dancing in a circle. Silly, silly girl. Opa would not have come. My parents had no nods to religion in their own wedding for that reason; Opa would not have come, refused to sit through such rubbish, all that God stuff. We recited the blessings, our friends held a chuppah over our heads, and my new husband stomped on a glass (the last time he'd get to put his foot down—ha ha).

"Ghastly," Oma would have told Opa.

"Absolutely crazy," Opa would have agreed. "What has come over that girl?"

❊ Now, in the church on Place du Jeu de Balle, organ music played on speakers, and more people syphoned in from the rain, filling the pews, more and more people. Of course—it was Sunday, so a service would begin at noon. Should I stay? But the service would be Catholic, in a French (and maybe Latin) I didn't understand. I made my way down between the pews and outside again. But the rain pelted down, and I hurried to one of the packed little restaurants along the street where I'd bought my dress. The place was full, and a waiter shuffled me to a small table in the corner by the bar. I managed somehow, in French, to order a glass of wine and an omelette. The wine came in a juice glass, filled to the brim, and the omelette was huge as my plate, with a mound of grated cheese on top. I was happy. Happy to be alone, because I didn't want to hear anyone explain, as Lev would have done, how wine should be served.

I touched the wedding ring in my pocket, slipped it onto the end of my ring finger and gave it a long look. When it had first arrived (in the mail; I'd ordered it, and its pair, online), I'd tried it on and felt elated. Once I'm married, I thought, I'll never take this off again; I'm safe now, forever. Actually, I soon found I couldn't sleep with it on, didn't feel fully naked, and took it off every evening. Before my next bite of omelette, I slipped the ring back in my pocket, stretched out my hands; I preferred my fingers bare. I took out my journal and my pen, but only for the armour they provided, and watched the other diners, all in big groups, in their jeans and sneakers and windbreakers. People smoked here, and women had feathered hair. Rain outside and wine inside, and all the tension fled my body.

Desperate for all the sleep I'd lost since leaving Canada, I hurried back to my hotel, the storm now eased to mist, and napped soundly. How had I until now forgotten the obvious and easy solution to my restlessness—alcohol?

When I woke, I went out for dinner in a pita sandwich restaurant I'd passed several times, then straight back to the hotel.

※ In the hotel bathroom—the toilet—I stared at my face in the mirror, my nose's odd shape, squashed on top and long at the tip. I leaned my head back and squinted at the faint scar that ran under my nose and up into both nostrils. The blemish was almost gone, both the burn of it and the pimple-ness. Then I smoothed on the cleansing mask I'd bought in Amsterdam. I couldn't help but find the phantom pains in my nose symbolic, regularly showing up in times of stress, as though my secret, real face was pushing at me from the inside.

The years I was ten and eleven, I had grown and grown, turbo-charged. Puberty hit me early, stretching my arms and legs like a rubber Gumby's, longer and longer, and skinnier and skinnier. By fifth grade, I had reached five-foot-six but not quite a hundred pounds. My limbs lengthened, and my once-smooth hair frizzed up and outward, as though my body were full of static. I tried to coax the hair down, but some switch had clicked, and it now obeyed an imperative more urgent than the ingredients of any conditioner. Oh, please, I begged my bones and my fuzzy mop, stop! Meanwhile, my nose swelled outward at a faster pace than any other part of me. I was not pretty, not pretty at all, oh, was deeply unpretty. Why couldn't I look like the popular girls, with their smooth pale hair and small symmetrical features? Prettiness seemed merely an absence of offending features, the way cleanliness is simply an absence of filth, and I longed to be clean, inconspic-uous, invisible. Or at least smart. I was smartish, but to make up for not being pretty I'd have to be much smarter than that, the smartest, a genius, and I just couldn't sharpen my mind that fine, not even close.

When we visited DC, one of Mimi's fancy American friends, with her bleached hair and button nose, looked at me, then at Mimi. "Look at her eyebrows."

"I know."

"Cheeks, too."

"I know. It's such a shame."

They meant my nose. My nose was such a shame. To hover so close to attractiveness, facial harmony undermined by the misshapen lump between my eyes and mouth.

The shameful nose was not the real shame, though. The shame was that I had not yet agreed to undergo the procedure to fix it.

"It's not a big deal," I remember my grandmothers, both Mimi and Oma, and my parents, assuring me. "Like having your tonsils out."

I developed a habit of holding my hand over my nose while I talked, pulling my sleeves over my hands and burying my face in the fabric as I sat at my school desk. I'd push the tip of my nose back and hold my finger over its bridge, trying to picture my face relieved of this burden.

It wasn't just my family. "Hey, Pinocchio!" a guy in my class yelled at me, all the way down the stairwell. He explained to me, angrily, as though I'd worn socks that clashed with my pants and offended his sensibilities: "Your face is tiny and your nose sticks right out like a carrot."

"A prominent nose is okay on a man," my orthodontist told my parents, right in front of me, "but unattractive on a woman." He referred them to his buddy, the cosmetic surgeon.

That could have been the clincher, or maybe the tipping point came on the day each student in my art class sat in front of a projector so that his or her profile was projected in silhouette on a giant piece of paper, for another student to trace. When my turn came, the projector switched on, and everyone laughed, involuntarily. Then some people felt bad, and stopped, but others just kept tittering the whole time, while I sat there, being traced, and then turned to face the result. My profile looked exactly like the Wicked Witch of the West. Even witchier, because of my untamed frizzy hair framing the pointy little face with a carrot nose. By the time I was fourteen, and Mimi offered me a nose job as my next birthday present, I said yes. It was all I thought about. A non-ugly future. The idea of surgery terrified me, but how could I turn down this offer, for life to be infinitely better?

In my Brussels hotel, the prescribed ten minutes over, I washed off the cleansing mask and leaned in close to examine my pores. Again, I ran my fingers over the broken bones in the bridge of my nose. At twenty-two, I'd made an appointment for a second nose job; midsummer, I was to fly to Maryland, where I'd get the surgery and then recover at my grandmother's house. Something must have gone wrong the first time, to cause the excessive bleeding; at the ER, they'd packed and packed my sinuses with gauze, trying to staunch the flow. Even after the bandages came off, my nostrils sometimes leaked blood, leaked and then poured. And the first time Mimi saw me after the surgery, she told me I needed a second one; I couldn't go around with a bad nose job in the middle of my face for the rest of my life. Too much bone had been removed from the bridge, and I could feel a gap in the middle, a hole where I'd previously had a bump. The cartilage in the tip was full of scar tissue, leaving me with a "polly-beak deformity," according to one surgeon, who took my nose between her fingers and gently wiggled it around. When I was twenty-two, seven years after the nose bleeds stopped, I decided, I can't, I really can't live with this weird face. This asymmetry, this mistake, distorting my features.

Mimi took me for consultations with several DC surgeons, one of whom told me the first surgeon had completely botched the job. Of course, he added, I'd started down nose-job road due to a classic "ethnic problem." Back when I longed to look like the other kids at school, it had not occurred to me that I looked Jewish. Only many years later would I read that in 1850, Scottish zoologist Robert Knox described the Jewish nose as a "large, massive club-shaped, hooked nose, three or four times larger than suits the face...thus it is that the Jewish face can never [be], and never is, perfectly beautiful." What was I acquiescing to?

And was that what I needed, wanted? A perfectly beautiful face? Once I started down that road, I would only want surgery after surgery, one more adjustment, just one more, like my grandmother's friend whose face was so tight she couldn't fully close her eyes and had to lubricate them from a little tube. Mimi had already told me I'd look great with bigger lips. What for, though? And who was I to be perfectly beautiful? Beautiful according to whom? Was my face really so abhorrent, that I should pay someone to take a knife to it?

Anyway, as the surgery loomed nearer, anxiety seized me hard. Two days before I was booked to fly to Maryland, I couldn't get out of bed, couldn't stop crying. I couldn't explain, only that it felt wrong. I cancelled the appointment for my second nose job.

And now, at thirty-nine, I was still thinking about it, or thinking about it again. My bent and broken nose.

In bed, I texted Matteo. 'See you tomorrow.'

He wrote back. 'I can't wait.' I tucked the white blanket tight around my body and sent one more text. 'Me neither.'

I was just closing my eyes when my parents phoned; I should have called earlier. I said I was fine, just exploring, and told my mother about the salt liquorice I bought her in Amsterdam. She said she didn't like salt liquorice.

"You said you ate it all the time as a child—"

But she said, "No. Uh-uh. Not for me."

I got out of bed, and plugged in my phone to charge, repacked my bag, then popped one of the hard black disks in my mouth, pressed my teeth down and sucked, gave myself a few seconds to adjust to the combo: candy, but salt. Oh yuck, a little longer, oh no. Ejected it, slick and goopy against a white hotel tissue.

※ Two years earlier, at thirty-seven, I had read Philip Roth's novel, *The Ghost Writer*. I thought it might be about a ghostwriter, and I was working as a ghostwriter myself, but the book wasn't about that. Set in the mid-1950s, *The Ghost Writer* was about a young American writer, Nathan Zuckerman, who meets a hot, mysterious woman whom he becomes convinced is Anne Frank, alive and settled in New York state under an assumed name, watching as her diary achieves iconic status. Roth's Nathan, meanwhile, has written and published a story about a family arguing over money, a story based on an embarrassing incident in his family history—a story that has infuriated his father, who feels Nathan has betrayed his people, showing Jews behaving badly and stereotypically. Nathan is undeterred, feels he's simply telling the truth, writing his experience. When his mother tells him his writing will provide fodder for anti-Semitism, and brings up the genocide in Europe, Nathan tells her, "Go to the office of the plastic surgeon where the girls get their noses fixed. That's where the Jewish blood flows in Essex County, that's where the blow is delivered—with a mallet! To their bones—and to their pride!"

I googled "jewish nose job." Twenty-five hundred hits. Ads and articles, both, galore. One doctor claimed to see "many Jewish patients who want to keep the natural features of their noses intact, while still improving their overall appearance." According to his fairly typical website, "Generally, the Jewish nose tends to have a large dorsal hump and a prominent over-projected nasal tip."

✳ It felt like a mallet-bashing, the surgery itself: two weeks before my fifteenth birthday, I counted backwards from one hundred: ninety-nine, ninety-eight, ninety-seven, and the voices went quiet. I lay unconscious, a tube down my throat, and a man cut an incision under and into my nose, separated skin and cartilage from my skull, and peeled my face open to break and scrape and slice and squeeze the stuff inside. Blood pooled in my sinus cavities; bone and tissue lay rejected in a steel bowl. I wouldn't remember any of that, of course, woke up sewn back together, my head wrapped in plaster, sinuses stuffed with gauze, but not enough to keep the blood from pouring down over my lips, my chin, dripping onto my white hospital sheets.

I called out for help, and the nurse shoved more gauze at me.

"Nurses don't have much sympathy for elective surgery patients," my mother explained, pushing me toward the car in a wheelchair.

"I can't believe I did this to myself." I wasn't quite crying, because crying would require contortions my bashed-up face couldn't manage.

My bandages and plaid shirt were stained already with copious amounts of blood. The shirt, I could shed. The bandages had to remain on my face for two weeks. My sister, twelve years old then, seemed afraid of me, with my black eyes and swollen everything. I couldn't talk or chew without straining the stitches between my nostrils. Laughing was torture. I had to breathe through my mouth, my sinuses swollen and jam-packed with cotton. I sequestered myself in my bedroom, and wouldn't let anyone turn on my light, because I didn't want to be visible. In two weeks, my mother returned me to the surgeon to have my face unwrapped and unstuffed. He held up a mirror, warning me that my lip and nose were swollen, and my eyes bruised. In that mirror, I saw someone who strongly resembled me, but was fundamentally someone else, like a close relative.

Shortly after I read Roth's novel, my parents visited Lev and me in Calgary, and I demanded of them—as they stared at me in bafflement over a restaurant table—why they let me get a nose job at fourteen. How could they have let me go through something so clearly insulting, and so racist? I regretted it, I said.

"But it was your idea," said my mother. "You were really unhappy. You said you didn't have friends. You said you didn't fit in, and you really thought it would solve those problems if you had this surgery."

"Didn't you think that might have been misguided? That maybe I needed a therapist instead?" I asked.

"Memory can work in strange ways," Dad told me. "I have always remembered, vividly, getting my tonsils removed, lying in the hospital room, unable to speak, the Jell-O they brought me, my parents visiting, and my grandparents. All the details. But then I went to the doctor as an adult, and he looked in my throat, and he said I had my tonsils. I remembered it so clearly, the whole thing. I asked my mother—Mimi—and she said, are you crazy, you were never in the hospital, what are you talking about?"

I stared at my curry, my water glass. I felt my features move into the expression that my father hated, the judging look, he'd say.

Lev put his hand on my arm in a way that meant, give them a break.

"You were a difficult child to raise," Dad said. "I didn't know how to deal with a child like you. I could tell you had secrets, even as a baby, as soon as you were born. I could tell you knew things I didn't."

My face scrunched further into the look. I stared at my plate. At the wall. At my mother's face, which bore her own familiar look, which I'd always interpreted as exasperated and baffled.

"Frankly," Dad said. "You think you've been harmed? Your aunt has suffered. And she never even had her teeth fixed, and I never did either—that's something—I always thought, I felt—"

He folded into himself, lowered his voice, said, "Are you very angry with us? Do you—do you still love us?"

At the condo after dinner, my mom and Lev and I talked about other things while my dad stared at me, close, it seemed, to tears. Before they left for Ottawa the next day, he said again, "Do you still love us?"

I tried to keep the "judging" look off my face, and before I had to respond at all, my mother said his name in a voice that meant, of course she does, get a grip.

✳ The idea of writing about my nose job horrified me. I hadn't even told many people about the surgery, and not only because I feared revealing that my face wasn't really my face. But I would try. Writing about rhinoplasty might give me distance—I could research the topic and gain some perspective.

I called my parents again and asked them, more calmly, how I ended up getting a nose job at fourteen. This time, I was ready to listen. I was a journalist. My father fell silent, but my mother said, perky and upbeat, "Oh, okay, let's see—"

She said again that the surgery was initially my idea, an idea that preoccupied me. "You said you'd have friends if you got this surgery," she added. I mentioned the nose-job idea to Mimi, Mum said. "And she thought it was a great idea, so she encouraged you, and she encouraged Dad and me as well. I guess because, in her circle, it wasn't a big deal, sort of like having your tonsils out."

"And what did you think, Dad?"

My father paused for a long time, then answered slowly and carefully. "I thought I wanted you to have what you wanted. And you felt it would make you—I mean you really—you really wanted it badly. And the surgeon said it was normal and safe." He added, "You were more than adamant. It was a passion."

I told Yael about the article I wanted to write, and she said she remembered seeing me at school with two black eyes. She said that was the first time we ever spoke, in Grade 9 typing—didn't I remember?— she'd asked me what happened, and I said my grandmother made me get a nose job. I didn't remember that, only telling Yael that I liked how she'd styled her hair, upswept and back-combed into a giant magical Sandman-comic inspired nest.

I called Mimi too, and asked how I decided to have the surgery she paid for, for my fifteenth birthday present. She hesitated. "I think you didn't like your nose."

My mother told me she didn't recall anyone, during her Dutch-Indonesian-British youth, getting a nose job or talking about it. She said the concept of cosmetic surgery was new to her in North America. But my father, and his older sister, Rachael, began their lives in London too, in a Jewish neighbourhood, before they left for America at eleven and fifteen. Rachael turned sixteen two days before their ship arrived in New York in 1960. When they began school in Silver Spring, Maryland, Rachael told me, she was acutely culture shocked. I knew this story already, a little. Rachael had only stayed in the US for a short time before Mimi and Grandad shipped her back to England to stay with their friend. She was that miserable. Rachael told me the girls in her eleventh grade classes had braces on their teeth and had their own cars. Meanwhile, my grandparents didn't even own a car. She felt ostracized, like a refugee, due to poverty, due to her unstraightened teeth.

Dad, who graduated from that same high school in 1968, said nose jobs were "very common."

"Do you remember who tended to get nose jobs?" I asked.

White girls, he said. "My impression, looking back, is that they were Jewish kids, but I don't know that for a fact."

I asked Auntie Rachael, too—she was living with and caring for Mimi then, and when I phoned, she happened to be in bed recovering from a neck lift. She knew for a fact, she said: rhinoplasty was the realm of sixteen-year-old Jewish girls, and judging by the experiences of her acquaintances' grandchildren, still was. "In these rich—not rich—but—Jewish families, having a nose job is like a coming of age. If you need it."

"But how do you know if you need it?"

"Well, if you have a bad nose."

"And why Jewish girls, in particular?"

"They were the ones with the bad noses," said Aunt Rachael.

"What is a bad nose?"

Anything bigger and bumpier than "a tiny little triangle," Rachael said, is less than ideal. Some people are born with those perfect little noses, she added, and named her (Anglo-Saxon) daughter-in-law.

Rachael, Mimi added, "needed her nose done, too, when she was sixteen or seventeen, but she wouldn't do it." They were taking turns talking to me, Rachael in her bed in Grandad's old room downstairs, Mimi up at the kitchen table.

"I always thought I had a hateful nose," Rachael agreed. "But when I had an opportunity to do it, I was too scared." I told her I loved her nose the way it was. I'd always found her face exceptionally appealing. She didn't seem to hear me.

She never heard about nose jobs in England, Mimi told me, but in the sixties, she saw American mothers taking their daughters for schnoz upgrades as soon as the girls turned sixteen. "Nobody thought it was a big deal." She denied that rhinoplasty was or is a particularly Jewish phenomenon, however. "It's everybody." Mimi said that she was "absolutely" a proponent of cosmetic surgery. If looking better makes you feel better, and you can do it, why not?

"My mother believes you should do anything you can to improve how you look," added Rachael, because beauty, or a close approximation, is vital for success, socially and in business. I asked Rachael what she thought about that, and she said, without hesitating, "I think it's true."

And Mimi was the evidence, an extraordinarily stunning and charismatic woman who'd achieved monumentally more, career-wise, than a female, Eastern European, Jewish immigrant with no formal education could ever have hoped, certainly only aided by her "movie-star-type looks" as Rachael put it, "and her glam and outgoing personality." Mimi knew intimately, though she would never admit it, the privileges bestowed upon the beautiful.

When Auntie Rachael asked why I was writing about rhinoplasty— what I was getting at—I said I wasn't sure, but added that nose jobs were invented by Jews, for Jews, that the first contemporary rhinoplasty was performed in 1888 by German-Jewish surgeon Jacques Joseph (born Jacob Joseph), to cure a hefty-nosed patient of the melancholy arising from social exclusion and ridicule. In 1933, one patient reported that "Nosef," as the surgeon became known in the German-Jewish community, sometimes provided his services for free when he felt that someone "suffered from a Jewish nose" but couldn't afford the surgery.

Was simply looking too Jewish the issue, attractiveness aside?

"Look at the propaganda and all of that," Rachael agreed. "It was really prevalent. All of the caricatures..."

In *The Jewish Body*, Melvin Konner includes an 1888 chart entitled "How We May Know Him" designed to help the unsuspecting spot sneaky Semites. The labelled illustrations include "ill-shapen ears of great size like those of a bat," and, of course, "curved nose and nostrils." As Sander Gilman writes, the Jewish nose's "nostrility" was at one point even believed a result of congenital syphilis. In any case, the Jewish nose was considered to embody a combination of racially inscribed characteristics which set Jews aside as an entirely different species—a dangerous combination of craftiness, avarice, and amorality. All this is summed up rather neatly in a joke: Why do Jews have big noses? Because air is free.

"I'm sure that was part of it," Rachael said. "The parents wanted their girls—their kids—to have a life without being made fun of, being called big nose, hook nose, Jew nose. And in the sixties, it was only twenty years after the war."

In 1933 Berlin, as Nosef performed his free rhinoplasties, looking Jewish was more than a minor social liability; it would soon become a matter of life and death. As Konner describes, in the Nazi era, German children were taught how to spot Jews attempting to "pass." And 1930s Berlin was exactly where Mimi grew up—until her parents managed to escape to England when she was sixteen.

My aunt intuited that rhinoplasty's popularity among North American Jews peaked in the sixties and seventies, and my research backed her up. Though no such studies have been conducted in Canada, statistics from the American Society of Plastic Surgeons reveal a thirty-seven per cent decline in nose jobs between 2000 and 2011. Moreover, the procedure's increased popularity among Asian and Hispanic communities implies that Jews were getting even fewer nose jobs than the numbers show. Melvin Konner told *Tablet* magazine in 2012 that the explanation likely lies in Jews becoming prouder of their heritage, and less anxious to assimilate.

"Is it ethnicity or is it aesthetics?" my aunt mused at the end of our chat.

※ It was a spring afternoon when I did my first interview with a non-family member for the nose-job article. "I have an appointment with a cosmetic surgeon today," I told Lev that morning, when he stuck his head into my office, which was in the condo's second bedroom, with a view of the alley, and Calgary's downtown skyline beyond that.

"What?" Lev leaned further into the room. He wore a dark grey suit; I was still in my blue flannel pyjamas.

"I'm interviewing him for an article." I laughed. "You look so worried!"

"Uh. What's the article about?"

"Nose job. The whole nose job thing."

"I don't want you to get another nose job." I knew he hated that I'd had the first one, because it made me look less Jewish, was part of my family's tendency toward assimilation. Ironic, considering that the point of the nose job had been, according to others, anyway, to get a husband.

"I'm not going to," I said.

"Well, I don't want you to." During our relationship, I had talked about wanting to get my nose straightened, the damage from the first surgery, at least, repaired. It was an urge that came and went.

"Not planning to," I assured Lev.

"Okay...Have a good day."

"You too."

He left, and I showered, then dressed in one of my skirt-and-blazer combos, my business-lady look.

"I'm writing an article about rhinoplasty," I told Dr. Greg Waslen a couple of hours later, after following my new smart phone's GPS the forty minutes to his office. But even as he took the seat across from me at his long, white desk, I had the distinct impression he was sizing up my features. I felt like he knew my secret: that, though I'd presented myself as a journalist, which I *was*, I bore a "bad nose job," as Mimi, my paternal grandmother, once called it.

I told him I was inspired to write this article because of my own experience. "I had the surgery when I was fourteen," I said. "I'm thirty-seven now. So, a long time ago."

"Mmhm." Towering and grey-haired, he sported a small moustache and a wrinkled forehead. His own nose drooped at the tip. I only noticed the facial imperfections because he was sitting there noticing mine. "You had a very basic rhinoplasty that I wouldn't do, because it's not sophisticated." He told me my surgeon just took the "hump" off, flattening my nose's bridge, "which doesn't make it attractive." And, he added, the doctor didn't do enough to the tip, leaving my face unbalanced. He retrieved a caliper, and proceeded to measure my features, explaining that in the golden ratio—1:1.618—lies the empirically demonstrated source of beauty, in everything from flowers to faces. My face, he showed me, was pretty well proportioned, except for my nose, which was out of whack in several regards.

"Have you had any cosmetic surgery yourself?" I asked.

"No." He smiled. "Not yet."

Wasn't trusting a wrinkled cosmetic surgeon a little like trusting a skinny chef? Before I'd decided whether that was a good joke to say out loud, he led me into another room and sat me in front of a camera, then showed me on his enormous computer screen how I'd appear with my profile adjusted for perfection, ratio-wise. "Looks cuter," he said. Then he made my nose bigger and hookier, to show me what I'd probably look like if I'd never had surgery in the first place. "More severe," he said. He was right, in a way, on both counts.

"Do you find you get a lot of patients of certain ethnicities?" I ventured. "For instance, I'm Jewish. Do you find a lot of people who get nose jobs are Jewish?"

"No," said Dr. Waslen. He denied any correlation between ethnicity and nose shape or relative beauty. It's just about math, he said. Design.

"What's your article about, exactly?" he asked.

"I'm not sure yet. I'm not exactly sure."

My nose job was one of a couple of topics I'd repeatedly tried and failed to write about. Every word came out banal or sappy, every thought *poor me poor me poor me*. Why did it upset me so much, almost a quarter-century later, this surgery I underwent twenty-three years ago? I didn't even know what the big deal was. Sometimes I stared at my face in the mirror and felt ready to pay anything to straighten the bones that the surgeon left crooked and squashed. And then I'd forget about my nose for months, years, looked at my face and just saw a face. And sometimes I just felt grateful to have shed that other nose, the more severe one.

Lev had worried that I'd visit Dr. Waslen and find myself unable to resist a second surgery. And I did ask the doctor, just out of curiosity: What would he say if I asked him to reconstruct my nose as it had been? He said he wouldn't do it. It would be unethical to make a patient look less attractive.

Easy enough to say, I realized, that I regretted the surgery when I haven't seen my first face in two-and-a-half decades, and couldn't quite recall just how gargantuan my nose used to be. For some reason, few photographs existed of me between the ages of twelve and fifteen.

"You didn't have a big nose," my mother had insisted, on the phone. "There was a bit of a bump."

"I remember you had a large bump on your nose," Dad added.

"Did my nose look like other people's in the family?" I asked.

"No," said Dad.

"What do you mean?" Mum asked him. "She had your nose." A pause. Nervous laughter. "No—Naomi, you had a normal nose with a little bump."

"And that was the issue," said Dad.

I asked what they thought about the outcome of my surgery. Mum was silent. Dad told me, after a long pause, that I looked lovely and looked equally lovely before. What bothered her, Mum said, was my painful recovery from the operation. Dad agreed: that bothered him, too. A far cry from the "no big deal" the doctor had promised.

A bump? So I never even had a disproportionate face? A "severe" profile? A Jew-nose worthy of free-air jokes? Would it truly have made no difference at all if I'd never gone under that knife?

☀ A couple of months later, I did write a magazine article about nose jobs and Jews and my own nose, and my own murky Jewish identity, but later that May day I interviewed Greg Waslen, and I forgot all about all my questions and queries and ideas and plans and complaints, and everything else running through my mind as I walked home. Because by later that day, I was getting divorced.

☀ Early evening, Lev told me, "I owe you an apology."

"For what?"

"What I said this morning, that I didn't want you to get a nose job."

"I don't want you to want me to get a nose job—what do you mean?"

"It's your body, and I shouldn't tell you what to do with it."

"Okay, I guess. But I don't want to get a nose job. I like it that you don't want me to change..." Some tension I couldn't name moved his body across the room, movements exaggerated. Something needed smoothing over. "C'mere," I said. "Want to cuddle?"

He sighed so hard his arms flailed. "Can't we just have sex?"

"Lev!"

"You're rejecting me!" he yelled. "You're always rejecting me! You're afraid of intimacy!" He stormed out onto the balcony and then back inside to hunch miserably on the far end of the sofa.

"What's going on?" I moved over, hugged him, tried to sit on his lap. He went rigid. "I love you," I said.

His body tensed even more. "I respect and admire you as well."

"You—*what?*"

By mid-evening, he'd drunk two-thirds of a bottle of wine, while I sat with a single half-filled glass in front me, my stomach tense and sick. He told me he could not be happy without children.

By sundown, he'd sprawled on the bedroom rug. He slammed his fist against the floor. "It's make or break!" he cried, baring his teeth. "It just is!"

I had never heard him use the phrase *make or break.*

"But we agreed—" I said. "Since when?"

"I can't give up my lifelong dream of being a parent!" He threw himself onto the bed.

"Your what? But you said you were fine with—you said you—why didn't you tell me you were feeling this way?"

"I couldn't. You're impossible to talk to! You get all upset!" He sprawled. He sipped and swallowed. He'd brought his glass, and the bottle, into bed with him.

"But we agreed—I mean, I asked, I wondered, and you said. You agreed that we were a family. A family of two."

"It just doesn't feel like a real family to me," said Lev. "I thought I could do it, but I can't. I was lying to myself."

At two a.m., I asked, "Is there someone else?"

"No..."

"Is there?"

"...No..."

"*Is* there?"

In this pause, my marriage tumbled out an open window. In this pause, I had time to think, this is how it ends, I'm going to hit the—

"You're still my first choice," he said. "But—"

I convulsed, gasping. This is real.

"Your *what?*"

My husband repeated that I *was* still his first choice. But this woman, they'd been talking, and her fiancé didn't want children either, and they understood each other, this woman and my husband, and it felt so good to be understood by someone, and they agreed that it was make or break, it just was. And they'd tried not to develop feelings for each other, and she really was a good person; in fact, she was the one who'd explained to Lev, earlier that day, that it was my body and that he should apologize to me, because I could get a nose job if I wanted, because some people had low self-esteem.

Then he closed his eyes and lay still, breathing evenly. I sat beside him, tears rolling down my cheeks and I sobbed and sobbed, but he didn't wake up, so I put on a coat over my pyjamas and went outside into the night and walked in the rain, because I couldn't sit still with this brand-new knowledge inside me, with my future ripped away, within the same walls as this man who'd reported to a stranger that I'd gone to see a cosmetic surgeon because I secretly wanted to rearrange my face, and who'd followed this stranger's instructions, this stranger who explained to him that some people have low self-esteem, and with whom he'd agreed *it's make or break, it just is*, and repeated the phrase until it became part of his vocabulary, and all the while, I was in, in for life, because we were married. I mean I'd thought about leaving him, sure, even looked at rental listings, and I'd had my infatuations, and even thought, oh, God, what have I done, but we were married, and I'd been all, come to bed, it's late, and he said, I'm still working, but he was online, text-talking to that woman, typing, 'make or break' and 'my wife had a nose job at fourteen and she's been crazy ever since' and 'my wife has issues with intimacy' and who knows what else.

Next night, Lev stayed with a friend. He phoned me in the late afternoon, and I left my office at the magazine to half-run a couple of blocks and then pace around in front of the old hospital by the river while I called him back.

"I'm doing this because I'm a romantic and an optimist," he told me.

All the frantic energy that had kept me going all day wafted through my skin and away, and my body crumpled onto a slab of concrete, some kind of public art piece. I lay on my back and thought, he and the make-or-break woman came up with that one, too. He and Make-or-Break agreed that they were both romantics and optimists, and that her fiancé and I were, what, cynics and pessimists? *It's make or break! You can't stay with a cynic when you're a romantic!* Fuck you, I thought. *Fuck you.*

He said, "I need a couple of weeks to decide what to do." I closed my eyes, felt the cool concrete against my neck, my shoulders. He'd told Make-or-Break that he couldn't talk to her for a while, until he'd figured things out with me. Wanted to come back and sleep on the couch while he chose. Or, he suggested, we could take turns staying with friends.

I thought, are you fucking kidding me, I can't believe this, where will I live, how will I live? I thought, did we ever actually love each other, did we ever actually listen to each other? And what about the mortgage and what about my medical benefits? I need a better job, I need several better jobs. I need to sleep with as many people as possible, immediately; no, though, don't do that, but why not? I can do whatever I want, I can do whatever I want. I thought, I'm going to have to check off *separated/divorced* as my marital status now. I thought a lot of things, I mean, a lot of thoughts occurred to me. I stared up at the wide blue sky. Calgary was famous for its wide blue sky.

"This marriage is over," I said.

He didn't come back until a month later, to get his things and move them into the apartment he'd found. His framed photo of the two of us, he left face down in a pile of dust.

I SPENT THE MORNING OF MONDAY, JULY 20TH strolling in
the drizzle to Brussels' famous Grand Place—a massive and fairy-tale-
magnificent square full of damp tourists taking photos of each other.
There, I sat in a coffee shop, sipping cappuccino at the only table
for one, lodged into the foyer beside the door. Matteo was in the air
between Rome and Brussels, on his way to see me. Out there, zooming
right through clouds, hurtling toward the same little bit of space as me.
We'd sit face to face soon, and soon after that we'd kiss and take off our
clothes. That part was the hardest to believe.

On Monday, July 20th, 1942, Jos woke in Brussels a single man on the
run. He wouldn't meet the beautiful, British, twenty-one-year-old ambulance driver Mary Elizabeth Skipsey until a year later. According to family
lore, Oma and Opa met up in Brussels early in their acquaintance;
maybe they walked these same streets. If only I had a time machine, I
could have stepped through a portal to find these same streets with all
the chain stores and tourists gone, little cafés and shops instead, and
soldiers in uniforms, and my grandparents, young, walking toward and
past me, hand in hand. I had a photograph of them from that time,
looking glamorous in their military uniforms, like movie stars in a film
about the war. Betty's hair is pulled back, brown and shiny, her stride
confident, head turned in profile, lipstick perfect. Opa, blond and
handsome, smiles at the photographer with pride, and almost a little
bashful; he looks surprised and pleased to have this pretty girl on his
arm, this lovely young girl in her early twenties, who moved to London

alone, from Yorkshire, to escape her small-minded family, who'd re-created herself as an urbanite, an army ambulance driver, who'd probably never met a Jew before. As far as she was concerned, Jos was Dutch, and left the Netherlands to help the war effort from England, as a translator, an interceptor of German messages. My grandparents, Jos and Mary Elizabeth—they were hot. No wonder they met up for a fling in Brussels. Who took that photo?

But on July 20th, 1942, Jos didn't know yet that Betty existed. He took a day-trip by train, from Brussels to a village in East Flanders, which he doesn't name in his diary. His colleague who helped him leave the Netherlands was staying in that village, and from him Jos received French cash. His hosts celebrated Jos's success thus far with "a large pre-war Dutch Gin, and an hour later an as-much pre-war meal." I would not take a train to East Flanders. I was disturbing the symmetry of our trips. Relaxing, walking, writing, and waiting for my lover. Isn't it funny, I thought, that I used to long for adventure? Turns out I love stories, reading them and inventing them, but not necessarily living them.

☀ Before I ever thought to write in a diary, I drew pictures of my favourite story. I drew Dorothy and the Scarecrow, the pale blonde good witch and the green, hook-nosed wicked one. Drew tiny houses blowing around in whirling crayon tornados. I'd discovered *The Wizard of Oz* one night when I couldn't sleep, and my parents let me watch this magical movie that happened to be on TV, which they kept in their bedroom to keep us from rotting our brains. It was late (after eight), my sister was sleeping, and I got to sit in my parents' bed by myself, with my dad in the chair beside me, saying, "Oh, this part's my favourite!" He imitated the Cowardly Lion's voice: "I didn't bite 'im!" Dorothy was far from home, and with a wicked witch after her, but she couldn't get lost as long as she followed that yellow brick road. One foot in front of the other—or sometimes just behind it, when skipping—and a story would swoosh up and all around her.

Even better than getting my dad all to myself was getting Oma. In any room, I manoeuvred myself close to my grandmother. I wanted her attention, to be like her—set out in sharp relief, not soft around the edges like Opa and my mother, neither of whom laughed much or made jokes, and not wavering unpredictably between playfulness and anguish, like my father. Oma offended people constantly, in a way I found brave and hilarious. She fashioned her opinions for maximum shock value, and she had the charisma, good looks, and proper English accent to get away with it. She'd taken elocution lessons in her late teens, she told me once, after leaving her working-class Yorkshire family and moving alone to London. Oma could be intoxicatingly kind, and she could be viciously mean, choosing her favourites and her victims seemingly at random. But I hadn't noticed, because, so far, I had been a favourite.

In the summer of 1985, when I was nine, Oma took me to see the new movie *Back to the Future*. Just Oma and me, at a matinee, and that was enough for a great day. But not only did I get Oma to myself—the movie was the best! By the end of its two hours *Back to the Future* had usurped *The Wizard of Oz* as my favourite film in the history of the world.

I loved Marty McFly, played by Alex P. Keaton from *Family Ties*, and his aviator sunglasses and electric guitar, and envied his friend-ship with the old-man scientist, Doc, who looked like Einstein and turned a car into a time machine. And Marty inadvertently drives back to 1955, where he *meets his own parents*, but they're not Mom and Dad yet, they're Lorraine and George, and Lorraine falls in love with Marty instead of George. And that's a paradox, and a paradox, Doc says, could destroy the space-time continuum. That means the entire universe! Of course, in the end Marty gets his parents to fall in love after all. He drives the DeLorean past the clock tower at exactly 10:04 pm, gets struck by lightning in the process, and goes back to the future with a fiery bang. He finds a slightly changed 1985—changed for the better, because he helped his parents make better decisions in the past.

The story was *perfect*.

After the movie, Oma took me for tuna melts at Casey's, where sandwiches came in baskets instead of on plates, and we debriefed.

"One thing I don't understand." I said. "Does Biff like Lorraine or not?" In the movie, Marty has to get his parents to kiss at the dance so they can fall in love and get married and have Marty and not destroy the universe. The plan is for Marty to take Lorraine to the dance and then pretend to do—something—to her in the car, and then George can save her, and she'll automatically fall in love with him. Only Biff comes along instead. The big bully. And Biff *really* starts doing something to Lorraine in the car. He pins her down and gets his arm right up her dress. So when George shows up and pretends to punch out Marty, he ends up *really* punching out Biff, and Lorraine falls in love with him, just as planned.

So, *does* Biff like Lorraine?

"That's a complicated question," Oma agreed.

"Why?"

"He likes her...in a way," Oma said. "But not much good can come of a man like Biff liking you in *that* way." She sipped her tea. "A man like that liked me once," she said. "Before I met Opa. I didn't understand, because my mother hadn't taught me a thing about being a woman. Even when my period started, I'd thought I was dying. I ended up— well. We have to be careful, darling. Men really are pigs. Not all men, mind you. Not *all*. But. Many."

"What about George McFly?"

"He was nice, wasn't he? But sometimes, even when they seem nice—it's not as obvious in real life."

I really had no idea what she was talking about. Well, I had a tiny bit of an idea of what she was talking about, enough of an idea that I felt too embarrassed to pursue the question further.

I took a bite of my tuna melt, opening my mouth wide to get around the mound of fish, bread, and oozing salty cheddar.

"What if I travelled back in time?" I asked, when I could talk again. "How old were my parents in 1955?"

"Well, let's see. Your mother was ten. Your father was five."

"Mum was one year older than I am now! That would be like if I ended up marrying someone who's four now! How old were you and Opa in 1955?"

"In 1955. I was thirty-four. Opa was forty-eight."

"That's like if I ended up marrying someone who's—twenty-three now."

"Yes, that's true."

"When you were nine, Opa was twenty-three."

"Yes."

"Did you ever think of that before?"

"I suppose I have," said Oma. "But once you get a little older, ages don't matter so much. You'll see."

"What were you like then?"

"Well, I don't know—I was the same as I am now, more or less. Let's see. In 1955, we'd just moved to England."

"From Holland?"

"Yes. After the war, in 1945, we went back to Holland. That's when your mother was just a baby. I had Auntie Karin soon after that, and then Jos got a job in Indonesia. Did you know, Shell flew him to Indonesia, but sent me and the babies by ship? We were at sea for weeks! And I contracted hepatitis on the ship. That was in the late forties, that we lived in the tropics. It was beautiful in Jakarta. We ate mangos, and we had servants. It was always hot, except when it rained in sheets. When we returned to Holland, life just felt grim. *Grim.*"

"Why?" I'd heard this story before, heard it and heard it, but I wanted to hear it again. The details seemed a little richer, a little different, each time.

"Oh, it was dark, grey. Cold. The food was bland. And Opa, you know, was terribly depressed—"

"He was?"

"Yes. Because of what happened in the war."

I nodded. Because of what happened in the war. I knew Opa had been depressed because of what happened in the war.

"When we went back to Holland, and his mother was gone, and everything that had happened—it was such a shock. You can't imagine the shock. You know, he went back a hero. He was awarded a medal by the queen. Queen Wilhelmina, and I went with him. The queen herself gave him the medal and told him, 'You were very brave.' That was really exciting."

"What was the medal for?"

"He was a translator," said Oma. "After he escaped Holland, he made his way to England and joined the army. He spoke English and German both very well, so he was a great asset. I was in the military too, you know. I drove an ambulance."

I nodded.

"Once I picked up a man in my ambulance, and then picked up his boot, which was lying nearby. I looked inside the boot, and his foot was in there."

She laughed. I'd heard the foot-in-boot story many times too, but laughed along with her anyway.

"But 1955," said Oma. "Well, it wasn't like that movie, maybe in America, but not in England. I moved to England that year with the girls, and Opa came a year after that. Shell agreed to transfer him to the London office." She wiped her hands on her napkin and pushed back the wave of grey hair that fell over her forehead. She was wearing a long-sleeved cotton shirt tucked into a long blue skirt, with a navy cardigan on top.

"What did your hair look like then?" I asked. "What did you wear?"

"My hair? It was long and brown, and wavy. And I suppose I wore— hmm. A blouse tucked into trousers, most often."

"Was your hair like mine?"

"Quite like yours. But not as curly. You have Opa's hair, I think."

I tugged at the ends of my hair. My hair made me miserable. So *puffy*, no matter how much I brushed it, no matter how hard I tried to flatten it with my hands.

"Oma?" I said. "Opa's a man, and he's not a pig."

"Opa's nice," she agreed. Then added, "But."

"Mum said he wasn't *always* nice...?"

"He wasn't always nice, because of what happened to his mother in the war," Oma agreed. "He wasn't *nasty*, and he wasn't mean. He just sort of didn't notice that other people were around."

"What do you mean?"

"Well, for instance, when we were living in Holland and had two babies, Shell offered him a position in Indonesia, and he just said yes, without telling me or asking me. He took the job and then came around to informing me: *I've taken a job in Indonesia, and you'll be travelling there alone with the babies, by ship.* They would only pay for one plane ticket, you see. For him. It simply hadn't occurred to him that I might have anything to say about it. He thought, oh, Indonesia, that sounds rather nice, and he said yes."

"Oh..."

"And another time. We were married during the war, and then the military promoted him, and he was going to be sent away, back to Holland. They telephoned, and he had to report for duty straight away. I drove him to the headquarters in London. I was pregnant with your mother by then, and he was being sent off, and we didn't know when we'd see each other again. Maybe never. Of course, you couldn't help but think that maybe you'd never see him again at all. I pulled up in the car, and he got straight out and went into the building. I thought he was going in to, you know, find out exactly what was happening, and that he'd come back in a minute for our goodbye. But he never came back out. He'd just forgotten about me. He hadn't thought to say goodbye at all."

"That happened before he found out about his mother," I pointed out after another bite of tuna melt.

"Yes," Oma said. "That's right. Good point. He was like that all along, wasn't he?" After a pause, Oma said, "If you take my advice, you'll live your own life, and don't think too much about men. The world has changed, and marriage is terribly outdated. In ten years no one will be marrying anymore."

I glanced at Opa throughout dinner that night, trying to imagine what he was thinking. He smiled at me, chewing a bite of chicken, made an appreciative eating sound, gave a quick acknowledging nod. The kind of smile and nod a person could deliver automatically, yes, without really noticing the person at the other end of it.

"The kind of man who just forgets you're there," Oma had said. "Which is different from a *pig*."

A pig, like Biff.

In bed that night, I thought more about Lorraine and Biff. Oma said it's no good having that kind of man like you, in that way. I mean, I wasn't an idiot. I knew: he wanted to have sex with her. You can tell Lorraine's the prettiest girl because the resident bully harasses her unremittingly, and finally tries to have sex with her. To make her do it. Would I ever be pretty enough for a bully to stalk and attack me, and for a good-looking nice guy to save me? Or would I end up with someone who wasn't mean, but who tended to forget I existed, who looked right through me?

※ When I turned ten, we rented the customary birthday VCR and I picked my birthday movies. *Stand by Me*, another long-time favourite, and *Back to the Future*, which I'd replayed in my head since I'd seen it the previous summer. We watched the movies at my party, and then, over the course of the weekend, I watched *Back to the Future* eight more times.

Each viewing brought me in closer to the plot's intricacies. Just like Dorothy, I realized, Marty's trapped in a humdrum locale with a washed-up family, and then gets whisked away to somewhere sweeter and brighter, only to find himself surrounded by familiar-unfamiliar faces. Like Dorothy, he spends the rest of the story trying to find his way back home. Like Dorothy, getting home involves a quest, and a riddle. Only—unlike Dorothy—Marty finds home transformed. Home's gone from gaudy to chic, parents from trashy to tennis-playing. By his own doing! He's explained to his parents how to quit being such losers, and they listened. He discovers he's changed other things, too, little things. Twin Pines Mall is now Lone Pine Mall, because Marty ran over one of the historic trees as he sped into 1955.

And like any burgeoning time-travel fan, I revelled in finding the plot's problems. At the end, Marty goes back early and watches himself leave, so shouldn't that version of Marty come back too? Shouldn't there be two versions of Marty in 1985, I wondered, and two DeLoreans? And wouldn't the other Marty be a totally different kind of kid, from growing up with those different parents? In which case, why would he have the same girlfriend, and the same clothes and guitar and skate-board, and most distressing of all, why would he be friends with Doc Brown, if he already had a super-cool nerd of a dad? Would Marty have to *kill* the other Marty? Or would the other Marty run him out of town? And if our Marty prevailed, wouldn't he spend the rest of his life with childhood memories his family didn't share. He'd move through the world with a constant sense of *jamais vu*, nothing familiar, everything *off*. And wouldn't his parents and everyone else notice he'd trans-formed overnight into the kind of boy raised by an alcoholic mother and a pansy-ass father, the kind of father who never got to slam his fist into the face of the town boor, saving his girl from attempted rape?

Between my fifth and sixth viewings, the implication of all this took a definite shape in my mind. Unlike Dorothy, Marty fails to get home, can never go home, has undone his home by leaving it.

☀ I'd placed my phone beside my coffee cup, and reached for it the moment after Matteo texted me: 'I'm here! Just getting off the plane!'

I arrived at the coffee shop by Louise Metro at least twenty minutes before Matteo said his train would arrive, ordered a coffee, and tried to read. Then, in the washroom—toilet—I peered closely at my face. The red mark on the end of my nose had faded almost to nothing, and with the makeup I'd applied that morning it didn't show at all. Back at my table, I tried to read again, but instead watched the window. Every time I saw a bald head, my heart leapt—despite that these bald men looked nothing like Matteo, not even at first glance: short men, round men, black men. I'd joke later to Matteo, one was even a baby. I never realized how many men had no hair.

To distract myself, I texted Yael in Singapore. 'There is a universe where I am in a Brussels coffee shop, and it is this universe! But there is also a universe where everything is exactly the same as this one, only there is no such thing as coffee, and I'm in a broth shop, drinking a hot mug of broth.'

She was awake. Three minutes later, she wrote back: 'There is a universe where coffee plants were made extinct years ago by invasive flamingos.'

And then:

'How's your trip?'

I peered through the window again. No Matteo.

'Good,' I told Yael. Then, 'There is a universe where I'm drinking flamingo broth.'

'Noooo,' she texted back.

'I wish it were not so,' I told her. Yael and her daughter loved visiting the flamingos at the bird sanctuary in Singapore. 'I'm meeting Matteo today,' I texted.

'Have fun!'

I thought, there are universes in which I'm here to meet each of these other, lesser bald men.

Finally I saw Matteo, his own bald head inside the hood of his green jacket. I ran to the door to hug him, and our arms got a little mixed up, our limbs not in sync yet. I took him to the restaurant where I'd eaten the day before, and we ate tabouli and hummus, both nervous, which meant he was quiet, holding himself still and composed, while I babbled and laughed too much, and we stared at each other like is it you? Then looked away shyly and back.

As we walked back to the hotel, he carried his bag in one hand, and squeezed my shoulder with the other. Our arms touched as we walked, and we held hands. We walked without speaking, just smiling. If Matteo were a colour, I thought, he'd be grey-blue. If Matteo were an insect, he'd be a grasshopper.

"If you were a texture," I told him later, lying face to face in the white hotel bed, "you'd be moss on a boulder."

Strengthened and refreshed, I make the return journey now with my complete travelling fund, besides which I have been able to buy a pound of clandestine butter—partly reinforcement of my stock, partly a present for my host in Brussels. On the way back by bus and by tram I learn that our Dutch ideas about overcrowding on public transportation are still ridiculously plutocratic. Pressed, mangled and in good health I arrive in Brussels; despite everything the butter was saved from a seemingly certain disaster!

That night I dreamed I sat in Oma and Opa's den, on the black leather armchair. Evening, dusky, and Opa across from me on the matching sofa. Beside me stood the iron wood stove, black as a silhouette.

"Opa?" I said.

"Hello, darling." He appeared eightyish, hair thick, blond, and curly. The skin around his eyes crinkled.

"Are you back?"

"Ja, ja. The situation was a bit precarious for a while. But I'm perfectly fine." He pronounced it *sit-uation*, not *sitchewation*. I sprung to the sofa and hugged him tight around his bony chest and shoulders, the knobbly weave of his sweater against my cheek. "Oh!" said Opa, waiting a few moments before gently but firmly removing himself. "Thank you, darling."

I stood with my back to the bookshelf. "I thought you had Alzheimer's. I thought—I thought you were dead."

"Oh, no. No, no. I had a bit of a scare."

"You mean you remember everything now?"

"Of course I do. I'm fine, darling. Perfectly fine. You needn't worry."

I leaned closer as we spoke, and realized his face had been disfigured, features knocked apart, flesh torn back to reveal skull—and then rebuilt. He'd found the best plastic surgeon in the world, and looked perfect, almost perfect. I could sense, if not see, the seams, so faint, so masterfully concealed. Anyone could look at his face for years without noticing a thing.

THE NEXT MORNING, Matteo and I went out for breakfast, then wandered around in the crowds. It was Belgian Independence Day, and I was grateful to be spending time with someone whose instinct was to get away from crowds, rather than to head further into them.

We stopped for lunch at the restaurant where I'd eaten the night before. I felt ridiculously proud that I already knew the place, as though this were my city, explained that it served only pita sandwiches, hundreds of different pita sandwiches. I ordered the chicken-apple-raisin, and Matteo ordered the chicken souvlaki. At a table nearby, a woman was speaking in English in a loud, confident manner, jarring in its out-of-place familiarity. I peeked over and saw that she was between twenty-five and thirty-five, with long curly blonde hair and freckly toned arms. She wore sports sandals with long slim shorts and a tank top that would not have been out of place in a yoga class. "This whole Europe thing's okay," the woman was telling her rapt companion, a similarly dressed guy, tall with shaggy dark hair. "But I don't know. For me, it's not what touches my soul. When I was in my early twenties, I think, Europe seemed like, I mean, that was travelling to me then. But now. The history is important and a privilege to witness. And it's so cool that you're here, and we can hang out!"

"Yeah! It's so good to—"

"But it just, it doesn't touch me in the same way. I mean—" she gestured around, at all the Belgians in their tee-shirts and jeans and sneakers, eating their pita sandwiches, speaking in quick happy French with their kids.

"Canadians," I whispered.

Matteo nodded.

"I drove a motorbike through Vietnam," the woman said. "The locals just flocked to me. They found me so full of light and positivity. They said they literally felt my light when I was around. They saw that everyone has the potential for possibility, no matter their circumstances. It's about inner possibility."

Matteo widened his eyes at me.

"Anyway," I said. "When you're at a party, do you prefer to stay near a wall, or stay in the centre of things?"

"Ha ha," said Matteo. "That's from the personality test, isn't it? With the letters? IQGB, or whatever?"

"Nooo."

"It is!"

"Introverted vs Extroverted, Intuitive vs Sensing, Feeling vs Thinking, and Judging vs Perceiving," I explained.

"Uh huh."

Since the spring, I'd been trying to convince him to do the Myers–Briggs personality test, which is based on Jungian archetypes, and though it had become a joke between us, I really did want to know his type. INFJ, the "counsellor" type, like me? Definitely not INTJ, the "scientist," like Yael and Opa and my mom, and not ENFJ, the "teacher," like my sister and my father. He certainly wasn't ENTP, the "inventor," like Lev, either. Matteo was some other type, that I didn't know well.

"My type," I said, "is the most likely to be interested in personality tests. You probably don't like them because of your type."

He laughed.

"Anyway," I said. "I know the answer. You prefer to stay by the wall."

"I was blessed to spend a month at an ashram in Bali," the blonde woman told her companion.

"It depends," said Matteo. "How big is the room? How crowded? Do I know the people? Where are the people I know? Am I tired? Did I get bad news that day? Where are the snacks, and are they good snacks, and am I hungry?"

"Ugh," I told him. "You're just being difficult." I could see that he was distracted, listening to the woman at the next table. We both gave in to eavesdropping.

"I don't even have words," she said. "I mean you just can't put an experience like that into words."

The guy friend nodded eagerly.

"The experience itself was wordless."

"Right, so how could you possibly—"

"I realized in the second week that I was letting go," she said. "Letting go of my self. My *self*, you know? We all have things we need to let go of. For me, it was my self."

The server came by. Matteo had finished his sandwich, and ordered each of us another glass of wine.

"I'd like you to visit me in the fall," Matteo said, "but I don't have a lot of stuff right now."

"Stuff?"

"Furniture and things. I don't know how long I'll keep this job, so I haven't settled in. I'm embarrassed."

"I don't need luxury," I said.

"But I never have people over."

"Okay."

"But I'd like to invite you."

"I'd like to visit you."

"I want to go back to Asia," said the Canadian woman. "I don't know why I've been given this gift, this light, this light inside me that everyone can see."

"I can see it," said the guy. "The light."

Matteo and I smiled at each other, squeezed each other's fingers.

✳ Late afternoon I lay in bed under the Brussels hotel's puffy white blanket, watching Matteo sleep. When he woke, we'd go out for dinner, and then in the morning we'd have to part ways again. I didn't want to part ways. I wanted to stay warm with him in that bed. The night before, he'd hugged me while he slept; he'd never done that before. When he woke in the night, I felt him run his finger along the bridge of my nose. He'd read the magazine story about my nose job, so he knew my nose had been all hacked up. I wondered what he thought, if he thought I must be spoiled and superficial, from a family that dished out the cash for a child's face to be prettified, enough cash to pay for a year of university.

I watched him, his long lashes, his long neck and lean, muscular arms. He had big hands, with long, straight fingers. What kind of man was Matteo? What kind of man would Matteo turn out to be? Would I really visit him in the fall, or would he soon forget I existed, out of sight out of mind? Or would he hold on too hard, or would some terrible secret bubble up? Or would he just reach a point he couldn't push past, the thought of me in his space too intrusive? Was he really a loner, solitude his natural and best state? Was that why his company felt so precious, a rare and special gift, this intimacy so hard-won?

Once upon a time, Betty must have lain in a Brussels hotel bed beside Jos. Watched him sleep, his big hands curled like a child's. Maybe she thought, *what kind of man is this? What kind of man will he turn out to be? He doesn't seem like a pig. Will he forget about me, will he survive this war, will I? Imagine if I never see him again. Imagine if we have grandchildren someday.*

✳ Jos didn't write much about July 21st. Half a page again. Though it was Belgian Independence Day, he managed to visit an associate's office and receive further assistance from "a little man with a small moustache but luckily of a better kind: neither fanatical nor malicious," who would arrange for Jos to cross the border into France. From these men, he received ration tickets, and used them to buy bread and meat for his travels.

> With this and with what was left of my original stock I can now provide for myself for two or three days.

ON WEDNESDAY, JULY 22ND, Matteo and I slept until the last possible moment, and checked out of the hotel at 10:00. My train would leave Brussels at 12:17. We found a sushi restaurant, then headed for the train station. Though I'd be alone with my little blue suitcase for the next ten days, I let him pull it down the sidewalk for me, toward the train station, while he carried his own small backpack as well.

"Do you try to answer your emails as soon as you can, because you can't stand a messy inbox?" I asked.

"Well, I don't wait *too* long..."

"Definitely agree, slightly agree, or moderately agree?"

"Ah!" said Matteo.

I shook his arm. "Why won't you do the personality test? Seriously. Just curious. Why won't you?"

"You want to figure me out," he said, after a moment, "and then you'll be done with me."

At the station, I bought each of us a coffee, and we stood up on the platform. I wrapped my arms around his waist, his cheek against the top of my head.

"Thank you—" he said.

"Thank you. For coming here."

"I loved it. You'll be fine," he said. "You'll have a good trip."

"I don't want to figure you out so I can be done with you," I told him. "It's impossible to figure a person out, anyway."

"I'm still not doing that test." He kissed my forehead. "I can see the light inside you," he told me.

"That's why no one can resist me. The light."

As the train (Brussels—Midi—Mouscron) pulled out, Matteo turned and headed back down into the station, where he'd catch his subway back to the airport, and back to Italy.

On the train, I didn't write or read, just slumped a little, watched the city then countryside outside the window, acutely aware of some strange discomfort, which I realized was Matteo's smell; that is the absence of his smell, and of his warmth, nearby.

On Wednesday, July 22nd, 1942, Jos travelled by train to a town near the border with France. There, he met his guide, Arbuste, who was "accompanied by someone whose role in this story has never become very clear to me."

Elsewhere, three hundred thousand Warsaw Ghetto Jews were sent to Treblinka extermination camp.

The three of us enter the town, and within five minutes we are in a pub. I am introduced to the pub owner, a fairly young man with a portly, clandestine appearance who turns out to be my guide until Valenciennes. He holds onto my money, leaves the business in the hands of his wife—and now four men strong, we make our way to the border. This time we follow the official road, a wide, bald street with messy and characterless houses on both sides, typical of the suburbs of a Belgian or a French industrial area. We are absorbed in a stream of people who have arrived on the same train and are all going the same direction. At a certain point we reach a barrier across the road: Belgian customs, and a couple of hundred metres further down the exact repetition: French customs. There is no passport control except on the rare occasions when the German police make a surprise check.

My guide simply dives underneath the barrier—I follow. He waves jovially to customs and at the gendarmes, who greet us in return.

We are past the Belgian control. In the no-man's-land between the two customs we dive into another pub. My guide disappears to the back to settle my money business, and I am treated to a stiff drink "to a happy ending." A bit later we go on, now in two groups of two. My guide takes my suitcase and approaches the French customs. Suitcase open: a quick search. In the meantime, a second customs officer asks if I have nothing to declare. I reply: "no." And otherwise, stay dumb; just when it seems that he wants to interrogate me further, the first customs officer, the one with the suitcase, gives him a sign that he should leave me alone. Apparently, I'm in such esteemed company that any question would be an indiscretion; and so we also pass French customs.

A little further on the tram is waiting, but when my guide catches the slightest glimpse of a German uniform, we go a couple of hundred metres past it to the next tram stop and its accompanying pub. I receive my money: twenty-eight-thousand French francs. A bit later Arbuste and his friend appear. We have a less potent drink by way of farewell. A moment later the tram arrives—overcrowded of course, I shake hands with Arbuste—and that's over too.

Instead of taking his next train all the way to Paris, Jos and the pub owner decided on a tram headed to Valenciennes, where they would spend the night. I changed trains in Mouscron, and in Lille Flandres I boarded a train to Valenciennes.

❋ In *When Paris Went Dark: The City of Light Under German Occupation*, Ronald C. Rosbottom asks why so many Parisians kept journals during the German Occupation, recording sentiments and actions that could have seen them punished or killed. "In a world where there has been a short-circuiting of normal connections," he suggests, "blank pages can offer the freedom that one misses." Opa waited until he arrived in Lyon to record his illegal and dangerous crossing, but then he packed the journal in his small suitcase and kept it with him, fleeing Vichy France before the Germans occupied the whole country in November 1943. He crossed Portugal and Spain, then ended up in England. He met Betty, they married, he left again for the Netherlands, where, days after the birth of his first child back in London, he drove into Delft, and straight to his brother's house, where his young nieces mistook him at first for an official come to arrest their father. All that time, he kept the thirty-page journal with him.

He'd written that account, and kept it safe, because he wanted to record what happened before his memories faded, while they were still true—that was the reason he gave. I so wished he'd recorded more than just facts and actions, and included more of his memories. Even references to his own emotional reactions came only in tiny accidental-seeming bursts. He recorded no anecdotes about his childhood, no reflections on his relationships, on the war itself, on his convictions, on anguish about the people he left behind. He never even referred to the Occupation or to his own status as a Jew, and certainly included no reflections on what his identity meant to him—oh, if only! If only he'd written with the desire to be *known*. If only he'd *lived* with the desire to be known. He'd never said a word about himself, or about the war, or about Judaism, except to Oma. I'd learned everything I knew about Opa through Oma. And how much was she repeating, how much was she guessing, how much was she inventing? On the train to Valenciennes, I read Opa's entry of July 22nd in frustration. I kept trying to see something between the lines, to see his *heart*.

I did understand the impulse to record events, to preserve the facts in the face of everything that will try to distort them. I was a compulsive diarist for years. I never received a regular allowance as a child, but sometimes one of my parents gave me a few dollars. "From now on, you'll get ten dollars a week," my dad would say, and then forget about it again for a few months. When I did have a big enough bill, I walked up the five blocks to Sunnyside Avenue, a block past where I normally turned to get to school, a block into the wilderness, to the corner store. They sold notebooks at that store, and I stood in the aisle turning through the blank pages, imagining what I might write on them: rhyming poems, stories about flying bicycles, misfit kids on epic adventures. Then, the Christmas I was ten, 1987, I received a blue cloth-covered notebook in my stocking. I balked at first at the word "diary," which sounded too close to "diarrhea," but finally the word found its own compartment in my mind, and I could say it without blushing. From then on, I always used that word for my notebooks, never the more sophisticated "journal." I started writing every day, with Anne Frank as my model diarist, which meant describing places and people, and my feelings and thoughts about those places and people, and my observations about the way people interacted with each other, all as clearly as possible. Mimi had given me a copy of Anne Frank's diary for my eighth birthday. I meticulously recorded the events of each day so that time couldn't beat the brightness out of them, I imagined that someone far in the future would find my notebooks, and travel back to me. I didn't have any good secrets yet, but planned to acquire some as soon as I could.

Before I slept each night; sometimes exhausted, longing to close my eyes, I penned out tens of pages, determined to capture my day before it faded. During the days, I focused on memorizing what people said, on noticing how they moved and held their faces. The harder I tried to record every moment, the more I feared I'd forget and lose them forever. I kept souvenirs, too, tickets, bus transfer slips, and receipts, silly flimsy things. I glued them onto my pages. Sometimes photographs, news-paper clippings. By high school, instead of recording details that would have actually interested me later, I filled pages and pages with angsty abstract musings, attempted humour, rage with my parents, and reportage about my friends, infatuations, and misguided romances. For whole entries, I catalogued pains and twinges in various parts of my body and lamented my impending death.

"Why doesn't anyone tell that child to put away her damned note-book?" Opa rumbled one summer day as he came into the kitchen.

Oma and I were at the table, me writing, she salting almonds to roast in the oven. I jumped, hadn't quite realized anyone could see me; my notebook always felt like an invisibility shield. I shuffled the notebook onto my lap. I'd never made Opa angry before. Looking back, I wondered what he had been thinking and feeling. A man with a secret diary. But after all, I was just a girl, just a little girl with a little-girl diary, no one anything had ever happened to, no one destined to be a man, no one who could have reminded Opa of himself.

❊ When I was twenty-four, all my old diaries drowned in Ottawa. I was soaking in an iron clawfoot tub two provinces eastward, in a ramshackle house off the highway when it happened. I had just finished my first year of grad school—I'd quit my eleven-dollar-an-hour job at a book distributor in Toronto to study creative writing in New Brunswick, having decided that I had to give writing a real try. I'd committed to my roommates before meeting them or seeing the place they'd rented. It was a house with half-decayed wood siding with peeling red paint, antique hardwood floors scratched on top of scratched, the clawfoot iron bathtub gradually easing downward to reveal its bottom through the cracked kitchen ceiling. The house flooded come spring, the Saint John River creeping across the yard to lap at the porch and seep in. As water fingertipped the edges of the foundation, leaking drops into the basement, I sank deeper into the bath water, rinsing conditioner out of my hair. We didn't have a shower, only this tub that took half an hour to fill.

When I re-emerged from the water, the ceiling over my head shook with a clatter and then a bang. Like a pot dropped in the attic. This rental house had no attic, though. The house itself shifted and creaked constantly, its geriatric joints groaning. But that was no house sound, I thought. Imagine if there was something alive in there, something with wings, something fluttery. But no—that crash sounded so much like a person, and the silence that followed had the quality of stilled breath, of someone hunched, holding as still as possible, hoping no one heard.

I was in creative writing school, and always looking for stories. *Anne Frank*, I thought. *Imagine there's a secret attic up there, and Anne Frank is hiding in it. Anne Frank, living in the attic, far from Europe, decades after the war.* (I never ended up writing that story, but someone else did, and did it perfectly—in Shalom Auslander's *Hope, A Tragedy*, a Jewish family living in an early-twenty-first-century American town they've chosen for its lack of history, find themselves saddled with Anne Frank, a foul-mouthed old woman, the Anne Frank in every Jew's attic, shuffling on the floor boards when you're trying to find some ahistorical peace.) Something shifted, under me this time. Something cracked. The kitchen ceiling, below, had been sinking. The bath sank again. I rolled inelegantly over the side, hair clean enough.

The phone rang.

"Naomi!" my roommate called up the stairs. "It's for you."

"We're going on an away mission," Dad told me, when I picked up the phone in my room, dripping in my towel. What he meant was, they'd decided to travel in Europe and see their relatives, their old friends. For the last couple of months, Dad had been entertaining everyone around him by pretending he lived on the Starship *Enterprise*.

"Oh—listen—" I said. "Can I stay in the house while you're gone? My house is falling apart. And I'm just working on my thesis this summer. I have a new place for September, with Val and Barb, but—"

"When do you want to come?"

"Next week?"

"Terrific," he said. "Wonderful, amazing. Oh, did we tell you about the warp-core breach? Engineering required a complete overhaul."

"What do you mean?"

"The furnace room. You remember the furnace room? In the basement?"

"Of course."

"Well, the furnace exploded, basically. It was as old as the house—remember? And it cracked right open and flooded the whole room. All those boxes, with our tax receipts and everything, were sitting in half a foot of water. We just threw everything out."

"But—except for my diaries, right?"

"Your what?"

A floaty feeling came over me, a preternatural calm. "All my diaries, my letters, all my photos and everything. In boxes. In that room."

"I can fix this," said Dad. "I'll call you back."

But he didn't call back, because he couldn't fix it, of course, and he didn't know how to state the shitty plain truth, that my boxes were gone. My piles of notebooks, the products of childhood and adolescent obsession with writing everything down, with pinning every memory to paper before it could fade. All wiped out at once.

"Maybe it's for the best?" he suggested, when I finally called him and made him admit that he couldn't actually find out where the garbage truck had gone, and go there, and go through all the garbage, and find my books. He went on, "A lot of people say it's more painful than anything, reading that stuff that they wrote when they were young..."

Then he said, "Your mother's so upset, just devastated, afraid you'll never forgive us."

He said, "Are you *terribly* angry? Do you hate us? Do you still love us? Can you—" his voice shook "—forgive us?"

All my muscles tightened, my stomach sucking into itself. "Sure," I said. "It's not your fault. It's no big deal. It's probably for the best."

The next Monday, somewhere over Quebec, I laid my index finger over a persistent tingle on the left side of my chin. A pimple was forming in there. A bad one. Gestating way down deep, by the roots of my teeth. I hadn't stayed in my parents' house for more than two nights since I moved out almost a decade earlier. I'd never stayed there alone.

"Airlock opening. Docking at shuttle-bay twelve," said Dad, we pulled into the garage.

"Bernard," said my mother.

"What?" said Dad.

"He thinks he's Captain Kirk," Mum told me.

"Give me some credit," said Dad. "Next Generation. Picard."

I wasn't staying in my childhood bedroom, but in the guest room across the hall, which my father now called my "quarters." A few minutes into unpacking, Dad beckoned me down to the basement.

He opened the furnace room door. "Check out engineering."

Engineering: lit so fluorescent bright, so futuristic white, the smallest dust mote would sparkle; but there's no dust in fake space and no insects or mould, nowhere for rodents or face-sucking aliens to hide. This room had once resembled the ship in *Alien*, but now it was all *Star Trek*. The once cluttered room stood empty apart from the light that violated its every corner, empty apart from the white warp drive, that is, furnace, turned off for summer.

"Cool, huh?" Dad hesitated, as though giving me a moment to absorb the sterility, the total wiped-cleanness of it, to wipe myself clean of the loss, the millions of words I'd written, the scraps I'd collected and glued, the thousands of hours I'd spent writing and adhering mementos to paper. I pictured the diaries, the blue one I received in my Christmas stocking at ten, the red one I began at thirteen, the white one with the lock, the green one with the tinted pages. All of them soggy and filthy, ripped open, lying in some landfill.

"Neat," I said, and went upstairs.

That evening, there was blood in the toilet. From my butt. My bowels. My insides.

Before I had time to consider the contents of the toilet at any length, Dad called upstairs that Yael was on the phone, from New York, where she was studying.

"I'm on my mobile," she told me. "In the bathroom of a restaurant." She was out with some guy from a dating site; she was trying to find a Jewish husband, and had dinner dates at least three nights a week all that year. "He just confided that he was recently on trial for murder," she said. "He wanted me to hear it from him, before I found out online. He was acquitted." She made me write down his name and phone number. "He says he didn't do it." If I didn't hear from her by midnight, I was supposed to call the police.

Yael called back at 9:30, and I answered right away. I was sitting at Dad's desk, googling "bloody stool." She was home, and fine, not murdered.

"Phew," I said. "I'm worried," I added. "Something's wrong with me."

"You're not dying," said Yael, automatically.

By then hypochondria was reaching its tendrils across my mind to strangle every other thought, and by the next morning, I was ready to call an ambulance. Over breakfast, I asked my mom to drive me to the emergency clinic.

"Why?" asked Dad.

"A personal thing."

"Hm," said Mum. "Are you being weird?"

"Who are you living with next year, again?" said Dad.

"Val and Barb."

"Polish Barb? And who's Val?"

"You know, Valerie? Tall? Art history?"

"Oh, of course. She's funny!"

"Yes, she's funny."

"*Very* tall," said Mum.

"Father's log," said Dad. "Daughter Naomi approaching the Valerian sector. The humanoids there possess unusually elongated limbs and a highly developed sense of humour, perhaps due to the unique gravitational and atmospheric dynamics on their home planet of Barberon-R."

"Bernard," said my mother. "This *Star Trek* thing is no longer funny."

I pushed the sore spot on my chin. It hurt more today, and had begun to swell.

"It *is* funny, though," I said. "Will you take me to the doctor, please?"

"He's obsessive," said Mum. "He can't make a joke once and move on."

"Will you take me to the doctor?" I said again. "Or I can take the bus."

"What happened to your chin?" she asked.

"It doesn't matter. There's something wrong with my—digestive system."

She drove me downtown, to the same doctor I saw as a child, and all through high school. But it wasn't him. A resident. Who poked around a little with latex-gloved hand while my heart pounded so hard it hurt, and I pictured my funeral.

He said, "You don't have cancer. Yes, I'm *sure*."

Did my file list every time I'd come here, every time I came, all through high school, ready for the death sentence? What worried me was, what if the doctor saw my file and thought I was a hypochondriac? And didn't take my symptoms seriously, as a result? And missed the fact that this time I really did have cancer?"

"No," he said. "You absolutely do not have cancer. And please don't search symptoms online."

I had to admit to my mother, in the car home, that I'd probably live.

"What is *wrong* with you and your father?" she said. "You're *obsessive*."

The pimple on my chin, meanwhile, kept growing.

"That looks really uncomfortable, Mum grimaced, the morning before they left for the airport. "You must have an infection festering in your skin."

"Set course for the European quadrant," Dad called out the window of their taxi. "Engage!"

"Bernard," said Mum.

"Have fun!" I called after them.

※ That summer, I was reading for the first time about the Holocaust, reading a lot, everything I could get my hands on, histories and novels, memoirs and poetry, everything. Starting research for my master's thesis. I was also reading about alien abductions; I thought maybe a flying saucer could visit my characters, maybe some long bony fingers in the night, like a metaphor. I piled my Holocaust books on one side of the dining table and my alien books on the other, checked the jam-packed fridge, freezer, and cupboards for supplies, and stayed in the house for five days, an old cashmere scarf of Opa's wrapped loosely around my neck and lower face in case I caught my reflection.

My chin continued to swell, and I brushed my teeth with my eyes closed, afraid of the deformed spectre of my own face. The left side of my chin ached like I'd been punched. My face featured not a pimple, but a disfiguring lump the size of a baby's fist. The touch of a fingertip sent tentacles of pain into my jaw. My skin had been more or less okay for a couple of years; I'd almost forgotten about the years of red lumps blooming bright against my too-white face.

I read John Mack's *Abduction: Human Encounters with Aliens* and Budd Hopkins' *Missing Time*. I read anthologies of first-person accounts, and memoirs of people convinced they'd been abducted repeatedly. One of the books offered a list of symptoms of repeated, repressed abduction. One of the symptoms was a sudden overwhelming interest in books about alien abduction. Anal pain or bleeding. Of course. Who were known for their anal probing? A feeling that something terrible has happened, but you can't remember what it was.

I sat in my parents' living room, the living room that had been my living room from the ages of seven to nineteen, and jumped up, peered out the window, where I was sure I'd seen a strange light out of the corner of my eye. I didn't believe aliens were abducting people nightly. And certainly not abducting me. But alien abduction was physically possible. It seemed far more reasonable to believe in aliens than to believe in, say, a Judeo-Christian God.

I phoned Yael. "I'm having an attack of hypochondria," I said. "Only, instead of a disease, this time I'm afraid of aliens. I feel like they're here, in and around the house, right now."

"But you know there aren't really aliens, right?"

"Yes. But I really feel like there are. I should do my CBT worksheets."

"Because you know you don't believe in aliens."

"Sure. A cognitive behavioural therapist would say there's no evidence for aliens. But a psychoanalyst would say the fear of aliens means something. It's a metaphor. It's emotionally true, or. I just read this memoir by Lauren Slater. It's called *Lying*, and through the whole thing she talks about her childhood epilepsy, and about lying, and it turns out at the end that she never had epilepsy; the epilepsy was a metaphor."

"Ugh. Sounds awful. I would hate that book."

"Maybe the emotional truth here is, aliens are abducting me nightly."

"Naomi," said Yael. "You understand the difference between fiction and nonfiction. Between truth and what's not true, and you know that difference is important. That's why you're not a weirdo."

"You're studying Hebrew," I said. "You're studying for a bat mitzvah."

"Yes, but I understand the difference between metaphor and fact too."

"So—do you believe in God in a literal way? Like, God giving Moses the mitzvot..."

"Of course not."

I bought Whitley Strieber's *Communion* at a used bookstore, put it in the freezer for twenty-four hours to kill any potential bedbugs, then settled down on the sofa. I read half of it before growing bored of the endless hypnosis sessions and vague impressions of various species of alien floating him out the window naked and paralyzed, and started skipping pages and chapters. The boredom eased my fear a little, but I was still freaked out.

One of the books suggested bravery, and I tried. Lying in bed, I said out loud, "Go ahead. Take me. Just don't hurt me, and bring me back rested, okay?" But they couldn't hear my voice, or if they could, they didn't understand English.

Was it possible that I had been abducted, nightly, all through my childhood, by aliens? No. I wasn't thinking that. I never believed in aliens.

I thought, there are no aliens but fear itself.

There is nothing crawling but my skin itself.

There is no cancer but these thoughts themselves.

There is no spaceship but this house itself.

I placed my alien books under the dining room table. Tomorrow I'd start reading the Holocaust books.

But first, in the morning, I phoned my former dermatologist's office, and they told me to come right in. After arranging Opa's scarf around my chin, I took the bus out past St. Laurent mall. The dermatologist had the same slight figure as always, same straight grey hair, blue eyes, and surgical mask covering the bottom half of her face. I had never seen her nose or mouth.

"Pretty bad," she said, "but I've seen much worse."

She injected cortisone into my chin. "You'll still have a cyst," she said. "But it will be flat. Invisible."

By the time I got home, my chin had shrunk back to its usual angularity, except for a tiny hill, a mogul at the centre of the former mountain.

At home, Opa's scarf in my hand, I stood in the doorway of the blanched furnace room. I told myself that I had, after all, taught myself to write. I had thought through the events of my young life, I had tried and tried to explain myself to myself. I had failed, yes, to deliver those letters I wrote to my future self. But the few occasions I had glanced into those notebooks as an adult had felt just like stepping out of my mother's car the day we visited my childhood neighbourhood in Maryland, everything smaller and just *less* than I remembered. I'd tried to preserve my memories like pickles in jars, but they lost all their flavour and all their colour and floated grey and shrivelled, and didn't resemble themselves at all. Perhaps this bright white basement was just as well.

❄ Jos and the Flemish pub owner arrived in Valenciennes. The pub owner led the way from the train station into town, and to a hotel where he knew the owner.

And then I can eat without ration cards and can sleep without identity papers. Here my friend meets two Quiévraing beauties, the four
of us have a lot of drinks, then lunch with a couple of bottles of wine,
followed by coffee and brandy, and when I get up to pay the bill,
because my guide wouldn't accept any payment for his services, he is
so touched that he buys another couple of rounds of brandy. Farewell.
Alone, I sail on rose-coloured "apéritif-wine-brandy-clouds" through
Valenciennes. The town, once an unattractive industrial centre, is
now horrifying, because the whole town-centre is wiped out by the
war: Rotterdam on a smaller scale but looking more sombre because
the ruins are only partly cleaned up.

I left the train station and followed my GPS into Valenciennes, saw
nothing of that unattractive industrial centre, nothing sombre, no ruins,
only a street of local business and then the tourist area, big restaurants
with sprawling patios jammed with people drinking beer and fruity
cocktails, the kinds of generic places along every main street in every
city back home. Still, as I rolled my suitcase straight through the town's
centre (my GPS pointed me straight on, straight on), I tried to feel my
feet touching the same ground that Opa's touched. Even if, after all, the
notion of same place, different time, and vice versa, fails to stand up to
scrutiny, if you ask a physicist. Or even if you just think about it a little.
For starters, the Earth is careening around the galaxy, which is also on
the move. That's the number one problem with time travel that I could
never get past; how did Marty's DeLorean always land in Hill Valley?
The car, along with H.G. Wells' time machine and Doctor Who's Tardis
and all the rest should have ended up floating in some lonely gap in the
galaxy, or even embedded in a planet or incinerated in a star or devoured
by a black hole. The spot that Valenciennes occupied in 1942 was now
most likely in the vacuum of space, if it was pinpointable at all.

At the hotel, I curled up in bed for a few minutes, nauseated with
missing Matteo. This was my first little French town, but all the longing
made me extra place-blind. My room, anyway, was tiny and charming,

with huge picture windows all around the bed, with its dainty coverlet and wooden frame with built-in shelves. The bed filled almost the entire room, the whole hardwood floor, white radiator to white radiator. One of my windows opened to a little piece of roof that I climbed out onto. From there, I could almost touch the massive old church next door.

I would have liked to talk to Yael. Or my sister, or Matteo. But none of them were online, were probably sleeping. I wanted to tell someone, I am sitting on the roof of a French hotel, and could reach out to touch the church next door. That's what Facebook was for. But I didn't post on Facebook, just wrote in my white notebook.

I wrote, *What am I supposed to be* doing *here?*

I thought, I'll call Val, she'll understand. My friend Valerie, who I lived with in grad school. She hated travelling too. She taught in Korea and then northern Manitoba after we lived together; she could move to a new place if she had a purpose there, but just travelling? No. Because what was she supposed to be doing? I thought, I'll call Val, and a microsecond later, remembered. Val was dead. She had died only four months before I left for Europe. She ordered a pill online, and someone mailed it to her from China. The pill came with a template suicide note, and suggested leaving a list of people who should be notified, with their contact information.

I had known Val was depressed, and sometimes manic, but sometimes I almost missed it, because we were both laughing so hard. Her parents lived in Ottawa too, and she came to town that summer before we moved in together. We met at a pub, and laughed and laughed, about my dad's *Star Trek* obsession, and about the alien books I'd been reading. We laughed and laughed about her cousin who kept getting arrested, and about her thwarted attempts to find a boyfriend. Over the next decade, Val and I talked on the phone or Skype, or in an Ottawa pub, and sometimes I'd be doubled over, ribs aching, and then suddenly stop, and she'd stop, and we'd stare at each other, both afraid. We laughed about illness and addiction, and about the appalling things men said to us. We laughed when I told her Lev had left me, and we laughed when she told me about a one-time date who'd hung around her building at all hours, whom she hadn't managed to shake off for weeks. Sometimes our laughter wound down to strained smiles, when we talked about our bodies, the parts we hated, or about our careers, and how they didn't seem to want to land anywhere, or about love, and how it always slipped away. Once I was so overcome with hilarity, I stepped into the street without looking and would have been hit by a car if Valerie hadn't yanked me back onto the sidewalk.

I had a psychiatrist from the ages of sixteen to twenty, two to four sessions a month. My family doctor referred me when I described the anxiety and depression that made me want to sleep all the time, and about the sensation that I couldn't touch the world or understand it, that I didn't understand anything at all. My therapist and I talked, and she never prescribed any drugs, but she was a doctor, and covered by health insurance, so my parents didn't even have to know. I told Val about my high school therapist, and how she didn't think I should be laughing so much when I told stories that weren't funny at all. "Why are you laughing?" she'd say. "Why are you smiling? What you just told me is horrible."

"But it's also funny, isn't it?" I asked the therapist. "Sort of darkly funny? In a *can you believe it* kind of way?"

"No," she said. "It's not funny at all." What she meant was, I laughed to avoid uncomfortable emotions, facial contortions, tears.

Val agreed she had that tendency too, and that we egged each other on. But Val and I were funny, we made things funny, and I do think some of the stories I told that therapist might have been a little bit funny too—for instance, the story about my dad making my sister's Christmas date shave off his moustache because it looked like Hitler's, and the story where my high school friend Lena dumped me for her drug-dealer boyfriend and then they broke into my parents' house to steal my camcorder and the yearbook with the bad photo of Lena, and the story where I stuck my gum to my high school boyfriend's wall by his bed, my DNA and thumb print embedded in each grotesque wad. Naomi was here, said the gum wall. Or, at least, someone was here. One night I went over, and he'd peeled it all off, and I knew for sure he didn't love me. For a second. Then I thought again that he might. Love! What did I think that meant? I'll be a published writer someday, I thought, and then he'll be sorry.

"Whaat?" howled Val, when I told her about the gum wall.

☀ I climbed back through the window into my hotel room, and went out, found some dinner at a small Chinese restaurant, where I sat at a bar at the window and ate dumplings. The French owner asked, as I was leaving, about my trip. I switched to English, trying to explain. My grandfather travelled through here during the war. I'm writing about his trip. His escape. He was Jewish.

"Ah, Juif," said the French Chinese chef. He had a Jewish friend, he said, in Paris. The Jewish friend was quite interested in the Resistance.

Back in my room, I emailed Yael in Singapore. Everyone close to me, I told her, was in a time zone so far behind or ahead, I couldn't find them online during my prime chatting hours. I had no one to talk to.

Seventy-three years earlier, Jos slept safe in his hotel room, I had no way of knowing which hotel—maybe the same one. Maybe the same room. Why not? Jos considered going on via Switzerland, but didn't know anyone along the border, and had heard passport checks were getting stricter. He decided the Paris route was probably safer, and went to sleep that day without contacting anyone. Contacting someone was not even a possibility to entertain.

I told Yael my trip wasn't amounting to anything. What was happening? Anything truly memorable? Mostly, I was sitting on trains, thinking, recalling more memorable times. I was writing in my white notebook the way I remembered writing in my old diaries, just rambling, falling back and forward in time, now the least interesting moment.

Was I using my family's misfortune to try to make myself more interesting? Was I engaging in "ruins tourism," gawking at suffering from the safe side of a temporal divide?

Was I failing to feel adequately crushed by the gravitas of the past? Was I appropriating a history not my own? Was I even a real Jew?

My high school therapist lit up when I mentioned that grandparents on both sides of my family had fled German-occupied Europe just in time, while their close relatives were murdered in, or occasionally survived, concentration camps. I'd already been seeing her for a year without even mentioning my Jewish heritage. She said, "Your grandparents are Holocaust survivors, on both sides. That's what your parents have in common—their parents are Holocaust survivors."

"No, no," I said. "No, you're making too much of this. They're not Holocaust survivors."

My therapist said they were. She even dug up a definition for me, from the United States Holocaust Memorial Museum: "The Museum honours as survivors any persons, Jewish or non-Jewish, who were displaced, persecuted, or discriminated against due to the racial, religious, ethnic, social, and political policies of the Nazis and their collaborators between 1933 and 1945. In addition to former inmates of concentration camps, ghettos, and prisons, this definition includes, among others, people who were refugees or were in hiding."

Well, according to that definition, then yes, my parents were both children of Holocaust survivors. But.

She strongly recommended I read books about children and grandchildren of Holocaust survivors, said a lot of questions about my parents had just been answered for her. For instance, why my parents had never rebelled against their own parents and remained unusually attached. "It's not uncommon," she told me, "in children of traumatized parents. To over-identify, to feel so responsible for the damaged parent that the child struggles to form his or her own identity. Read the books," she said. "I'll recommend some titles. I think you'll find a lot that feels familiar."

I insisted that none of that had anything to do with me. My family did not care about that stuff, and neither did I, and it didn't have anything to do with anything. And anyway, my mother's mother wasn't even Jewish.

"But she's a veteran. And she married and lived with a Holocaust survivor, a veteran himself."

A *veteran*? Yet another word my family never used.

My Oma's story about finding a foot inside a boot, my therapist added, was not funny. Why did I laugh when I told it? Oma laughed when she told it. It was supposed to be funny. But Oma drove an ambulance in wartime. Imagine what she must have seen. She was traumatized, my therapist said.

But, no. No, no. All that happened in the past, and my parents didn't dwell on it—we weren't one of those families—it wasn't happening now, and it didn't happen to me. I lived in the present.

WHAT DOES IT MEAN TO BE AN ADULT, and how do you get to be one? What if you're thirty-nine and checking out from a hotel as late as you can because you love to sleep in, and you're pulling your sky-blue suitcase back to the Valenciennes train station, where you'll buy vending-machine coffee to go with a granola bar from your backpack— all without, at least, using a GPS? On Thursday, July 23rd, I bought a ticket to Paris, then sat with my coffee and granola bar to wait.

On Thursday, July 23rd, 1942, Jos wrote, "This journey is a good remedy for lazy people. Got up at half past four and went to the station at a quarter past five after the hotel owner saw me off and fervently reminded me that I am immediately to forget that I had ever stayed in his hotel." Maybe his journey really was a remedy—a remedy for the youthful, almost-lazy quality Josette remembered her own mother describing in my grand-father. Opa left the Netherlands while his brother hid in his own house, because Sam had a wife and children, and Opa did not—still lived with his mother. According to Josette, her own mother was surprised when Opa returned from the war all man-like, with a wife and baby, no less. He'd been taking his sweet time growing up. But maybe he became an adult, finally, because he had to leave home without looking back. Or maybe he became an adult only when my mother was born. Or maybe Jos never really became an adult, and that's why Betty—Mary by then—left him in 1955. I thought again of Rabbi Gerry's conviction that adulthood simply cannot occur until you have children of your own. Become a parent; that's the only way.

At least I'd become a better traveller. Travelling alone! And small things that were really big, such as packing efficiently and carrying snacks, and knowing what to put in my suitcase and what in my small backpack, which I'd decorated with a pretty scarf. The scarf, beige silk with little orange and brown flowers, I'd never managed to incorporate as clothing. Finally, a use for it.

❈ Jos arrived at Gare du Nord. I arrived at Gare du Nord. In the 1946 book *Paris pendant la guerre, 1940–1945*, Pierre Audiat writes that the feeling "of Paris during the Occupation…changed from one year to the next, one month to the next, and, in critical periods, one hour to the other. No one, no matter his or her learning or his or her intuition, is capable of evoking that atmosphere if he had not himself breathed it." Still, I tried to imagine the scene Jos witnessed as he walked, "soul-contented, along the Boulevard Montparnasse, and with some astonishment observed a Paris void of motor-traffic." I took the subway six stops to Gare de Cité Universitaire, walked fourteen minutes along streets thick with pedestrians and cars and bikes and buses to my hotel.

I took a tiny, rickety elevator up to a tiny room, in which the tiny single bed barely fit. Alone was okay. Alone was better than being, than travelling, with the wrong person.

I had never been good at being alone. I was not an alone kind of person.

I missed Matteo. I needed a chance to recover from factors over-ruling reason. Then I could trust myself. I longed for—a perfect union of souls. Well that was stupid. I'd be disappointed and pained forever then, wouldn't I? When souls remained, as they do, separate, distinct, virtually unknown to each other as well as to themselves.

Anyway, I just wanted to kiss his face all over for an hour and be happy. That's all I wanted, Matteo's face there to kiss. His face smelled better than any other face in the world.

What if someone else was kissing his face? I didn't know. It was possible. We hadn't made any promises or commitments. What if I was lying there thinking about his fragrant pretty cheekbones while someone else kissed them? We would visit each other, we'd said. But had either of us bought a plane ticket yet? I thought, I have other things to think about, by the way. Fuck him! What's the point, anyway? Elizabeth Gilbert broke up with the guy she met at the end of *Eat, Pray, Love*. The *Love* guy, the guy played by Javier Bardem in the movie. She wrote a whole follow-up book about marriage, how she didn't believe in it but then changed her mind for this guy. And now they'd broken up. That was not encouraging. I mean, after all that publicity, couldn't they just stay together for the sake of the people? I would not text Matteo or write to him again. Not today. I would stop thinking about him.

※ Jos found he had nowhere to stay. The friend he'd planned to connect with was not only out of his house, but out of town.

> In the nearby Jardin du Luxembourg I sit down on a bench to think matters over and to have a snack out of my own stock as it is now lunchtime and I haven't a ration-card to go to a restaurant. The sun which was shining cheerfully in the morning has disappeared behind a heavy cloud and a few drops of rain are falling. I feel like a beggar or a tramp, as alone as an orphan, with my suitcase on a little bench somewhere in this immense Paris.

The Luxembourg Gardens were a fifteen-minute walk from my hotel. But which bench, Opa? There were so many. I chose one near a fountain. He sat there, on one of those benches, looking, at least, blond and blue-eyed and not Jewish. There were German soldiers everywhere, of course. But not just soldiers—occupied Paris had become a tourist destination for German and Austrian civilians, who wandered around snapping photos of "their" new city, equipped with the guidebooks published by the Occupation authority.

Opa had reason to feel anxious.

In *Sophie's Choice*, William Styron's narrator, Stingo, tortures himself remembering the details of his own cushy life at the very moments of his beloved Sophie's most appalling misery. Stingo quotes the postscript to George Steiner's *Language and Silence*, in which Steiner writes about the "time relation" between such "irreconcilable" simultaneous experiences and remarks that "their coexistence is so hideous a paradox...that I puzzle over time."

But what about the space relation, what about returning to the same place, at a different time? What about Opa and me sitting in the same place seventy-three years apart, he risking capture, internment, his life, me concerned with my own heart, and my own art? Wasn't the coexistence of these two times—July 23rd, 1942 and July 23rd, 2015—a hideous paradox as well?

I thought of my creative writing student, a thirty-something *Twilight* fan, who told the class she'd travelled to Forks, Washington, where the teenaged-vampire series is set. "I realized when I got there that I'd made a big mistake," she admitted. The author, Stephenie Meyer, chose that town as her backdrop after googling which American town had the most rainy days per annum, that's all. It's a tiny, dumpy town, and Meyer never even went there.

"I thought I'd find the feeling of the story," the student said. "But I found nothing, just nothing. A crappy little town I'd travelled all the way to for no reason."

"I totally understand!" said another student. "I went to Bali after reading *Eat, Pray, Love*." She'd confided in me that she worked as a flight attendant and could travel wherever she pleased for next to no cost. She laughed. "I was looking for the feeling of the story too. So were a lot of people. There were tons of start-up gurus there, selling the *Eat, Pray, Love* experience."

"At least you were in Bali!" said the *Twilight* fan.

Elizabeth Gilbert really *was* in Bali, unlike the teenaged vampires and Forks, but the feeling was still in her story, not in the place itself.

And Anne Frank really did write her diary in her Secret Annex, which was why people flocked to the house and tried to feel what it had been like.

Not just the Anne Frank House—Auschwitz had tourists lined up around it, too.

When I travelled in Spain with Lev, he woke me early one morning to take a train into the countryside. I hadn't slept enough, and didn't want to take a train into the countryside. The train seemed sinister to me, full of humans and full of the accessories that can be pulled and peeled off humans and piled up—coats and rings, shoes and hair. Actually, I spent that whole trip in a heightened state of anxiety. I'd never travelled with Lev before, and hadn't realized he'd spend the whole time talking about his previous trip to Europe, which he'd taken alone, equipped with a giant backpack and camera. I hadn't started taking anxiety medication yet then. I couldn't blame him for my anxiety. I could never blame him for anything, because I'd been diagnosed with an anxiety disorder, while he was supposed to be perfectly normal.

As we sped through the Spanish countryside, Lev was all revved up for a full day of adventure. "Okay," he said, "I'm thinking of someone we know." I was supposed to ask: If they were a tree, what kind of tree would they be? If they were a dessert, what kind of dessert? A shoe? A colour? A political system, a fabric, a tool? Chloe and I had invented the people-guessing game as children.

"I'm too tired," I told him. "Okay, um, what weather system would they be?"

He tapped his chin and tipped so far sideways, in thought, he seemed about to fall into the aisle. "Hmmm. Sunshine, with intermittent lightning."

"Um," I said. "I'm too tired, I'm sorry, I don't know, who is it?"

"Ask more things."

"Later."

We sat in silence for a while, and my eyes were starting to close when Lev said, "Okay. I'm going to describe the person as a wine. This white wine has a sophisticated mouth feel and high alcohol content, and has been aged for many decades. It begins bold and fruity, and gives way to citrusy bursts, zingers you could say, before it burns the throat. The grapes were grown in the British moors and processed in the Netherlands before—"

"My grandmother? Oma?"

"Yup."

I felt nauseated with fatigue, and horrified about what a terrible travelling companion I was turning out to be.

"I love trains," Lev said.

"Yeah."

Then Lev told me he'd taken a train through Poland on his previous trip to Europe, and visited Auschwitz, taken the tour. He said he'd met two young American men travelling to the former concentration camp too, to "get it out of the way," so they could enjoy the rest of their trip without that obligation hanging over them.

"That's horrible," I said. "That's—so horrible. It's become this—this—obligation for tourists? One of the sights on their lists? When in Poland must-sees?" My eyes stung with tears. "I don't know how people can go there at all. I couldn't do it. How could you stand it?"

Lev said, "It's different for me than for you. I went to Jewish schools. I grew up talking about it."

"So?"

"I was the only Jewish person on my tour of Auschwitz," he said. "And I was the only one who didn't cry. The others even asked me how I could be so unaffected. I just grew up with it. I'm used to it. I'm desensitized."

"But those piles of shoes, of hair—those are my great-grandmother's shoes, that's my great-uncle's hair, and *your* great-aunts' and uncles' hair." I no longer had damp eyes, but was sobbing, grimacing, and hiccupping, soaking my cheeks. "Don't you get it? That is *our hair*." I grasped a handful of my own hair in my fist, yanking at it painfully, and gestured at his own similarly unruly mass of curls with my other hand. He abandoned me to my bawling, not even putting a hand on my arm, just leaning away and eyeing me like, here's more proof that I grew up immersed in Jewish culture and you didn't. I was not a big crier, normally, I cried like that maybe once every two to five years. I must have been tired. Tired and, whatever else, disappointed. I was disappointed to the point of despair. When I married a Jew, a grandson of Holocaust survivors, I didn't want someone who wouldn't cry at Auschwitz. I wanted the one who'd cry the hardest.

❄ Jos sat on his garden bench feeling increasingly desperate. He didn't want to risk dropping in on his friend at work, but he did know other people who worked there too. He had to do something, so he tried the office. There he found another acquaintance, who said he'd consult with his boss. Jos wandered for another couple of hours before returning for the good news that he could sleep in the office building itself. His contact and the company's managing director also cheered him up by approving his plan,

> Namely: to go on to Dijon and to try there to get the necessary information to cross the Swiss border. Thus, they give me the address of the manager of their branch in Dijon, and when I have also received sufficient tickets for bread and butter rations to be able to eat in restaurants for the next two days, I take my leave, both grateful and satisfied.

In a restaurant near the Jardin du Luxembourg, a restaurant with high ratings online, I ate dinner, a delicious cut of lamb, my only meal of the day, which might have gone partway to explaining my anxiety. That, plus a migraine creeping up my forehead, premenstrual.

At the station I get my ticket for Dijon in advance, and deposit my suitcase in the depot so that I can go to my "hotel" without attracting any notice. As a revenge for my drifter's lunch, and as an amusing interlude before going to my very humble shelter for the night, I have dinner in a chic restaurant surrounded by a team of waiters and all the outward appearance of wealth.

I walked for an hour back past the Jardin du Luxembourg all the way to the Seine and to Shakespeare and Company, the bookstore everyone talks about when they talk about Paris. Front and centre sat Alison Pick's memoir *Between Gods*. The memoir of a woman raised Christian in Toronto, only to learn that her father's family was Jewish and decimated in the Holocaust. She wrote a novel about the Holocaust, then this memoir, which describes her journey from paralyzing depression to conversion. The memoir includes her experience in the year-long conversion class. Pick was now an observant Jew, raising Jewish children. Reading her book filled me with empathy and envy. In one scene, a devout man tells her at a Seder that she has a "Jewish soul." I was afraid I didn't possess such a soul. Why didn't I, though; why was I born without a Jewish soul? Had Opa and his brother Sam been born without Jewish souls? Why did Lev get a Jewish soul, and Yael get a Jewish soul, and Alison Pick get a Jewish soul, but not me? What was I asking?

Then I descend to the basement of the office building of the company P. The night watchman receives me and brings me quickly and quietly to the second floor to a large room full of unused furniture. In a corner between a row of steel filing cabinets and a heap of desks with a lovely view of a number of revolving chairs I find an iron camp-bed with a straw mattress and a horse blanket. The watchman warns me in a whisper that I must be silent as a mouse as the remainder of the floor has been requisitioned for German offices, and that part is under the surveillance of a different night watchman. I receive the key of my room to protect myself against a possible raid.

That day, Thursday, July 23rd, 1942, the gas chambers at Treblinka extermination camp began operation, killing six-and-a-half thousand Jews newly arrived from the Warsaw Ghetto, and Hitler gave the directive to occupy Stalingrad.

The night has passed without any incidents. I have slept reasonably well, although I heard the enemy watchman on his rounds once or twice when he stamped through the corridor, which was separated from my room by a thin partition of glazed glass. At precisely a quarter to six, I am fetched.

What is your name?

What city are you in?

How old are you?

What year is this?

Who is our prime minister? And who is the president of the United States?

Will you draw a clock, please? A clock-face.

The morning of July 24th, a Friday, I lay awake in my tiny bed somewhere in Paris, running through the Alzheimer's test questions.

Naomi Katherine Lewis. *Josua Samuel van Embden.*

Paris. *Paris.*

Thirty-nine. *Thirty-three.*

2015. *1942.*

Stephen Harper. *William Lyon Mackenzie King in Canada. Winston Churchill in England. In the Netherlands...?*

Barack Obama. *Franklin D. Roosevelt.*

I drew a circle in the air. Twelve at the top. Six at the bottom. Three here, nine here. Or, 00:00.

I reached for my computer.

In 1942, Pieter Sjoerds Gerbrandy was prime minister of the Netherlands. Today it was Mark Rutte. Okay.

The night watchman gives me soap and a towel so that I can spruce up quickly and tells me confidentially when he sees me off that during the previous war he was also on the lam after he had escaped from a German prisoner of war camp. I give him a packet of cigarettes, and then at six o'clock in the morning I sashay along the Parisian asphalt.

I checked my email. Yael had responded to my message about being alone, with no one in the right time zone for online chatting.

'Maybe this is an opportunity,' she suggested. 'For unmediated experience.' She went on, 'your grandfather had no one to talk to while he travelled, and had no way to contact anyone he knew.'

Yael and I had a similar conversation when I took the Jewish conversion class in 2010 and 2011, determined to write a book about it. I even had a title: *Jew School*. Yael insisted my experience would be more authentic if I just lived it, instead of trying to shape it into some kind of narrative as it happened. When she rediscovered Judaism herself, in her thirties, learned to chant in Hebrew, and even had the bat mitzvah she'd resisted at thirteen, she didn't do it for the story. My conversion class refused to take on a satisfying shape, I failed to have a year full of ever more profound epiphanies, I failed to remain as fascinated as I'd hoped. I didn't do all my homework. I never even went through with the conversion. Other people, other Canadians, had already written that book in the last couple of years, anyway—Alison Pick with her gravitas-steeped *Between Gods*, and, on the other end of the heaviness spectrum, Benjamin Errett with his light-hearted romp, *Jew and Improved: How Choosing to be Chosen Made Me a Better Man*. The authors and their books couldn't have been more different, but Pick and Erret ended their stories with conversion, and both would begin Shabbat dinner that very night, a Friday, by slicing the challah and pouring the wine, and reciting the blessings for each.

❋ Outside the hotel with my suitcase, a little after nine, I made it only a few metres, peeking at the racks of second-hand clothes all along the sidewalk, before a middle-aged woman with short, dun-coloured hair and a dry tanned face above her leopard-print pantsuit stopped abruptly before me on the sidewalk, face to my face, and widened her eyes. *Américaine*, her eyes said. *Touriste imbécile.* She looked a bit like my Grade 8 French Immersion teacher, Madame Méchin, or reminded me of her anyway, with her long thin bangled arms. Startled, I laughed.

I headed back toward the Luxembourg Gardens, the same route as the day before, a chance to start working a groove in this city, to engrave a few familiar sights. As long as I ended up near some subway station, I could find my way to Gare de Lyon in time to leave for Dijon.

Maybe, I thought, when I was a baby, before I acquired language, maybe that was unmediated experience, though I doubted that jumble of neural stimulation counted as experience at all. I'd failed to mediate experience during previous travels, too overwhelmed or stressed or overstimulated to put what I experienced into words. That way, I failed to retain whole days, wandering lost through streets and museums and forest hikes ending at cool bright water. For instance, I was pretty sure I'd been to Orlando, Phoenix, Ithaca, a camp site in Algonquin Park, an amusement park near Montreal, and another camp site somewhere in Ontario, by a lake. Each experience had fallen right out of my brain just as my senses let it in, data washing over me without taking on any shape or meaning at all. This sensation had always come accompanied by guilt and anxiety, because each time, someone walking beside me; no, truthfully, someone walking slightly ahead of me, had a lot invested, financially and otherwise, in my getting something out of it.

✳ I ate breakfast at a corner café, watching traffic and passersby. A chocolate croissant and an espresso. Parisians, I noted, were not all that stylish. What a naive notion I had, that people here dressed better than at home. Why did I expect that?

The day before—I mean, the day before in 1942—Opa composed a poem, in French, before he fell asleep:

A midi, au Luxembourg, déjeuner de chemineau

Le soir le diner, comme il faut, chez Ramponneau

Pour finir la journée, c'est sur un lit de sangle que je dors

Et le tout ensemble s'appelle: changement de décor

Lit de sangle means cot (or folding bed), but it also means, literally, bed with straps, and when I googled the term and clicked on "images," cots appeared, alongside hospital beds with canvas straps for securing patients. Decades later, Opa lay strapped into a bed like that before he died, so ravaged by Alzheimer's that he might roll out otherwise, or try to stand, and fall.

In his early eighties, Opa had been ageless, his hair still dense, vertical, and blond. But once the greying began and the curls thinned, slipping from his scalp onto his armchair and his pillow, his memories went with them.

Oma and Opa had moved down their street to a bungalow, because Opa couldn't handle stairs anymore, let alone a pool to maintain all summer. Whenever Oma left for longer than five minutes, he asked, "Where's Mary?" We told him she'd gone to the store, but a few minutes later, he asked again. "Where's Mary?"

He had a new favourite joke: "I don't buy green bananas anymore," to which my mother just grimaced and my father laughed too loud.

"Where's Mary?" said Opa.

"She went to the store, Jos," said Dad, kindly.

"I thought we'd travel," I heard Oma tell my mother. "I didn't think I'd end up caring for a retarded child."

My sister and I no longer had an air vent to eavesdrop through, but Oma stage-whispered this comment right on the other side of the door. That was around the time a neurologist diagnosed Opa with Alzheimer's. *How old are you? What year is this? Who is the president of the United States? Draw a clock.* Alzheimer's patients can't draw clocks. Oma described his effort, with the numbers all bunched up together in tiny, shaky handwriting that she didn't recognize.

Oma took care of Opa for as long as she could. She hired a nurse to come and help with bathing a few times a week. But he forgot more, and started methodically ripping the pages from his favourite books—Goethe and Shakespeare. Oma locked the rest of the library behind glass. He sat in his chair while she tried to keep everything moving forward, just sat there, leaning forward to comb the Persian rug's fringe with his fingers, pulling each strand straight, again and again. He emptied the contents of drawers and piled them in strange places. He became incontinent. He was heavy, and Oma couldn't lift him. After a couple of years, she had to move him into a nursing home. For ten years, Oma visited Opa almost every day. When we went to Barrie, we visited him, too. Mum sat in silence, didn't know what to say, except, "Hi, Dad!" Dad and Oma were better at keeping the tone almost normal, joking together, laughing, and sometimes Opa made a comment that fit the tone of the conversation, if not quite the content.

Opa died during my third and final year of grad school. When Dad told me on the phone, "I'm sorry, darling, but poor Opa passed away last night," the volume of my world decreased with a bang, a pressure change that creaked my ribcage inward and squeezed my lungs so they wouldn't fill. Opa had been absent with Alzheimer's for ten years, yes, and he was ninety-six, but still. He was the only dead person I knew. I mean, he was the only dead person I loved. I cried on my boyfriend's futon-couch, and he put his arm around me. When I lifted my head, he was fiddling with the edge of some embroidered fabric he'd hung on the wall.

Oma said Opa wouldn't have wanted a funeral or a wake or any kind of gathering, but then we all met in Barrie after all. We scattered Opa's ashes in the woods near my aunt and uncle's old house in the country, and my aunt said, "So long, Dad." Oma held a wake at her house, and a group of old men I'd never seen before drifted in. Veterans. Opa was a veteran and had attended a club with other veterans.

"Your grandfather was a war hero," one of the old men told me. Then he talked for while about Opa, calling him "Josh."

"My favourite story about Opa," my cousin Zarah told the room, "was that he liberated Delft. I love that story. They let him go first, ahead of the troops because his brother lived there. He got to drive through in a tank, and tell everyone, 'the war is over!' Did you know they had a parade, and celebrated him as the city's liberator?"

After Opa died, Oma moved to Ottawa, into the same condo building as my parents. She stayed home more and more, annoyed by almost everyone she met, especially my parents' friends. She almost befriended a neighbour, but then the woman gave Oma white chocolate as a gift, proving her unworthiness. That wasn't all though. "I offered her potato-leek soup," Oma told me, "and she said no. She said she doesn't *like* potato-leek soup. Have you ever heard of not liking potato-leek soup? Silly girl; she must be mad."

She began telling the same stories again and again, tweaking them as she told and retold. One of these was the story of Opa's death.

"Opa told me on his death bed that he was sorry he'd never known how to be a husband," she said one afternoon over tea in her living room, when my sister and I were both visiting.

"Really?" said Chloe.

"No," muttered Mum between her teeth. "She's started telling this story, okay? It's one of her stories. Of course it's not possible that—"

"He said he'd always loved me," Oma went on. "But hadn't known how to be a husband. He hadn't spoken in months. You remember. But right before he died, he spoke, and that's what he said."

"She keeps saying that," said Mum. "But it's impossible." She found it unbearable to see her mother lose consistency this way—she wanted her mother back, firm and solid, the way she was meant to remain forever.

"Just leave her alone," I whispered. Which was ridiculous, because Oma was sitting right there. She squinted at Mum as though realizing something for the first time.

"He told me he'd always loved me," she repeated, "but just hadn't known how to be a husband. And that was true. He just didn't know. But he was a lovely man. Jos was the kindest man you could ever meet."

"Yes," said Dad. "He was. And we think it's so, so touching, so *very* touching—"

Mum frowned. "Maybe *you* do," she muttered.

"Yes," said Oma. "He said, I didn't treat you how I ought to. But it was never because I didn't love you. It was just that I didn't know how."

"I'm sure that's true," Dad said.

"Hmm," said Mum.

"Jos was a lovely man, you know." Oma smiled, folded her hands in her wool-trousered lap and gently touching her ruby engagement and wedding rings. I'd never seen Opa wear a ring. He never had his wedding ring properly sized, Oma told me once. Shortly after they married, they spent a day at the beach; he tossed a stone, and the ring followed it, arcing into the waves.

"He was lovely," said Dad.

"Eccentric though." Oma pressed her palms against thighs, lengthening her spine. "He was strange, wasn't he? An absolute madman!"

"But so loveable," said Chloe.

"Yes!" said Oma.

"He was *just wonderful*," said Dad.

"Well!" said my mother, briskly standing. "Shall I make us some tea?" She stood, feet apart, arms by her sides, with a strained smile, and Oma stared at her again, that same puzzled expression, lips moving over her teeth as though she were speaking inside her mouth.

"All right," Oma said. "All right." As Mum headed to the kitchen, Oma added, "Jos was a strange man, but the kindest person you could ever want to meet. And clever! And you know what he told me, before he died? They had him strapped to his bed then; he didn't know where he was, thought he was back in the Netherlands, young, and then he just didn't know, didn't think anything I suppose, but he opened his eyes and looked right at me and said—"

"Okay," said Mum. "So. Herbal. Mint?"

"—I always loved you, but I *didn't know how*. To be a husband."

"So," said my mother. "Five cups of tea."

"And I'm sorry," said Oma.

That year, Oma began accusing my parents of stealing her possessions and moving them around so she couldn't find them. She told stories about her life, on repeat, and some of the stories seemed to contradict others. She turned cruel, then vicious, sneaky and Iago-like, planting seeds of conflict. She didn't like anyone. She couldn't understand a word of what anyone said to her in Canadian accents, barely opening their mouths, and she didn't like people who believed that Canadian French was French or who wore synthetic fabrics or who believed in God. When I was engaged to Lev, she told me my parents didn't want me to get married but didn't have the guts to tell me. She told me that she and Opa hadn't wanted Mum to marry Dad, couldn't bear him—though Oma did, she admitted, like Dad now—just like my parents secretly couldn't bear Lev. She competed with my sister for her husband's attention. Everything got all mixed up.

Then one afternoon, at the grocery store near their building, Mum realized her mother was no longer by her side. Couldn't find her anywhere in the store, and searched frantically down each aisle and up again. She had a cashier call over the store's intercom: "Mary van Embden, please come to the information desk by the main doors," just like three decades earlier, when Mum had lost track of me in a Toys R Us. Finally she decided to check the car, and found Oma in another part of the parking lot, lying on the concrete floor, just lying there, conscious but disoriented.

Shortly after that, Oma underwent the Alzheimer's tests, the same ones she'd described to me herself when Opa failed them. *What is your name? What year is this? Who is the prime minister, the president?* She didn't much like that they called her Mary, instead of Mrs. van Embden.

She knew. For a few days, at least. "The doctor says I have Alzheimer's disease," she told me on the phone. "I'm quite all right with it. I'll be all right. It's worse for everyone else, you know. Remember Opa? He didn't suffer so much. The person with the illness doesn't suffer so much, I think—it's everyone else."

Everyone else did suffer—everyone else meaning, especially, my mother. And Oma's descent into madness was so much more spectacular than Opa's. You couldn't really have called Opa "mad" at all. Gentle and stoic as always, he wilted and wound down, slowed and slowed and forgot and forgot. He lived more and more in the present moment. Long before Oma's temporal existence shrank down to the present, she lived in past moments, obsessions, rehashings. Childhood memories and adult memories too. Retelling, reliving, reworking, and finally replacing. My mother heard neighbours refer to Oma as "that old lady who won't stop talking." She couldn't stop. As though trying to explain herself to herself. As though trying to ask everyone she met, *Who am I? What happened, and why, and what does it mean?* Opa had never told stories when he got sick. He just grew lost and quiet, tore the pages from books and bent in his armchair to straighten the fringe of the rug he and Oma had bought together in Turkey. Then again, he'd always been quiet. Never seemed curious about the lives of the people around him, or even, seemingly, about his own.

After she moved into the place dubbed, euphemistically and ironically, a "home," all Oma wanted was to get out of there. My parents convinced her to use some of her savings to renovate her room, which was really more like a one-bedroom apartment. They had the carpet replaced with hardwood. They moved in her furniture, and her books on her very own bookcases. They hung her art on the walls. This only seemed to confuse her more. What were all her things doing in this hospital room?

"I fell and hit my head in a parking lot," she told me, when I visited. "And it turned out I'd had a stroke. I'm recovering, though, and soon I'll move back to my condo. I really can't bear it here. Just waiting, hanging around doing nothing."

"But that's why you moved here," I said. "So you wouldn't spend too much time alone. Isn't it better to have people around, to talk to?"

"*These* people? No. I don't know who told you that, darling, but it's not true. I had a stroke, but I'm nearly better now, and soon I'll be going home."

"Okay," I said.

"I've been thinking a lot about Jos," said Oma. "About Opa."

"Yes?"

"Yes. And you know, the more I think about him, the more it dawns on me that he was an absolute bastard."

"What?" I faltered. "Really?"

"Wasn't he? He had a way of charming people, of course, and he was awfully clever. But when it comes down to it, he was a—just an absolute bastard. He told me when he was dying, that he never figured out how to be a husband. And that was true!"

"But he always loved you."

"He was a bastard, really. An absolute bastard. Wasn't he?"

"I don't really—"

"We met during the war," said Oma. "We didn't think we'd survive, and everything was terribly exciting. No one ever tells you that, do they?"

"You mean—that the war was—*fun?*"

"Yes!" said Oma. "Well, that those were exciting times. Life seemed dull afterwards, in contrast. No one would ever admit that you *did* things when a war was on; you had a romance in Belgium, because you never thought that in a year, in *sixty* years, you'd still be alive."

"It was romantic? With Opa?"

"Mm. Yes. And then—"

"Yeah?"

"Well, we got married. The war ended, and Trish was born. Do you know my daughter, Patricia?"

"Patricia is my mother. I'm Naomi."

"Oh, yes, darling. Yes. My memory is still a little affected at times, after my stroke. Your mother was born. She was born the week the war ended. So we went to the Netherlands. And that's when he learned his mother was gone."

"Isabella, right? You named my mother after her."

"No."

"But my mother's first name is Isabelle. Isabelle Patricia."

"I know what her name is, darling. I liked the name. It had nothing to do with Jos's mother. I supposed that was her name too. But, no—I didn't even know Jos's mother's name when I named Trish."

"But. Oma."

☀ My train, like Opa's, would leave from Gare de Lyon. And my train, like Opa's, was packed, so packed that I sat in the corridor between two cars. Cross legged on the floor, I checked my phone, and found a text from Yael: 'There's a universe where all conflicts are settled by limbo contests.'

In our corridor we soon form a club of four, bound together by the strong train-friendship of one journey: a young lady, a sales-clerk of ladies' wear by my guess; a business traveller; a prisoner of war recently returned from Germany; and myself. When I have had my breakfast in the restaurant car, and by chance, on a tip from the conductor, am able to secure seats for the four of us halfway to

Laroche, we are sworn friends. The business traveller starts to tell of all the black-market food he brings home from the various parts of France. The hams, sausages, and cuts of meat grow larger with every kilometre, and half an hour out of Dijon, his most outrageous stories appear. First about a good friend of his on a farm in Bretagne where they grow everything themselves—even the coffee which they serve after dinner. I want to tell the story about my garden at home where I grow my own kale and sausage, but before I can remember what kale is called in French, he is busy with his next story. This time about a hotel where he had to accept a loft when all rooms were suddenly requisitioned by the krauts, and how he found a large barrel full of pure white flour. In order to bring a load home for his wife, he put knots in the bottom of the legs of his pyjama pants and then filled them up with flour. And the delicious pancakes they ate!!!

There were four of us on the floor of this corridor too, one in each corner, me and three men. One, middle-aged with a thick brown moustache, kept his eyes on his newspaper; another, black and skinny, in a white tee-shirt and jeans, kept his eyes on his phone; and the third, red-headed and freckled, earbuds dangling their wires into an oversized hoodie, stared as though fascinated at the floor in front of him. And me with my notebook. No train-friendship there. I thought, some people make friends when they travel. They have spontaneous life-altering conversations. That never really happened to me; people didn't speak to me. Or if they did, they were not people I wanted to speak to. They were men, and I was afraid I wouldn't understand anything, wouldn't understand what they wanted or expected. Afraid of some a secret language among travellers that I didn't know.

I texted Yael: 'In the limbo universe, I guess saying someone is "flexible" means they will go to any length to win an argument.'

✳ The train eased past the platform, through a mass of tracks heading away away away. We passed graffitied concrete walls, passed apartment buildings that must have rattled and hummed all through the days and nights, but never had faces in the window. I'd always imagined that living beside train tracks I'd spend all my free minutes watching travellers zip by, but I'd never seen a face in one of those windows, not in London (where I rode the train with Chloe), nor DC (where I rode the train with my aunt and my cousin, and my mother, and Lev), nor Chicago (where I rode the train with Yael, when she lived there).

Despite my resolve to notice the transition out of the city and into the countryside, it happened with no discernible flash, without crossing a threshold, like passing from one dream to another, and we rumbled smoothly through gentle greenery, as though Paris belonged to another universe.

THE STORY I WROTE ABOUT MY NOSE JOB was first published in 2014, in the *Calgary Herald*'s weekly magazine insert, *Swerve*. My editors titled the story—unfortunately, we all came to realize—"A Bridge Too Far: The Story of My Big Jewish Nose." The magazine's cover featured a photo of me in profile, with dotted lines drawn on my face in black eyeliner, suggesting surgical incisions. The photograph hurt my pride a little; I wasn't wearing any other makeup and looked haggard, my face still too thin post-divorce. But I was happy to see the story in print, and received a flood of responses. Women, especially Jewish women, told me that my story was just like theirs. One Jewish woman told me her parents hadn't let her go through with the nose job she craved, and that she was grateful to them now, thanks to my article. Friends I hadn't heard from since high school wrote too, telling me they hadn't known about my surgery, or that they had known, and had found my decision baffling; now they understood. Other readers were simply surprised and interested in the history of the nose job, and of the Jewish nose job in particular. I'd never received so much feedback for an article; I'd certainly never received close to so much positive feedback for an article—usually people only wrote when I'd pissed them off—by disparaging detox diets, for instance, or by arguing that parents should be required to vaccinate their kids. But why (I thought) would anyone be pissed off about my nose job? At first, the most critical remark came from some guy who told me, pretty tamely, "Don't blame your parents, girl."

But just a few days later, a full-page op-ed appeared in the newspaper: "Fixation on Noses Plays into Worst of Stereotypes." Written by the local Conservative synagogue's rabbi, whom I'd never met.

"Against the genocidal backdrop of the twentieth century and recent outbreaks of racism and anti-Semitism," Rabbi Rose wrote, the magazine "saw fit to re-introduce the much discredited and dangerous assertion that one can identify a person's religious or cultural affiliation by their physical attributes." He claimed that none of his congregants had big noses, though some were Holocaust survivors—survivors who had suffered untold atrocities rationalized by stereotypes. "In all of her self-deprecating and neurotic musings about her nose job," the rabbi wrote, "Lewis fails to see beyond her own face in the mirror that her article only serves to perpetuate such harmful stereotypes, thereby doing an incredible disservice to the Jewish community and the decent and moral citizens of our city."

There was more. I was ignorant and badly educated, which explained why I thought Judaism was a race. The rabbi explained: "What truly defines a Jew is that person's commitment to the values, wisdom, and moral vision that emerge from the Torah...and the subsequent teachings of the rabbinic tradition." And the final judgement: "Had Lewis seriously dealt with real issues concerning body image among teenage girls, sexist norms of beauty present in society, or minority assimilation into mainstream society, her inclusion of her own story might have been both relevant and instructive. Instead, we were subjected to an embarrassing and self-indulgent personal story."

Rabbi Rose seemed to accuse of me saying the very opposite of what I thought I'd said. I thought I'd written an article about Jewish identity, about my own slippery hold on that identity, which was surely not unique. I thought I'd addressed the deep entanglement, for Jews, of race and religion, partly because of the identities thrust upon us from the outside. I'd meant to write about embodiment, about my Jewish body, my female body, and about the violence history had inflicted on that body—"real issues concerning body image among teenage girls, sexist norms of beauty present in society, or minority assimilation into mainstream society"—yes, exactly.

My editor told me that another reader, a congregant of Rabbi Rose's, had sent a similar letter. This reader was particularly offended that I'd included the "air is free" joke (why do Jews have big noses?), saying I'd caused him pain by putting such hateful words in print, as though I'd provided the joke to Jew-hating readers, for them to use as a weapon. My editor informed me that Rabbi Rose had devoted a whole Shabbat sermon to me and my anti-Semitism. The thought of a Jewish congregation shaking their heads in grief over the bigotry in their own city—over *me*, a traitor who'd provided anti-Semites with fodder, flooded me with nausea. And the way the rabbi alluded to me in his letter, not as a writer, not as a serious person, but as some *girl* who'd more or less sent her diary to a magazine editor, who misguidedly published it. Rabbi Rose's whole letter was addressed to the magazine, not to me at all.

I was invited to talk about the story, and about the rabbi's letter, on a national radio program. The show's producer was a Jewish woman, and said half her friends, growing up, had nose jobs when they turned sixteen. She suggested, off the record, that perhaps the rabbi hadn't noticed the phenomenon, or didn't think it important, because it only affected girls and women. I jumped at the chance to explain myself on the radio, and after the interview I received more emails of support. And though everyone knows not to read the comments online, I did; one afternoon, I couldn't resist. Most of them were on my side, but I was dismayed to see that some were on my side in a racist kind of way. They said things like, "That rabbi's so typical. Those people think *everything* is anti-Semitic—they're *obsessed*." The rabbi's letter had provided fodder for anti-Semitism, just as he and his congregant had accused me of doing in my article. What a mess.

And of course I couldn't help but ask myself: was the rabbi right? The rabbi called my story, and by extension me, neurotic and self-indulgent. Fine. I could live with that. I had come by my neuroses honestly, and, yes, indulged a fascination with the self as an object of inquiry and art. I didn't think writing should avoid the personal or the embarrassing. I'd never questioned that the personal was political, and had often told my creative writing students that our most embarrassing memories, memories of losing our dignity, of accidentally transgressing unspoken edicts, often make for our most compelling and important material.

But worse, far worse, was I an anti-Semite? *Was I?* Growing up, I'd loved and admired Oma more than anyone. Oma, who once refused to attend a party at my cousin's house when she learned there would be observant Jews in attendance. And Opa—he and his brother Sam did not want to be Jewish, but it went deeper than that. They didn't *like* Jews. It wasn't that they believed Jews possessed essential ugly traits, though, Oma and Opa clarified. They believed that Judaism was a religion, not a race at all, and they didn't believe in organized religion, *period*. And they especially didn't like it when a group segregated itself, forbidding outside marriage and declaring itself special, chosen, even. It was all backwards, Oma and Opa insisted: observant Jews were racist against everyone else, which was why no one liked them.

At least there was no question that Dad was Jewish. I would have liked to show my father and his mother to Rabbi Rose and say, *see?* How can I be an anti-Semite with a father and a Mimi like these? Plus, I'd tried so hard, I'd married a Jew, and I'd worked to become a real Jew, and when people made cruel remarks about Jews, I felt like they were insulting *me*. Once I was at a bar and a man came over and told me, "I love Jewish women." And once I was at another bar, and a woman came over and said, "You think you're so smart, don't you? I know what you people are like." Then she said, "Do you know Dan Bernstein? I was supposed to go to my prom with him. If you see him, could you tell him I'm sorry I stood him up? And that it wasn't because he was a Jew?" No, none of this amounted to anything. People called Noam Chomsky an anti-Semite, and Sarah Silverman, too, and Hannah Arendt, and every Jew who'd ever criticized the State of Israel. Jews who allegedly didn't like Jews were called self-hating Jews. Opa would have said he wasn't a self-hating Jew; he didn't hate himself; he wasn't a Jew. But according to Rabbi Gerry, a Jew is a Jew forever, so if say you're not a Jew, you're just a bad Jew, the wicked son from the Passover Seder, the one who says *they* were enslaved in Egypt, instead of *we*. Because whatever has happened to the Jewish people has happened to each of us, personally.

What have a lot of flat-footed peasants wandering through the desert to do with me? Opa had said.

Months passed, but people I hadn't seen in a while still looked a little too long at my nose, and sometimes a stranger, a member of Rabbi Rose's congregation, recognized me in a coffee shop, but couldn't say from where. I just played along, said, "No, I don't go to that gym or that synagogue, do you spend a lot of time at the library, yoga studios, are you from Ottawa, well I don't know then, but nice to meet you," never clarified, "I'm that anti-Semite from the newspaper." Then, during the Days of Awe, the week between Rosh Hashanah and Yom Kippur, when Jews are meant to atone for all our (their?) sins of the previous year, I wrote to Rabbi Rose, expressing my regret that we'd never spoken to each other, only addressed each other through the media. My apology was a little disingenuous; I really wanted to elicit a reciprocal apology from him. Instead, he invited me to visit him in his office at the synagogue.

Rabbi Rose was an enormous man, over six-and-a-half feet, and heavy. If he were a tree, he would have been a redwood. If he were an animal, he would have been a bear. In contrast, I felt like a chipmunk scuttling past him, as he ushered me through his door. We sat across from each other in comfortable chairs, in a tidy, spacious office that contrasted markedly with Rabbi Gerry's jam-packed space with its piles of books.

"I decided not to reread your article before you came," he told me, gesturing toward the computer on his desk, indicating where he could have read the article if he'd been so inclined. "Because," he said, "I didn't want to get into a debate about details. I thought it would be better for us just to chat."

Faced as I was with this imposing man, a rabbi, in his own office, I could only nod. Already, this wasn't going as I'd pictured. How could I defend my work if it wasn't fresh in his mind? How could I explain my position so rationally and intelligently, and with such grace, that he'd see his glaring error and apologize? I'd worn my most official-looking grown-up woman clothes to combat whatever it was about me that made strangers mistake me for a teenager. It hadn't worked. Our whole dynamic was learned gentleman versus ingenue before I'd even settled into my chair. I wanted to stop him, to clarify that I was in my late thirties, that I'd published several books, that I was a respected professional in my field, which was writing. Instead, I answered his questions about my upbringing, then nodded gravely as he explained that my Opa, and my father in turn, had tried to erase their own Jewishness by marrying outside the community and raising non-Jewish children. He told me, in a sympathetic avuncular tone, that my parents had managed to keep me from Judaism culturally and religiously, but that my appearance had seemed to undermine that effort. Changing my nose had been the last step required to create a wholly assimilated child. Only, he went on, it didn't work. By withholding contact with Judaism, my parents had only piqued my interest, drawing me back toward my roots and my history. Rabbi Rose said all this kindly, as though he wanted me to see that he understood my plight, and wanted to help me, a lost lamb who'd wandered into his sanctuary. I noted only silently that he'd contradicted his own letter, the part where he'd claimed Judaism wasn't a race, that it was impossible to look Jewish.

Then, somehow, he was talking about my article after all, describing how hurt his congregants had felt when they saw the headline—"The Story of My Big Jewish Nose"—and the dismay I caused them by putting the dreaded joke in print. *Why do Jews have big noses?* Why would I do that? Why would I disseminate such hatred? As though the world didn't have enough ammunition already.

The joke, I tried to explain, I'd cited as a cultural artifact. To illustrate the stigma, the racialized body—to illustrate—I mean—wasn't it obvious?

"The problem," Rabbi Rose said, "is that you're not one of us. From the perspective of my congregants, you're an outsider, criticizing us in public, when we've already been through so much as a people. Your mother's not Jewish, so you're not Jewish, but it's not just that. You weren't raised in a Jewish home and weren't taught about Judaism, so you don't understand what it's like to be persecuted over your identity. My congregation knows what persecution feels like, and when they saw your article, they felt persecuted again, *by you.*"

"I'll think about what you're saying," I told him. "That certainly wasn't my intention." I did not want to continue the conversation by arguing, and I really was trying to understand. I understood that Rabbi Rose was making a decision for me, a decision about my identity that I did not agree was his to make.

"I suppose people have been telling you that it was brave to write that story," he said, and sighed.

✳ Throughout the bus ride home, I chewed over and wrote down my conversation with Rabbi Rose. I tried to take what he had said seriously, but in my gut, and also in my head, I really just thought he was being a jerk—a jerk who hadn't bothered to prepare appropriately before we met because he'd assumed I wasn't very smart. We hadn't discussed the matter, we hadn't tried to find common ground; he had never considered budging an inch.

In *Foreskin's Lament*, his memoir about growing up a juvenile delinquent in an Orthodox Jewish home, Shalom Auslander writes about the rabbis who taught him that it was a sin to embarrass his people. Though the adult Auslander doesn't believe in God, he can't shed his gut-level terror of God's wrath—is terrified, then, of writing frankly about his own life. But Rabbi Rose hadn't exactly accused me of embarrassing my people; I didn't face the same dilemma as a Shalom Auslander or a Philip Roth. Worse, the rabbi had said the Jewish people weren't mine to embarrass—and so the Jewish God, presumably, wasn't mine to betray, either. I didn't even get to be a self-hating Jew; I was just a shit-talking goy, a plain old anti-Semite.

In Rebecca Goldstein's book, *Betraying Spinoza*, she argues that Baruch Spinoza, the philosopher excommunicated from Judaism and whose ontology precluded any essential quality that could distinguish one group of people from another, could not, in fact, ever quite shake the trauma of losing his place in the tribe. "What is it to be Jewish?" Goldstein asks. "Is it a matter of creed, of culture, of family or blood— or, as we would now put it, of genes? Having once been Jewish, can one then cease to be Jewish? Or is a Jew essentially a Jew, no matter what religion he might practice or even think himself to be a member of?" Spinoza couldn't sort it out, and neither could Goldstein, and certainly, neither could my grandparents or my parents, and neither could I. But, according to Rabbi Rose, this question was none of my business anyway, because I simply wasn't Jewish at all. I was back where I'd started, before my master's thesis, before Lev, before Rabbi Gerry.

"You're Jewish," Yael assured me, whenever I asked. "You look like a Jew, you have a Jewish name, you even have the sense of humour and the neuroses. And you have a Jewish best friend, by the way—me. You're a Jew."

Because air is free, I wrote in my notebook. Leaning against the bus window, I circled the words, then filled in the circle until my pen's thick black ink bled through the paper, ruining the next page and leaving a mark on the one after that.

ON SATURDAY, JULY 25TH, 1942, Jos met his contact in Dijon, and learned that his planned route had become too dangerous, with strict military controls. But this could be the day—the day that he'd escape into unoccupied territory.

> To be able to do this, I have to go to Chalon-sur-Saône, 70 kilometres south of Dijon, which is still in the occupied territory but right on its border...In Chalon I'll have to visit Mme. T. who has some relatives who can help me across the demarcation line into free France.
> I receive a password with which to introduce myself.

✵ I woke on my Saturday to someone pounding on my hotel room door, a migraine pounding inside my eyeballs and head. My period must have started in the night, bringing its usual full-body torment.

"Please come back later," I called. A woman's voice responded, though I couldn't make out her words, and I heard her move away down the corridor. In the bathroom, one eye open the merest slit, I groped around in my toiletries bag for my four precious migraine pills in their blister-pack. These pills cost over ten dollars each, and weren't painkillers, but something to do with serotonin. Technically, taken together with the SSRI I swallowed daily for anxiety, this drug could cause serotonin syndrome—that is, could overload my nervous system and maybe kill me. But the chance of that was very low, and nothing else touched the pain that afflicted me on the first day of my period each month. I swallowed my pill with a small plastic cup full of water, and crawled back into bed, pulled the covers over my head to block out the sunlight, beams of bright agony streaming through between the curtains onto my pillow. I breathed evenly, relaxing my face as best I could. The woman returned within minutes, for more knocking and muffled French urging.

"I'm sick," I called, pulling the blanket off my face. My own voice swelled and jammed against the inside of my skull, then escaped down my spine, spreading out into nauseating waves through my stomach and gut. The knocking and muffled voice continued. "J'ai mal à la tête," I tried. I groaned pathetically. "Malade. Please."

Within half an hour, my thighs went numb and my head hurt more sharply, the pain concentrated in my right temple and between my eyebrows. The pill was working; this phase came right before the pain began to fade, leaving my whole head and musculature full of static and sadness but otherwise functional.

In the shower, massaging my head and neck with shampoo, I heard someone puttering around in my room. A vacuum cleaner. What the fuck? Some stranger was in here with me, vacuuming around my mess? I thought of my dad, how he'd yelled at service people when I was a kid, and pictured myself emerging from the bathroom naked, eyes wild, hair full of lather, to chase this intruder from the room I'd paid for. Mimi wouldn't have stood for it either, but she wouldn't have yelled, would have delivered some cool and devastating insult instead. I badly wanted the person and the vacuum cleaner out of my room, but I couldn't summon sufficiently terrifying rage, nor sufficiently intimidating elegance, especially not with a migraine.

I knew I should take a bus or a train from Dijon to Chalon, as Jos had seventy-three years earlier, but I couldn't. Though the pain in my head was receding, I felt like shit. I'd have to follow Opa the next day, behind schedule.

Under a heavy grey sky, limbs loose with medication, I spent forty-five minutes rolling my suitcase full of dirty clothes along narrow sidewalks. I was trying to find the laundromat a few blocks away, but somehow ended up back at my hotel, then on the wrong side of downtown's main drag. Finally I found the place on a deserted-looking narrow street. There was no one else inside. In the sloshing white noise, I sat on the thin wooden bench with a book open on my lap and my eyes closed, feeling the slosh, slosh inside my body. The druggy numbness had spread down my arms and back now, but numbness was the wrong word. More like, my muscles relaxed so insistently that I missed their normal tension. The migraine remained, but transformed into a painless pressure that sucked at my eyeballs and sinuses, that pressure with its familiar adolescent flavour of dread and tedium, incompatible components whipped together to form a greasy emulsified paste. I stepped outside, considering a walk, but I didn't want the stress of getting lost and having to find my way back, so just stood there on the grim grey pavement and then went back in. By the end of the washing cycle, my body was completely limp, and, loading the dryers, I took a break to flop over in a forward fold, stretching out my back and neck. I leaned into a downward-facing dog and remained there for a couple of minutes, feet and palms flat on the worn floor, then washed my hands in the sink. Each dryer bore warnings in French and English to check for large objects, pets, and children before closing the door. Finally, I slouched on a washing machine and watched the cyclone of fabric, my shorts and dresses and underpants flashing past in grey, black, red, and blue, a flash of white underwear, tears oozing down my cheeks.

My clothes did not emerge all that clean, but I folded everything, repacked my suitcase, and dropped it off back at the hotel, then wandered into the touristy centre. Jos didn't describe Dijon in his journal, except as "charming." German officers hanging around, of course. These streets in the old part of town would not have teemed

with tourists, and these old brick building would not have housed
clothing store after clothing store—plus the mustard store, with
its pyramids of Dijon jars in every size and variety—each with its
perpetual 60% Off Everything! sales. I ordered lunch on a terrace,
packed despite the overcast weather, beside a carousel with a red
wooden platform and an array of fanciful seating. It was not in motion,
and sat silent, its colourful carriages, cars, and horses, even a cow,
a monkey, and a plane, at ease. The waiter, young and tall and tired,
repeated, "Crêpes," and rolled his eyes.

Oh, my head. My drugged and throbbing head. My insides sluicing
loose and oozing out. I couldn't muster any charm, could barely muster
any facial expression. And, as Matteo wrote to me the night before, you
lose most of your personality without language. Since I couldn't speak
to anyone in France, my experiences were limited, interactions basic,
and stressful. How did I fail to learn French properly despite growing
up in bilingual Ottawa?

The day was ugly, and the waiter weighed down by his own problems, no doubt. Much ruder to me than to anyone else, though. He'd
probably taken me for an American. *I'm Canadian!* I should have told
him. No, of course, I thought, I'm the only person here alone, the only
adult without a partner and small children. I am occupying a table
that could seat four, with kids ordering crêpes and juice and eggs.
All these tourists, travelling just to travel. Just to wander around and
look at clothes and eat, and buy Dijon mustard at the mustard store.
Tourists of all nationalities and ages, often young or rather old, the
ones my age with kids in tow. I pressed my hand to my heart, feeling
for the wedding ring in my pocket. It was still in there, hard little
lump between palm and sternum. My eyes filled with tears again,
watching toddlers climb all over the immobile carousel, sitting on the
metal chicken, calling out for their parents to look, the parents all,
"Wonderful, wonderful, okay, be careful, don't do that," only in French.
The parents looked tired. I wasn't crying out of envy or longing, or even
out of loneliness. I thought, Lev and I could have had a family like that,

and family vacations like that too, and I felt only amazement and relief to have escaped such a fate—Lev would almost surely take his family vacations with another wife, and how strange that picturing it failed to hurt. Rabbi Gerry had said, repeatedly, that without children, you're stuck in a perpetual adolescence. By now I was meant to reminisce, a little or a lot wistful, about times I felt free: when I was young, and travelled alone, fell in love with a poet, stayed in bed with him for days in a hotel room—what business did I have doing such things *now*, at thirty-nine? Without the drudgery and the relative calm that come later, that came, as it did for Oma and Opa, as result?

Matteo didn't want children either. Matteo seemed like such a thoughtful person, a person who acted with great care and grace, and whose idea of a good life matched mine. Maybe he and I could have a relationship back in the real world. Maybe. I longed to contain and be contained by a perfect love, still longed to give my whole heart and to hold a whole heart in my hands, to find another soul to meld around and into mine. I entertained romantic notions! And this is why people lived unhappily, why people had affairs, why people moved from relationship to relationship. Looking for home in another person. Chasing the longing.

If Matteo and I became a couple, then we would argue, and would reject and hurt each other. I would annoy him with my hypochondria and my inability to read a map, and he would annoy me somehow too, though I couldn't imagine yet how. Maybe sometimes it would bother me that he never wanted to join crowds, and that he was always the first to leave a party, and that he really didn't believe in marriage. (Or worse, what if he decided that he did believe in marriage after all, and wanted to make babies, too?) I wondered if he'd be willing to come with me to Seders, and to light the menorah on Hanukkah. I didn't want to stop doing those things. Wouldn't it worry Matteo when he realized I had bourgeois values and an anxiety disorder, and wouldn't he see that despite all the therapy and the medication, I could never get enough nurturing? One of us would want more sex and one would want more security, and both would probably be me, since I always wanted too much from people, too much of everything—and I would ask, again and again, *do you still love me?* Unless I could somehow stop myself, maybe I could stop myself. Maybe we would both wonder if the other could ever really understand. We'd likely struggle financially, since we were both writers, and after a while the crazed craving for each other's bodies would ease, and the hotel bed in Brussels would assume a prehistoric halo glow. Maybe it would be better, then, if our romance remained just that, a romance, with no trajectory into the future, the ever more complicated and adult future.

How many times had Oma thought, of Opa, if only our romance had remained just that, a romance?

The waiter glared at my now empty plate, and grabbed it with another sigh.

※ I found a bench in a small park and sat with my white notebook in my lap. My steel fountain pen was running out of turquoise ink, so I took two cartridges out of my wallet—a black and a burgundy. I chose the black.

Seventy-three years earlier, in a suburb of Chalon, Mme T. told Jos she didn't have any connections anymore and couldn't help. He told her that he was almost out of ration tickets and didn't know what to do next.

The crazy part about it is that internally I am dead calm whilst I tell this tale of my woes just as if it doesn't concern me at all. Mrs. T. perfectly understands the situation, but it seems that she really can't do anything for me. The only thing she is able to do is to swap cigarettes for bread and butter rations.

He tried a café where she said he might find people who could help, but was kicked out. He should go back to Dijon, he knew, and then back to Paris on Monday to regroup and find a better plan. He was still stuck in occupied territory, still a fugitive, illegal, his life considered a threat to the German state.

> But it really rubs me the wrong way, now that I am standing at the edge of the promised land, after having crossed two frontiers and travelled nearly nine hundred kilometres to admit half a defeat by turning right back around. Is it not better to go all in, hang good sense on the coatrack, and try to reach the free zone all on my own? If I stay for dinner in Chalon, and afterwards look for a little wooded area or a barn on the outskirts of town and hide there until dark, then follow the railway tracks south, I should be able to reach the free zone within half an hour, and if I walk along the tracks for the whole night, I'll be in safety. The trouble is that I know absolutely nothing about the local conditions, so that I have no idea when and where to look for danger. Whilst I am still in doubt, it has become half past five, a quarter to six—and still no bus. When I enquire, I hear that some-times the bus gets so crowded in the town itself that it doesn't come to this stop near the station at all. I decide to leave my fate to destiny: if the bus arrives, I'll return to Dijon like a good boy, if not, I'll visit Mrs. T. once more in the hope that she can give me some more infor-mation, and will set out for a crossing tonight.

As Opa waited to see if the bus would come, it almost certainly did not occur to him that it was Saturday, Shabbat until sundown.

It occurred to me, though, in 2015, on my bench in Dijon.

While enrolled in Rabbi Gerry's course, Lev and I had half-heartedly attempted to observe the Jewish Sabbath by shutting down our computers and phones each Saturday. We soon gave that up—distressingly enough, neither of us could bear a whole twenty-four hours without our devices. Before Lev, I never knew the word *Shabbat*. Shabbat is the Hebrew word for Sabbath; my father's family used the Yiddish, Shabbos. Shabbos was why, when I was seven, six, five, in Maryland, Dad packed us all into the car each Saturday and drove the hour to his parents' and grandmother's house. There, our great-grandmother pinched our cheeks hard enough to hurt, speaking English with an accent and a lot of words we didn't know, *Pesach* and *tchotchkes* and *mishegas*, words that sank down a hole where meaning should have blossomed. Grandad lived in the basement, where he had his own bedroom, bathroom, and living room, with a player piano—a piano played by invisible ghost fingers. He looked exactly like my father, only balding and bigger and more worn down, and came upstairs in a haze of cigarette smoke, tired and worried—vibrating, really, poisoned by a potent emotional brew that would soon kill him: heart attack. He must have suffered from the anxiety and depression that afflicts so much of that whole side of the family (his mother had, famously, received electroshock therapy), but without the benefit of any treatment at all. I don't remember him speaking to me directly. And Mimi, the world's least grandmotherly grandmother, the heart of the household, glamorous and gorgeous with her blazing red hair and perfectly made-up face, didn't cook exactly, but sliced peaches, chopped eggs and pickles, tuna and celery, for sandwiches.

After lunch, we sat in the living room, with its potpourri and china figurines (just tchotchkes) and framed family photos. Melancholic paintings by Mimi's uncle, murdered in the Holocaust, hung on the walls. Sometimes Mimi took Chloe and me to her bedroom, where we leaned against innumerable pillows of varying shapes and sizes— sausage-shaped the most fascinating and least practical of all. She filled our pockets with lipstick and perfume samples, fastened Coco Chanel belts around our waists and stepped back to admire, let us apply lady-smelling powder to our faces with a giant puff.

On the way home, my mother called my great-grandmother a "racist old woman" and my father said, vibrating at exactly the same frequency as Grandad, that she had survived the Holocaust. She wasn't *exactly* a *Holocaust survivor*, my mother said, since she was never in the camps. And my father said her sisters were all taken, and only one survived.

Her husband—Mimi's father—was taken away too, to one of the camps for a few weeks, and then somehow sent back home; that was before they escaped Germany to England. He never talked about it.

"I grew up surrounded by the sounds of grief," Dad said, his voice so sorrow-laden, he seemed to be overacting in order to elicit a sympathetic response.

"But she's still racist," said my mother. "She thinks of me as a shiksa."

"Then don't *act* like a shiksa. When she wishes you a good Shabbos, just say it back."

"But I don't celebrate the Sabbath."

"*Keep*, not *celebrate*. You just *say* it. Good Shabbos. Not Sabbath. *Shabbos*. Like that."

"Stop it."

"Say it!"

"Stop it!"

"Just say it!"

"I don't speak Yiddish. Stop it."

※ The hormones in my body had me ransacking my mind for my worst memories, as though to find an excuse for how depressed I felt. I knew it was happening, but barely wanted to resist, was sinking into the poor, poor me as into a feather duvet. But after about forty-five minutes of aimless writing in the Dijon park, an urgent pain in my belly had me pushing my notebook and pen into my bag. I stood from my bench, and hurried to the automated public toilet on the other side of a row of trees. A pristine one-stall affair that opened at the press of a button, with robotic clicks and whirrings. The toilet itself featured no handle or button; a sign explained that once I left, the stall would lock, flush, and clean itself.

When I did open the door, however, a man waiting outside tried to dart past me inside, a young boy in tow.

"No, no," I said. "Wait, I just have to close the—"

"Laissez-la ouverte," the man commanded me, as we tug-of-warred with the door.

"Mais la toilette." I stumbled over my words, frantic. "The toilet won't flush unless—"

The young boy urgently needed in, probably, I understood, but young men didn't necessarily know that women bled copiously and chunkily once a month. I mean, men had confided in me that before they had girlfriends, they didn't know women even shit or picked their sweet little noses. It wasn't my dignity I worried about. The toilet might pose a real trauma to the boy. He might remember it forever, the way I remembered visiting my mother in the hospital after her tubal ligation and peering into another room to see a man with no legs prostrate on a stretcher (he didn't see me either).

"Do. Not. Close. The door," said the man.

"Okay, fine." I stepped past him and the boy to depart decisively, without looking back. I let it go. I didn't let it go. I'd still worry a year later, still wonder what scene unfolded between the man and the boy, confronted with the bit of my body I'd left behind in the unflushable toilet. But temporarily, I let it go. Returned to my hotel.

☀ I napped, then went out looking for dinner around ten, though the hotel concierge told me I wouldn't find anything open. Everything was open. I found a tiny restaurant outside the tourist sprawl, on a quiet street. Ordered a delicious stew with salad and then pear cake. The sun had set. No more Shabbat. The odd thing was, just in the past year my parents had started attending services almost every Saturday—a fact I only fully realized when I visited them a few months earlier, and they took me with them to a small room in the basement of a Unitarian church—the congregation was far too small to afford their own synagogue. My parents were defensive about their new congregation, and referred to it, jokingly, as their "cult." They made light of the whole thing because everyone they knew was baffled, including dad's own mother and sister. They'd become *religious*? After all *that*?

The congregation they'd joined was Reconstructionist—a big step more liberal than Reform, and their rabbi was a woman from Baltimore, a lesbian with long greying hair, who played the guitar and the piano, and sang Leonard Cohen songs as part of the service. Sometimes they did yoga. The other congregants were retired professors and civil servants with an air of pot smoke around their fleece sweaters, who wore wool socks with sandals and talked about their vegetable gardens. When I went with my parents to the Saturday service, I dressed painfully inappropriately, in a dress and high heels, expecting something like Rabbi Gerry's temple. My mother and father and I sat in a row with prayer books open on our laps, chanting the Sh'ma. My mother knew the Sh'ma? Since when? It occurred to me that Oma was too sick now to disdain the congregation my parents had joined, or to understand that it existed. Would Mum have dared to do this otherwise? When the rabbi invited my father and me to the front to read together from the Torah, Dad slung his arm around my shoulders so that I was supporting his weight, his hand on my arm, tears in his eyes.

At home after the service, Dad said he'd been led to Rabbi Green by fate; he had googled the name of his great-uncle, the artist who'd died in Auschwitz, whose paintings hung in Mimi's living room, and discovered an independent scholar who'd received a Fulbright to study him. That researcher happened to live in Maryland, near Mimi, so he went to see the paintings. He'd also written a book with Rabbi Green, in nearby Baltimore, and she happened to be moving to Ottawa. Dad said God had brought him to Rabbi Green, and told me that he and Mum were in the midst of a "spiritual crisis."

"I'm not having a spiritual crisis," Mum corrected. "Bernard may be having a spiritual crisis. I just like the people." They'd become such close friends with one of the couples from their congregation that they'd travelled together, to New York.

"They're so different from your usual friends," I said.

"You're being so judgemental," said Dad.

My voice had sounded that way, but I didn't know why. I liked my parents' friends from the temple.

"I don't mean to sound judgemental," I said. "I'm just curious what it means to each of you, being part of a congregation. How you came to this, when you were so opposed for so long."

"We've come to believe that things happen for a reason. That there's a higher power of some kind," said Dad. "And that Rabbi Green was sent to us, as our guide."

"You *have*?" I gaped at my mother.

"I have *not* come to believe that," said Mum. "I just like the people."

"So you have different reasons," I said. "Mum, I didn't know you knew any Hebrew."

"Well, I just read the phonetic version—Bernard, what's *wrong*?"

"I feel judged," said Dad.

I did still sound judgemental, or angry, or something. There was a nagging edge to my voice. Why?

As I finished my dessert at that little table in Dijon, I swallowed around guilt that I hadn't phoned or emailed my parents to acknowledge Shabbat. I imagined Dad's reaction, his "I'm so touched that you would think of me today. Shabbat shalom, darling." The thought of it annoyed me intensely. I didn't want to acknowledge my parents' embrace of tradition, even the hippified version they'd chosen. It wasn't fair of me, I knew: they'd chosen to raise secular children, had done it on purpose, for all sort of reasons. And people change throughout their lives, change their minds a million times, change completely. I hadn't lived with my parents for twenty years, half my life, and so much had happened during that time, for me and for them, too. Turning to tradition and faith were really not so strange. I had tried hard to do the same myself. The way each of them characterized their attraction to the Reconstructionist congregation was not, I knew, a final statement of fact. They must have had complex reasons, hard to pin down, harder to explain. And Dad had never really been on board with the post-religious lifestyle anyway, had seemed tortured by it. But to me it felt like both my parents had withheld vital information—my mother could pray in Hebrew? It would have been so much easier if I'd had a tradition to reject, instead of having to seek it out for myself first. I'd had to venture so far to learn the Sh'ma, when they'd known it the whole time.

✳ Back in my room, I made reservations for the next few more days, googling the name of each hotel along with *bedbugs* before committing.

I googled my own name, as if to confirm that I still existed. I did, according to Wikipedia and my own website. On the first page of hits appeared the article I wrote about my nose job, and Rabbi Rose's op-ed calling me an anti-Semite.

What's my ethnic background? I asked myself. *I'm a goy.*

An email appeared in my inbox, from Matteo, still in Italy:

Lil N. of my Heart (Italianism): I'm walking back to my aunt's apartment from a night in piazza mostly with my pal Luciano. The best thing I ate was a "crespella," basically a chunk of fried dough that somehow was way, way better than it sounds. I like all the things you ate yesterday (Nutella and a tomato) but together they are comical. You're funny! (I've had two very strong drinks). I hope you found a solid base food for your condiment. Crickets be chirpin'. A cat meows. Everyone seems to be returning home at 3 o'clock. (Car doors slam). I'm just standing outside the building now, thinking of you.

✳ The bus came, so Jos abandoned his plan to escape that night alone. Back to Dijon, and the next day, back to Paris.

Later I hear from experiences of other refugees that if I had perse-
vered, I would have stood a good chance of falling in German hands
and ultimately in a concentration camp as the guard near Chalon is
one of the strictest.

It seems to be very difficult to go against one's nature: some people have a strong fancy for tourism, others haven't, I belong to the first category.

And I belonged to the second. I hated tourism, hated moving through places with no time to absorb anything, hated how tired I felt from all the newness, unable to absorb any details except for the details of the meals I ate. I lay in bed Sunday morning, sleepy from the rain, still with a migraine, though the initial blast had faded to an insistent buzz. I pictured buying a plane ticket from Dijon to Calgary for the next day. Screw this trip. What was the point? I didn't want to follow Opa to Chalon any more than I had the day before—but I took a migraine pill, and mid-morning headed for the station, telling myself the train schedule would dictate my plans. A train was scheduled to leave within five minutes. I bought my ticket, half-ran to the platform, "and soon afterward I pass through the land of the Bourgogne, where the names of the towns and villages awaken the sweetest memories: Gevrey-Chambertin, Veurey, Nuits-Saint-Georges, Beaune, Meursault and all the rest." I caught glimpses of all those little towns, well, signs with their names—but *what* sweet memories did they hold for Jos? Once again, the journal seemed a tease, so withholding, the anomalous thirty-page confession of someone who otherwise lived inside his own experience with no desire to make himself known to anyone. And if Jos had made himself known to anyone, it wouldn't have been one of his three granddaughters, and it wouldn't have been one of his two daughters, either. I thought of *Back to the Future*—the irresistible idea of encountering one's own parents as peers, as *people*. The desire to meet one's own grandparents as people seemed even more prevalent—I was far from the first to try, with a pile of old papers, to reconstruct for myself the person, the zeitgeist, the perspective of my parent's parent. The world Jos had occupied seemed a different world, as magical and mythical as Oz, but also, in a very real way, my origin. I was knocking against the past, trying to get in, trying to find what made me—why? Because of some Freudian notion that unearthing unspoken trauma would set me free?

In Chalon, I found a street performers' festival underway. Despite the clouds and drizzle, everyone from the town and surrounding area had apparently come out for the day with their festival maps and their folding chairs, enjoying the inexpert hoop dancing, breakdancing, a brass band, and a park full of pianos. Some functional pianos, some only half there, one with a fish tank inside, one dangling from cords halfway down the low-rise apartment building across the street. From a bench, I watched children playing on a slide, and considered taking a nap right there. I badly wanted to. Just lie down on the bench and close my eyes. Who cares what people think? But I stayed upright, because I was an adult, I was a thirty-nine-year-old woman. I couldn't just curl up on a bench. This grey and rain would stick with me for days, according to the forecast.

I felt in my bones how tired Opa must have become, and how frustrated. Of course he was tempted to just push through, and almost didn't listen to the woman who told him the guards had become too vigilant. Almost tried to make his way during the night, alone. And if Jos had gone on alone, he may have ended up in a concentration camp and died, or survived but never met Mary Elizabeth Skipsey, survived but ruined, survived but someone else. "No way back," he wrote.

I followed my GPS to the Saône river, and followed the path alongside the water, passing only a few other pedestrians and one jogger.

People had pitched a long row of tents on the other side. It wasn't raining hard enough to open my umbrella, wasn't really raining so much as an ozone-and-shrub-smelling cloud had settled over the ground. The river was flowing left—more specifically, according to Google Maps on my phone, south, toward Lyon, where Jos would end up, though he didn't know it yet, and where he would write his journal throughout the next two months, August and September.

I watched the water and thought of Winnie-the-Pooh's game, Pooh Sticks, where you toss sticks off a bridge into a river, then run to the bridge's other side to see which stick will run the race. That was one of my favourite Pooh stories, Pooh and the gang waiting for their sticks, only to see poor Eeyore floating down the river instead. Though it wasn't as good as the story about Eeyore's birthday, and the honey jar and the balloon. What ever happened to those old books? And then, as the whiff of crumbling pages fluttered though me, a nostalgia gripped me, longing, or was it regret, or was it loss? That feeling, whenever I smelled gasoline like the gasoline in Opa's motorboat when I was five, or cherry Chapstick like the cherry Chapstick my new Canadian school-mates wore in Grade 2, or incense like the incense I burned in Grade 7 until my parents said I wasn't allowed, or rubbing alcohol like the rubbing alcohol my non-boyfriend applied to his body piercings in high school. This feeling had always baffled me because each memory, whether sweet or boring or miserable, evoked a longing just as potent and painful as any other. Just the past, and the fact that the past was in the past, hurt, oh hurt, hurt my bones and made it hard to breathe.

The feeling passed, and I closed my eyes; the movement of the water was making me a little queasy.

I had swum across a river once.

I was sixteen, and though my nose never healed perfectly and looked a bit broken, like a boxer's, I felt by then that adolescent ugliness had retreated from me. It wasn't just my nose. I'd stopped growing at a reasonable height, and my skin problems had taken a demotion from acne to a few red bumps, thanks to my dermatologist. I'd learned how to tame my hair from frizz into curls. I wasn't beautiful like my lab partner Tatiana, who looked like Milla Jovovich and had hordes of boys waiting by her locker for a glimpse, and I wasn't one of the just-plain-pretty girls, like Lena and Tanya, in long-sleeved tee-shirts and jeans, with shiny straight hair that looked perfect in a ponytail. But I no longer hated mirrors. And non-ugliness was just as good as I thought it would be.

Ugliness (or belief in my own ugliness) had been a heavy mantle, and its sudden lifting rendered a lightness I couldn't have prepared for, a lightness that floated me right off the ground. I was relieved, but, at the same time, I felt like an imposter, like I might be found out, an ugly person hiding in a non-ugly person's body. But one thing that came with newfound non-ugliness (or belief in my own non-ugliness) was attention, attention from men, attention I inhaled like laughing gas, and for which I would be, for many years, to my ongoing detriment, surprised and grateful.

Throughout that summer when I was sixteen, I dated a drummer five years older than me, with blond dreadlocks and a California drawl even though he'd never been to California, which was amazingly cool. I met him at a punk show in July, and he talked to me all night, *flirted*. And I flirted back, amazed that I knew how. I laughed at his jokes and made my own, head full of helium from the attention. At the end of the night, he kissed me. My first kiss. All summer, I told my mother (my father was in DC for work) I was out with friends, and made out with the drummer on his smaller-than-single cot. The first time we had sex was late September. I'd started Grade 11 by then, and sometimes had a three-hour lunch; that day, as I often did, I went to the drummer's apartment for a mid-day debauch. I'd planned to shed my virginity that day. I marked my day planner with a big star. For the occasion, I dyed my hair pink and dressed extra-cool in my purple ten-hole Doc Martens and a white tutu-like skirt.

We took a bath together before the big event, and my Manic Panic hair dye tinted the bath water red. Symbolism, I thought. It wasn't just the first time we'd have sex, but the first time I'd have sex, ever. I needed to do it, to get to the other side of that threshold. For one thing, I'd told Tanya, my friend with the shiniest ponytail, that I'd slept with someone during the summer, so that I could begin the school year free of her constant teasing about my virginity. I hated that I'd lied, and could see only one way to fix it. Also, the drummer was tired of stopping just short of the real action. I was more than satisfied with what we'd been doing; more than satisfied times a million. The first time I'd gone to the drummer's house, back in July, I'd made the most incredible discovery. Later I'd read accounts by alcoholics of taking their first drink; the first time the drummer and I got naked was like that. Suddenly I was beautiful and wanted, my skin and my bones, and my bad-skin face and my skinny ribs and my long weird toes. Suddenly I fit in the world *perfectly*, no awkwardness, no self-consciousness, just effortless grace. I'd found *my thing*, as though I'd never known before what it really meant to be alive.

Actual sex, it turned out, was painful and brief in all the clichéd ways. Next time, I told myself, would be better. The drummer took the elevator down with me and walked me outside. I had to get back to school, where we had a compulsory afternoon assembly to discuss the upcoming national referendum over whether to revise Canada's constitution as laid out in the Charlottetown Accord.

"Well, I hope that was an interesting experience," the drummer said.

That night, I taped into my diary the wrapper from the condom we'd used, as though we'd taken a trip together and I'd saved the train ticket. I had to use tape rather than glue because the wrapper remained a little slimy with spermicidal lubricant. Under the tape, the lube smudged into a greasy-looking stain, making the paper transparent and smudging the top line of careful blue cursive into a purplish stain. I wrote a full account of the experience. I don't remember now—the full experience or my account of it.

A few days later, I had my three-hour lunch again, and we did it again, and it was a bit better than the first time, and then he broke up with me, right then, before I put my underwear back on. He said he just felt too guilty because I was so young. Also, he had to get serious, and start looking for a wife. "I'm twenty-one-years-old," he emphasized. "I can't just keep fooling around."

At home that night, I stood naked in front of the bathroom mirror. Too skinny, ribs too visible, butt too small. Fuzziness where I should have been smooth. My breasts were big for my body, and that had to be good, but I had too much hair, everywhere, even on my arms. How was I supposed to get rid of it; wouldn't shaving be worse? My knees looked knobbly. My hair was long and curly and still dyed pink. And despite all the goop I'd loaded into it still frizzy at the back, where it always seemed to form a dreadlock. My skin looked oily, and I had three pimples, two on my chin and one on my forehead. I turned my head, ran my finger down my nose's crooked, asymmetrical bridge, and pulled at its weirdly extended tip. Was it because of my bad nose job? I was nothing to that drummer.

I felt hollow and heavy all at once, all through my bones. That's what it feels like to have shared a bunch of intimacy with someone who's remained a stranger, but I didn't know that then. I didn't know that I was going through withdrawal, that I was addicted to the drummer's smooth muscular arms and tanned face with actual blond stubble, and even the smell of his unwashed dreadlocked hair, that I was addicted to the feeling he gave me, that smooth, fluid feeling, a feeling I didn't know was akin to being high on heroin. Shortly after the whole "I'm twenty-one, I need a wife" conversation, I saw him out at an all-ages show and he said hi to me all casual, as though we just knew each other a bit, when mere days earlier, and all summer, we'd been so *naked*.

The next days at school, I sat in class in a daze. The problem, I thought, was that the making out (if not the actual sex) had involved so much kissing and so much hugging. The actions of sexuality had been physically identical with kissing and hugging, and kissing and hugging meant love. They meant tenderness. It's not that I imagined I loved the drummer. I barely knew him. It was just so *weird*, to go from all that stuff with our faces pressed up together to acting like nothing happened at all. And the fact that he had made this switch so easily meant, with glaring clarity, that I would be alone forever, just drifting, bumping into this person and that, to bump off and float away again, never successfully latching. The combination of dejection, rage, and *esprit d'escalier* occupied every bit of my brain, and only after about half an hour did I notice that nothing outside looked familiar at all. I was on the wrong bus.

And was lost, so lost. I was too tired to do anything about it, so I just stayed in my seat, and waited to see what would happen. Finally, I saw something familiar—the university campus where I'd hoped to end up in the first place. Without thinking, I rang the bell for the bus to pull over at the next stop. And there I stood, on some busy road I couldn't name. Carleton's campus close by, comfortingly familiar because I often volunteered at the radio station there after school. The only problem was, I was on the wrong side of the river. Right there, concrete buildings, red, gold, orange, yellow trees, one brown brick tower against the cloudy sky. So close.

On that university campus was an office with a man in it, a man with a blond mohawk, whose company I craved, ever since I'd heard he had ended a workplace argument by picking up his stapler and driving a staple into his own palm, his face still and steady. Then he marched out of the room, everyone stunned silent, and caught a taxi to the ER. He was twenty-four, a real *man*, he flirted, held eye contact, called me cute and hot and seemed to listen, rapt, when I spoke. I needed him to tell me the drummer had been crazy-lucky to have me, and crazy to let me go. (And he would say those things, and I would imprint on him hard. In a few months he would become my on-again, off-again lover, never acknowledging me in public, for four years—until I was almost twenty-one.) My limbs ached with fatigue, as they often did, and I could see a bridge off in the distance. To walk to that bridge, cross it, and walk back to campus would take at least an hour. Or I could cross the street, catch a bus heading the other way, and go back to where I started, all the way downtown, then start over. That would take approximately forever, and I'd arrive home for dinner and miss my opportunity.

I slip-slid down the escarpment, knees bent in a surfer's crouch, sometimes skidding to sitting in the slick fallen leaves, grabbing at branches for leverage, reaching into shrubs, scraping my palms. When I reached the bottom, I found my dress and tights covered in burrs, and I pushed my hand into my hair to feel the dense little balls in there, too, buried and barbed in tight. The river's opposite shore seemed further away now than it had. But there was no way I could climb back up the way I'd come—I just wasn't capable of it. I unlaced my Doc Marten boots and tied them together, looped them over my shoulders like skates. My black tights, I put in my purple backpack. I dipped one foot in the water and felt for the bottom. Stepped out into the river. Frigid, but shallow, barely reached my knees. Took a step, and another. The current lapped my calves, pushing firmly, caressingly, in the direction of my house, northward, toward downtown and the Ottawa River and Quebec.

The drummer had said, "Sex with you is fun, but..." *Fun?* I'd never had fun in my life. I did not do fun. This was serious business, what we were doing, not fun. Not *fun*. This was, I don't know, *art*.

No, I'd made a mistake. Sex was not *it*, sex was a distraction, a way to feel better. I needed something else, something for my life to be about. Once I'd longed to become an astronaut, to find the answer out there. But it wasn't space I wanted. I wanted to be wise. I wanted to pass a threshold and find myself whole and dignified, my head full of maps, an adult.

I'd made it practically to the middle of the river. Easy peasy.

And then I was underwater.

And swimming. Spluttering, gasping. Kicking, pulling with my arms, legs, every muscle, against the current. I didn't even register the cold, just the sudden sodden heaviness of the fabric drenched and tugging all over me.

I thought, move move move move.

Drop my backpack and boots and jacket? Only if my head goes under again. If my head goes under, the boots and backpack and textbooks and jacket and wallet are goners, better them than me.

Help! No one's here, no one can see me, no one to grab, move move move.

Die? Drown? Today?

No, I have to live!

Or they'll search, and the police will get involved, they'll find my body somewhere up-river, and it'll be on TV, and kids I've never spoken to at school will cry, like when that girl died of meningitis. The police will try at first to solve the mystery but find no clues. My parents and my sister and my grandparents and my friends and maybe even the drummer and maybe even the guy on the other side of the river will wonder forever but find no answers, will run through scenarios in their minds, but they'll never come up with this one, that I got lost, so lost I walked into the frigid Rideau River.

My poor parents. They would not know how to deal with this.

I pulled myself out, onto the grass, on the other side. I lay panting and shivering on the muddy ground. Alive. I'd swum across the Rideau River.

It took me some time to drag my soaked bag and clothes, as well as my soaked self, up the steep hill and onto the university campus, and went straight to the office of the man whose attention I so craved, ignoring all the glances on the way.

He said, "Whoa—is it raining?" then accepted my story about falling in the river without apparent judgement—if anything, my showing up soaked to the bone with a nonsensical explanation seemed to make him like me more. He gave me a tee-shirt from his desk drawer, let me change in his office and call my mom from his phone.

He walked me downstairs, hugged me, and hurried back inside before my mother showed up.

The family Volvo pulled up to where I stood soaked and barefoot and wearing an XXL men's tee-shirt instead of a dress. The tee-shirt was powder blue and read, *I'm so fuckin' happy*. My dripping purple back-pack sat beside me on the ground. My textbooks would be wrinkled and purple-tinted for the rest of the year.

"What are you playing at?" my mother said, through gritted teeth, as I climbed in. "Are you trying to get attention or something?" She waited until we got home to say anything more, and didn't say it to me, but to Oma, on the phone. "Why is she doing this to me?"

"I can't just keep fooling around," the drummer had said. I hadn't known we were just fooling around. I mean, I had known that, of course I had. But at the same time, I hadn't.

That feeling, the feeling that pushed me out into the Rideau River when I was sixteen, and that had never entirely left me, it washed back through me as stood on the bridge in Chalon, washed through my mouth, a taste. That feeling I'd hoped would meet its antidote in Lev, in the conversion class, that would wash off in the mikvah. That feeling, that *Oh God, oh fucking help*. I couldn't keep my head up, was so tired, but so light, like the wind could just blow me away. I was an ant under a magnifying glass, with the entire universe focused on frying me, but the universe didn't know I existed, I wasn't even part of the universe, was extraneous, not even an I, I mean, I didn't mean anything, just nothing, I was just *nothing*. Teen angst, my chemistry lab partner Tatiana had called this existential horror, all ironic, I mean, the horror we thought we had in common, and that, while distressing, also somehow made us sophisticates. That was before she was run over by a taxi and hospitalized for a whole month.

Over homework, Tatiana had told me in her broken English (which was improving weekly) that she'd been taken away by the state (communist, I vaguely understood) when she was twelve and forced to appear in propaganda films and posters because she was so gorgeous, but then her father, a diplomat of some kind, got her back and got himself posted in Canada. Gorgeous, tall Tatiana often wore a lot of makeup in a way that Canadian teenagers did not consider cool, with blush and eyeshadow and lipliner, and still modelled a bit, except now she got paid for it. Thanks to the weekend modelling career, she met lots of jerks in their twenties, and even in their thirties, to sleep with, not just one twenty-one-year-old drummer.

I visited her in the hospital shortly after the river incident, when her collarbone and pelvis had all but healed. She'd been moved up to the psychiatric ward a few days earlier, because, she'd told me on the phone, her father was convinced she'd stepped into traffic on purpose, and had convinced her doctors as well. I took the elevator to the right floor and rang the buzzer outside the ward's locked doors; not for the first time—she wasn't my first friend to spend time in that part of the hospital. A nurse led me to a room with Tatiana inside, sitting on a single bed in a lime green and black velour tracksuit, in full makeup and a neck brace.

"What do you call Jew flying plane?" she asked, by way of greeting.

"What—?"

"The pilot. You are racist."

"What? No. What? I meant what—what?"

"Tatiana," said the nurse.

"Relax. It's a joke."

There was nowhere to sit, so I just stood in the doorway.

"Ridiculous," Tatiana said, of her ongoing hospitalization, right in front of the nurse, who wasn't going anywhere. "I am run down by idiot taxi driver. My father searches my bedroom to find teen angst poem composed when listening to depressing American music. So what? I am bad poet, fine. I deserve prison?"

"Tatiana," said the nurse. "Why don't you take your friend to the common room?"

"I only make a joke. Come," Tatiana told me. "I show you."

We watched TV for five minutes with a skeletally skinny girl with a feeding tube up her nose and a ponytailed guy in a black Nirvana tee-shirt. The ward's walls were painted a friendly sky blue, with sporadic puffy white clouds and even a rainbow. What would I have to do to get locked in here for a while, watched day and night by a staff of nurses whose job it was to keep me safe, safe from myself, and assigned a psychiatrist devoted to helping me? Tatiana signed out with a different nurse and was allowed to take me down to the hospital cafeteria, where she smoked about a pack of cigarettes and complained in her sexy accent about the other patients, one of whom had fallen in love with her and kept writing her songs. But some were all right, she had to admit. One or two were among the smartest people she'd met in Canada. One of them had told her the Jewish pilot joke; he told it about a black pilot, but Tatiana thought a Jew would be funnier. (I did not mention that I was sort of a Jew). Why were those extra smart teens in here? Canada. She did not understand Canada at all.

I told her about the river. "All my textbooks got soaked and dyed purple." I felt my voice go high and hoarse as Tatiana blinked her dilated blue eyes at me. She was still on some serious pain killers, and who knows what else.

"So eccentric," she said. "Why not take bus back other way?" I'd hoped she would be able to tell me that; didn't she have some special insight into crazy-seeming impulses? Tatiana put out her cigarette and said, "I will tell you something strange. I feel safe in this place. In some way, I wish to stay. Perhaps forever. Institutionalized." She struggled only a little over the last word.

It turned out she wasn't psychotic or even clinically depressed, but a genius. (She went on to make important scientific breakthroughs, not in chemistry, but in the area of haptics, which means she made artificial skin that can feel textures.) It was just teen angst after all, though Tatiana must have suffered a lot more angst than I did, because I was never kept under medical observation for two weeks, and none of my therapists ever diagnosed me with anything more serious than anxiety, but then, I was no model and no genius. Goddammit, why couldn't I be a model or at least a genius?

After a couple of weeks, Tatiana was back in school, and we were lab partners again, but once the semester ended, we did not remain friends. She stopped me in the hallway once, a year later, and asked in nearly perfect English if I'd visited her in the hospital. Her memory of that time was blurry, and she thought she remembered talking to me, but wasn't sure if it had really happened. She'd toned down her look quite a bit, wore hardly any makeup at all, and was even more beautiful than before, though she'd quit modelling to focus on her new role as president of the school's debate team. When I confirmed that I'd visited her, she asked me not to tell anyone about her month up in the sky-and-cloud ward, and though I couldn't imagine anyone holding it against her, I said of course.

A few months later, Tatiana gave an award-winning speech in front of the whole school, in which she said that each of us should think of our life as a story, and that we should make that story beautiful, a work of art. I thought of the request she'd made of me in the hallway, and I guessed I understood. After all, we create narratives of our lives, create meaning that way, create our selves, and sometimes elements—scenes or chapters, or even whole characters—have to go, because they mess with the story's flow, or contradict a major theme, and can't be tweaked enough to fit. Sometimes an anomalous episode stands out awkwardly, a tangent. Much worse, it can threaten to take over, to point all arrows at itself—here I am, the secret, the answer, the cause—when the story is just not about that, not at all.

※ The train back to Dijon passed again through Jos's beloved holiday towns—Meursault, Beaune, Nuits-Saint-Georges, Gevrey-Chambertin.

※ Back in Dijon, I went to watch *Le Petit Prince*, which I'd seen advertised throughout France as the film event of the year. Sitting in the cinema, I could have been at home in Calgary, or anywhere. The same scattered audience, the same upholstered chairs with the cup holders. The film's protagonist was a contemporary little girl. I didn't understand much, though I gleaned that the girl's mother was a type-A perfectionist, and that the old-man aviator next door, who embodies lively chaos, befriends the girl, and shares his story of the little prince from another planet, whom he met long ago in the desert. At the beginning, the girl is terrified of growing up, of losing life's sparkle to grown-up tedium. The aviator tells her that the problem is not growing up, but forgetting. Just like Saint-Exupéry writes: "All grown-ups were once children, but only few of them remember it."

Jos sat in a Dijon cinema too, seventy-three years earlier, and realized he hadn't seen a movie in more than two years, since the Occupation. He didn't mention in his journal that Jews had been barred from entering cinemas throughout Holland. Only:

Actually, it is absolutely crazy that, although my situation is not very rosy and not free of danger, here I am leading the contented life of a tourist with a timely aperitif and my most pressing concern is when and where to have my meals! But after the last twenty-four hours it seems that I am more or less immune against nervous tensions—at least that is what I imagine.

MONDAY MORNING IN MY DIJON HOTEL ROOM, I laid out my
clothes on the bed. Polka-dot underpants, grey shorts, black tee-shirt,
black sports bra. After showering, I stepped into the panties, picked up
the bra, put it down. Took the pink lacy one from my suitcase, slipped
my arms through the straps, took it off again. The sports bra was more
comfortable, and cost fifteen dollars at Winners. The pink bra had cost
a hundred dollars at a specialty lingerie shop, and fit me perfectly,
hugging and supporting just so. I pulled the sports bra over my head
and placed the pink one back in my little suitcase. I'd bought that pink
bra over a year earlier during a trip to Ottawa, and I visited Oma the
next day at her retirement home to find that she wasn't wearing a bra at
all. She told me that she'd come to despise her ninety-year-old breasts,
and wished she could have them removed. She wanted her chest flat
and smooth as a baby's. Not long after that, she had started telling
anyone who'd listen that she needed a double mastectomy, and that the
surgeon had agreed to let her keep her breasts as a memento, pickled
in a jar. That's when the retirement home's administrators began to
suggest that Oma would fare better in a nursing home, where she'd
receive more attention and care. The other residents had found her
breasts-in-jar story extremely disturbing. Oh, come on, I thought. It's a
great story, it's a genius story! But she'd already been branded a trouble-
maker for insisting the other residents call her Countess, then Doctor,
and because she grabbed her nurses and told them, "Look at the big
juicy bottom on you!"

On Monday, July 27th, 1942, Oma, that is, Betty Skipsey, had perfect breasts: firm, young, big-for-her-body breasts. On Monday, July 27th, Jos took a crowded train back to Paris, where he visited the same friend who'd sent him to Chalon for advice, only to hear that there had been a crack-down, with all the French obliged to

inform the occupying authorities of any persons whom he sees acting in a suspicious manner. Although personally I am not plotting—I have to be extremely careful. They do not dare to let me stay in their office and they must urgently advise me to disappear as soon as possible out of Paris, which, as a main centre of administration, is guarded even more strictly than anywhere else.

He made a plan to go on that evening to Bordeaux, where he didn't know anyone and had never been before.

Well, I must try to make the best of it. By way of consolation, I get a quantity of ration-tickets—sufficient to live on for the next eight or ten days like a king, and in addition a parcel which, as I find out later on, contains meat, cheese, and tins of liverwurst and half a dozen hard boiled eggs, certainly a valuable present.

On my train back to Paris, my phone rang, someone calling from Fredericton, to arrange an event for after Christmas, when I'd be writer in residence at the university there.

"I don't have my calendar right now," I told the woman from the New Brunswick arts organization. "I'm on a train. In France."

"You *are*? What are you doing in France?"

"I'm—I'm doing research, actually, for the book I'm going to be writing during my residency."

I hung up feeling disoriented, my feeling of being away tarnished. I turned off my phone's ringer, but kept the device itself turned on for the GPS.

Three young Brits sat near me, a boy-and-girl pair with another girl, who sat across from her friends, a waterproof green backpack occupying the seat beside her.

"Want to hear something *mad?*" said the guy.

"All right," said the girl who wasn't his girlfriend.

"When I moved into my own flat, I started doing this thing when I stood at the kitchen counter chopping vegetables or whatever. While I was preparing dinner I'd reach into my pants, pull out a pubic hair or two, and put them in my cutlery drawer."

Both girls laughed.

"Do you think it was because I was living alone for the first time?" he asked.

"Could be," said the non-girlfriend. "Could be you're a freak."

"I know, right? So the first time Pammy came over for dinner, we cooked together, and she opened that drawer looking for a knife and there was this *pile*, this *drawer full* of pubic hair. And she was like, um? What is this!"

I glanced over to see Pammy lean toward him affectionately and nod, with a wistful smile, while their friend laughed showing all her nice white teeth. Well, I wasn't sure—Pammy may have always looked wistful. She was the kind of very blonde girl with resting-wistful face.

I squirmed on my seat, imagining some previous passenger reaching into his pants to pull out a hair and drop it onto the upholstery. Along with a pubic louse, a crab, a creepy-crawly now waiting for a new home. I breathed deeply.

I put on my headphones and played Leonard Cohen's "The Partisan," five times in a row while I read the book I'd downloaded onto my laptop, about Paris during the German Occupation. When the Nazis occupied France, I learned, they set the clocks forward an hour, to Berlin time.

✳ At Gare de Lyon, I caught the Metro. I was staying in an Airbnb in the 7th arrondissement this time, strangely inexpensive. I got off the Metro at the Louvre, and I thought I'd just take a quick look upstairs, since I was underneath the most famous museum in Europe. I stepped through a portal into another world, a writhing mass of people, thousands, it seemed, all waiting in line to buy entry tickets. I had pictured a big museum, not a vast museum, not the population of a busy international airport mashed into a magnificent hall. I'd even thought I might have time to buy a ticket and take a look around. I approached the crowd, stood at the end of the line. Within minutes, a new mass of people had gathered behind me. I stepped forward, my first step forward, in a stupor—was I really prepared to spend hours in this line?—and then hours more moving with the crowd through some tiny portion of the museum before I had to leave again. I had no idea how much a ticket even cost. But I was here, in the Louvre—what kind of person goes to the Louvre but doesn't venture inside? Behind me, still more people gathered, each family speaking in a different language, one child already screwing up his sweaty face to cry: he knew how long this was going to take.

I shouldered my way back out into the open and took the elevator up to the food court. There, I ate an absurdly overpriced thimbleful of hummus. I visited the fancy bathroom with multicoloured toilet-paper rolls piled in pyramids, and attendants who darted into the stalls to clean by hand after each person finished her business. What a horrendous job—wiping cooties off toilets in the Louvre. Wiping the cooties of tourists from all over the world. Wiping pubic hairs of all colours, and wiping herpes viruses and dead skin cells with every stripe of DNA and—could a bedbug end up on a toilet seat? If it had been hanging out in the seam of some lady's pants, say, and dropped off as she shimmied the fabric over her haunches? Oh, God, the cooties were moving in, little parasites everywhere. I longed for a bottle of disinfectant. I longed for home, clean sweet home.

Out in the rain, I pulled my suitcase through the streets so famous they were familiar to me though I'd never been there before. Across the bridge, I paused to look behind me, and ahead. On the narrow street ten minutes away, I rang the bell for my Airbnb, and texted my host. No response. I sat at a small purple table sheltered under a canopy. Was I allowed to sit there? Whose was it? I wanted to get inside and regroup, to sit alone in a room and close my eyes before heading out again without my suitcase, to wander around and take in details, one by one. After an hour, my host texted. He'd been in there, it seemed, the whole time, setting up my room. My "room"—a bed with panels around it, and not even proper panels, but sheets and towels strung up on a wooden frame.

My host, a tall thirty-something hipster with shaggy hair and tight jeans, watched me attempt to arrange my things, and talked about a dance club where he seemed to be employed. Maybe he was saying he owned it, or managed it? He said something about a rooftop and a DJ. I nodded as he told me I should come by later for a cocktail and handed me a business card. As I packed my small backpack for the evening, on the other side of my "wall," my host chatted with a woman who appeared to live there. From the sound of it, they were moving furniture while they talked.

She was telling him something in rapid French. "...too young," I made out. "I want to, but I can't, just can't. Too innocent, too young, too young."

Were they debating whether to murder me? Whether to rob me? Whether to sell me into some kind of slavery? People often mistook me for younger than I was, even much younger, especially when my face bore the blank blink-blink of confusion, which it must have as I peered through the strung-up sheets into my digs, and said, "Ooh...okay."

"Je voulais aller avec lui, mais..." the girl said. "Il me plaît, je sais..."

She was talking about a guy. She was talking about a guy she'd like to sleep with. But can't, just can't, because he's too innocent, too young. Thank God.

Before I went out, a man in dress pants and a white shirt emerged from a bedroom down the hall. He looked a little Mr. Bean, and we'd be sharing the bathroom, which included a shower with a mere drip of water pressure. He eyed my so-called room. "Is this what you were expecting?" he asked in a Belgian accent.

"Not exactly." I'd been trying to convince myself that there was nothing odd about the situation. That I should have known what to expect from the Airbnb posting and the inexpensiveness of this perfect location.

"I am very disappointed," he said. "I thought I'd have my own flat. I'm here on business. I am here for meetings. I am not a backpacker."

"I thought the same," I said, relieved to discover that the problem lay with the hipster's misleading description of the space, and not with my naiveté. "I'm also here for work," I added, which wasn't exactly untrue. What I meant was, I'm also an adult. "At least you have an actual room."

"Yes." He frowned at my bed, which was right there, where you couldn't help but see it.

"I'm a financial analyst. For an importer," he explained. "And you?"

"Journalist." Journalist always sounded better, more concrete, than writer. We nodded at each other, each trying to look as though we now had some idea of what the other did for a living. "Well, I have to go meet someone." It felt good to say it, and it was true. I had someone to go and meet. Danica, a friend of Valerie's whom I'd met before in Toronto, had invited me to a reading, some English author I'd never heard of, at Shakespeare and Company, which I had heard of. I walked along the Seine, a route that was impossible to screw up, and looked back across at where I'd emerged earlier in the day. Matteo had lived here, he'd said, in this neighbourhood, before he decided to apply for grad school. He'd been trying to learn French, teaching English to get by. He hadn't enjoyed his time in Paris at all, had been lonely the whole time.

I found Danica standing outside the bookstore; I'd been afraid we wouldn't recognize each other, afraid I'd forgotten what she looked like, but of course I knew her face as soon as I saw her. Thick black hair down to the collar of her blue blouse, sharp black eyebrows, disapproving mouth. She looked skeptical even as she smiled in greeting. "Do you want to stay for the reading?" she said in her faint Eastern European accent, after kissing me like a real French person. "Or just go for dinner?"

"I wouldn't mind dinner, actually."

"Me too," she agreed.

I glanced at her profile as she led me along the river again. She had a large nose that looked perfect on her face. Valerie'd had a nose like that too. Val had hated her nose, though, believed herself ugly. Danica did not seem like the kind of woman to entertain such a silly concern as whether she was pretty, and to what extent.

Having a dinner companion seemed like permission to eat and drink as much as I liked, and suddenly hungrier than I'd felt in days, I ordered a salad and pasta, and agreed to share a bottle of wine. Of course, she asked what brought me to Paris, why I was passing through so quickly like this, and I explained how I was following my grandfather's journal, day by day, spending most of my time on trains, dashing through cities so quickly I had no time to take them in.

"Nothing is happening," I told her. "Just hotel rooms and trains."

I told her that I was getting divorced, since I'd been safely married last time I met her, and she said she'd spent the day moving in with her French boyfriend. I told her how'd I'd met up with Matteo in Brussels.

"So, it's not true that nothing is happening," she said. "Love is happening."

And that's what we discussed over dinner. Love. Her newish love, my new love that was not officially love. Her desire to have children and my lack thereof. I stuffed myself with salade niçoise and spaghetti marinara and red wine. We confided in each other the way women do, though we didn't actually know each other all that well, inexplicably spilling our guts about the most unexpected things.

"Don't talk about what it means," Danica advised. "And don't talk about love. My boyfriend and I, we have never said that. We've never said, I love you. We have never said, what does it mean that I'm moving to Paris for the summer, that we're moving in together? What about the fall, when I return to work in Toronto? No. Have not discussed it. It's better that way. You don't talk about what it is, you just let it happen."

Not my style. I could never keep it up—not for months, not to say years. I needed cards on the table, and I'd want to write dramatic love letters, I'd want to roll onto him and say I love you I love you I love you. Did I love Matteo? It wasn't exactly that I loved him, but that I was falling in love with him, that I would love him if the circumstances allowed. Danica's advice was good for the moment. The same way you don't want to cut into an avocado before it's ripe. You know it will ripen, you know it will be spectacular, but only if you treat it right, if you're patient, if you resist messing with it before it's ready.

"It's not hard to find a boyfriend," said Danica, "but it's hard to find one who's halfway human. The last man I moved in with vanished one day."

"Vanished?"

"I mean, completely. He was gone, all his things gone. He quit his job, changed his phone number, gone from social media. My emails bounced back. He completely vanished."

"*What?*"

"Yes, everything was fine, and then one day, *gone.*"

"But you—you felt like you knew him?"

"Well, we lived together, cooked and ate and slept together."

"Wow. That's—How does a person even—"

"I think he'd been using a fake name the whole time I knew him."

"Did you have friends in common?"

"No, none. I never met his family or anyone he knew, either."

"God, that's really—" Was she making this up? I didn't feel like she was making it up.

"You never really know a person. That's what I think. You just have to go with it, whatever's happening, and at the same time understand that you don't know this person at all, and have no idea what he might do."

My pasta and salad wolfed down in minutes, I let Danica pour me another glass of wine.

"Dessert?" asked our pretty, red-lipsticked server.

"Just coffee," said Danica.

I ordered a piece of chocolate cake.

"Valerie could never find a boyfriend," I said. "Her relationships never lasted for more than a week, or a day. I don't understand why. It depressed her so much."

"So we're talking about Valerie."

Yes. I needed us to talk about Valerie. That's why I'd contacted Danica about meeting up in Paris; Val was our point of connection.

"I've had to accept that it's not real to me," Danica said. "To me, she's out there somewhere. I can't convince myself she's not. To me, I could send her an email if I decided, and she'd respond."

"It's so hard to believe," I agreed. Though—what was she saying? That Val was alive *for her*? But Val was not alive.

"I just can't understand why she would do it," Danica went on. "What was wrong? What was so wrong? We all have times when we feel bad about ourselves, lonely, depressed. But we don't do that."

"I think she felt bad in a way we can't imagine," I said, as though possessed of some special insight.

"But when so many people want so badly and try so hard just to stay *alive*. And she *decided* to die? I mean, I have friends who are refugees. I have friends with cancer."

"Yeah. It wasn't just that things weren't going well. She was ill, too, her illness killed her. She was mentally ill."

Val died at thirty-three, I realized. The same age as Jos had been when he ran for his life.

"*Was* she, though?" said Danica. "Did you think that, when you lived with her? Did she seem more mentally ill than you or me?"

"She seemed manic. And then depressed. She did."

"But so does everyone. I don't know. Should we have known? How bad it was?"

She asked her questions as though she really wanted me to answer them.

"I just don't believe it," Danica said again. "She's alive. For me, she's alive. I feel bad," she added. "Because we hadn't talked in a long time. Things went strange between us, because of a guy. I was jealous because I thought something happened between her and my friend, this guy I was interested in at one point. Just stupid, I was jealous, and mad at her. And I don't think anything ever even happened between them."

The story sounded familiar. I'd heard it from Val too, and though I couldn't remember details, I knew her version had been slightly different; she hadn't actually been so innocent as Danica was making out. That didn't seem like a good correction to make, so I just nodded sympathetically. They'd fallen out over a man neither of them actually had that much invested in. That much was clear, anyway.

The first time I'd met Val, in a grad school creative writing workshop, I thought, she's so aware and awake and alive, and there's something wrong with her. Val and I ate dinner together that night after class, and our conversation built up to a kind of hysteria, every sentence a joke, her huge grey eyes so wide with mirth she seemed not dangerous exactly, but endangered. And then, after we moved in together, came days when she just blinked, trying hard to focus but lost somewhere inside her own head. Some nights she came home from the bar and pounded on my bedroom door at two in the morning, wanting to tell me about her night, and some days she took everything out of the kitchen cupboards and put everything back in, actions jerky and quick, arranging our glasses and mugs into a grid. And then her diagnosis (of bipolar disorder), more schooling, careers and relationships that started strong but combusted. She came to see herself as some kind of alien. That's how she described herself to her mother, in the days before her death, when she'd already ordered her suicide pill from China. A perpetual adolescent who couldn't bridge the gap to adulthood. Weren't we all failing to bridge that gap?

I realized that Danica was asking about Val's cooking; I had stopped listening for a moment.

"Yes," I said. "I remember her guacamole." God, she really loved guacamole. How could someone who loved eating so much rather be dead than alive? Someone funny as any stand-up comic. Someone I'd seen laugh until she had to lie on the floor gasping for breath. In a cafeteria!

"Yes," said Danica. "She'd put in tomatoes and red pepper and onions and everything. It was great guacamole."

After dinner, it had grown dark, and Danica led me around the corner and another, along narrow streets, people packed into the café verandas glowing under their canopies, pedestrians strolling among the blackboard menus and postcard displays, vegetables and chocolates and Paris-themed tchotchkes, multilingual tourist hum pressing in on all sides.

Danica stopped in the middle of the thrum, and pointed up at a window on one of the brick walls. "That's my apartment."

We stood there in the crowd, craning our necks.

"It's like living in Disneyland," she said.

❄ I walked back to my Airbnb slowly, back along the Seine. I thought I understood what Danica meant, not that she refused to accept what had happened, but that it was hard to believe, to really know, that Valerie was dead. I found it difficult to know that Valerie was dead too. A decade earlier, Opa had died, and he was the first person close to me I'd ever lost. He was ninety-six. But I hadn't been prepared to start losing friends.

Then, when Lev and I had been married for about a year, his childhood best friend, Frieda, was killed in a hiking accident. Frieda, a social worker who looked a little like Anne Frank, only with crazy curly black hair. When we first met, Frieda seemed to resent me for monopolizing Lev. But eventually I got to know her better, and found that she was fiercely idealistic, funny, and good-hearted. She and Lev weren't as close as they had been in high school, but they'd known each other since they were five, and had attended the same private Jewish school. They had sort of dated for about a month once. It was that kind of friendship; Lev and Frieda were close as family, only closer. When she fell to her death, she was travelling in South America with a group of women she'd met through Lev, some of whom she'd met at our wedding.

I was shaken and confused by others' reactions to Frieda's death, and by my own. For weeks after the funeral in Ontario, I wanted to talk about her. I wanted Lev to tell me stories about Frieda. I asked what she was like as a five-year-old, a ten-year-old, a seventeen-year-old, and whether she'd ever talked about death, and what he thought she'd have said about someone who died so young and so suddenly. I asked Lev how he saw things differently now that he'd lost a close friend. But he said the time for mourning was through; death was a part of life. Frieda's parents' house had been packed with her family and friends and clients, seemingly hundreds of friends and clients, for seven days, everyone hugging and talking about the time Frieda made them eat kale every day for a month, or about the year they had a spiritual crisis and how only Frieda listened and knew what to say, or about Frieda's crazy, infectious laugh. Her parents and brothers sat on the couch in torn clothes, talking with guest after guest, squeezing hand after hand. There was a big guestbook in which everyone wrote notes about Frieda, wrote notes addressed *to* Frieda, and I did the same. The same crowd had gathered at the synagogue and then the cemetery, where each of us shovelled earth into the grave, Frieda's mother sobbing anew with each distant, deep thud. Those seven days had passed, though, and Lev was not interested in discussing the matter any further. He was mourning, he said, in his own way.

I'd talked to enough therapists in my life—a psychiatrist for four years in my teens and early twenties, a cognitive behavioural therapist for a year in my early thirties, and a Jungian for three years in my mid-to-late thirties. I hadn't talked with any of them much about death, except as it related to my own hypochondria. When I saw those therapists, none of my friends had died yet, and I still thought none of them ever would, or not until we were all very, very old.

After Frieda's funeral, I decided to visit not a therapist, but my rabbi. I'd never had a rabbi before. But here I was, part of a congregation, and wasn't this what religion was for—for offering wisdom and solace in the face of mortality? I phoned the temple and explained to Rabbi Gerry's assistant that my friend had died, that I was looking for counselling. When I showed up at the quiet temple on that Wednesday afternoon, the assistant hugged me and said she was so sorry, said she'd read about Frieda's death in the newspaper, and led me to the rabbi's office.

Rabbi Gerry shook my hand warmly and offered me an armchair. He sat behind his desk. Not so different from visiting a therapist, so far. "I'm so sorry—horrible—just horrible. I'm going to say first, Naomi, before I say anything else, that I'm not here to tell you Frieda died for a reason, or that her death makes sense in some way. She died senselessly, and it shouldn't have happened."

I already knew the rabbi was an atheist, but his words surprised me. I assumed he was revving up for a parable about finding meaning in meaninglessness, or something like that, and then quoting the Torah and offering perspectives from a series of ancient and revered Talmudic scholars.

"A tragedy," said the rabbi.

"She was much more Lev's friend than mine," I explained. "But I seem to be having more trouble than he is knowing how to deal with her death. It's so overwhelming—one moment she was alive, she had plans, was about to start a new job. She was dating, like not having the best luck dating, but really wanted to get married. She was having a great day, the day it happened. Her friends who were with her said she was having so much fun. And the next moment, she was crossing a stream and fell in, and the current dragged her over a cliff."

The rabbi shook his head in horror.

"I went to her funeral," I said. "I'd never been to a Jewish funeral before."

"Never? Haven't any of your Jewish relatives died? Your grandparents?"

"My paternal grandfather and great-grandmother died within a month of each other when I was about ten, but my sister and I weren't allowed to go to Washington for the funerals. Our parents left us with our other grandparents."

"Why? Didn't they think you'd need closure?"

"I don't know," I said. "I guess sometimes people don't want children around when they're already so stressed."

The rabbi nodded. "What about the shiva? You didn't go to that either?"

"I don't know if they sat shiva. I didn't even know what sitting shiva *was* then." Seeing that the rabbi was too confused and dismayed to respond, I added, "My Opa, my maternal grandfather died too. But he didn't want any kind of funeral. He was cremated, and we scattered his ashes, then had a kind of wake at my grandmother's house. My Oma said she doesn't want a funeral when she dies either. Just to be cremated, and scattered under the same tree. It did bother me, not that he was cremated, but how we just scattered his ashes and stood there and didn't say anything, and then went home."

"Your Jewish grandfather was *cremated*?" said Rabbi Gerry. It occurred to me, dark unbidden thought, that Opa's mother, Isabella, had been cremated too, almost certainly cremated after her murder in the gas chamber of Sobibór. She had no funeral either. According to Oma, and to Mum and Josette, Opa and Sam had never spoken of their mother again. No wake or memorial, certainly no seven days of sitting inside, in rent garments.

"Well, remember? How I told you? That he didn't want anything to do with organized religion? That he didn't consider himself Jewish?"

"No wonder," the rabbi said, with deep pity. "No wonder—you've never known what it is to be part of a community."

Involuntarily, I mirrored his sad face and nodded. Then it occurred to me, fleetingly, that I was part of a community—the writing community—but he was already explaining that growing up without a community and without a narrative, without the *we* of Judaism, we came out of Egypt, we received the gift of the mitzvot from God, a child ends up with a shaky sense of identity, confidence, and morality. I hadn't grown up with a sense of community, or with any such narrative. He was right about that. Poor me, I thought. *Poor, poor me.*

"Frieda's funeral," I said. "I was impressed by the ritual of it, how everyone knew exactly what was expected of them. I mean, I didn't *like* it, it was horrible, of course. But her parents and all her friends knew what was expected of them, and they knew exactly how to spend the next week just completely devoted to the work of mourning."

"Yes," the rabbi nodded. "Ritual is so important. You see it now, don't you? Being part of a tradition, a community. What it offers."

I nodded. "It made me think that I should convert. I should be clear about my identity. Otherwise, when I die, no one will know what to do. Lev won't know, my parents, if I die before my parents. If I'm Jewish, if everyone knows I'm Jewish, then there'll be no question. Frieda's parents— at least they knew what to do—at least it was laid out for them."

"Yes, it's important. It's so important. To be clear, that you're Jewish. And to understand that rituals around death exist for the sake of the living. But Frieda's parents—don't fool yourself. Their lives are ruined. You'll understand when you have children. You never recover from something like that." I let the when-you-have-children comment pass. My eyes settled on the poster hanging beside the rabbi's bookshelf. John Travolta's dancing body with Rabbi Gerry's head Photoshopped on top. *Friday Night Fever*, the poster read. Then, in smaller letters, *Staying alive...for Shabbat.*

The rabbi said, "Her friends and family should never have encouraged her to take such a risky hike into the mountains—she had a physical disability, didn't she?"

"Well, sort of, but she never let that stop her from doing anything. She was a very adventurous, fearless kind of person. That's how her parents raised her, how they encouraged her to live—"

"A senseless tragedy," he went on. "My dog fell off a waterfall once. My wife and I took him hiking, and we weren't watching him. We should have kept him closer to us. I felt completely responsible for his fall, it was my fault, and I admit it. He wasn't hurt, though."

"Your dog?" I couldn't help but stare at the poster. Rabbi Gerry grinning like a maniac, with a tight white bell-bottomed jumpsuit hugging his—John Travolta's—muscular body.

"But a child," he went on. "As a parent, there is nothing in the world except protecting your children, and if anything happens to them, you're ruined." He crossed his thin arms across his chest, as though to protect himself from the spectre of children dying before their parents. "You'll see, you'll understand when you and Lev have a family."

"We're not planning to have children," I blurted. "We're a family of two."

"What do you mean?"

"Lev and I have chosen not to have children. We already consider ourselves a family."

The rabbi blinked. "You—what?"

"Well. Having children is not for everyone, right? I've just never wanted to be a parent. There are other things I want to do, and I think people who have kids should really, really, want them. Like my best friend, Yael—she's an observant Jew, raising a daughter, and that's what she's always wanted. And even she tells me I should not have children unless I want them more than anything else."

"I'm sorry." He blinked, as though trying to process an intractable problem. "I don't know what to say. I've never heard of anything like that."

We stared at each other. I shouldn't have brought it up. But this had been bothering me all through the conversion class, his seeming conviction that raising children, ensuring the continuation of the race and the tradition, was the whole point of conversion, of Judaism itself.

"I want to be a Jew because *I* want to be a Jew," I said, as I'd said before, in class. "Doesn't that make sense? I want to be a Jewish *adult*."

Rabbi Gerry considered this. "You're a writer," he said. "My wife used to want to be a writer, but then she realized it was unhealthy, spending all that time alone, just *thinking*. She went to law school. Now she's a prosecutor, and we have three children. It's very hard on a marriage not to have children, you know. And to spend all that time alone. Our life is so rich now. Between you and me, we haven't slept without a child in our bed for ten years."

Rabbi Gerry went on to tell me that Lev did want children, needed children, that he was a good guy and needed a family to be happy, even if he didn't know it. He said that without children, one remains in a perpetual adolescence. He repeated that his wife had once published a short story, but then realized writing was for weirdos and went to law school, and now she had a rabbi husband, a thriving career, three kids, and a dog.

"I think it's a good idea for you to convert," the rabbi concluded. "Just let me know when you're ready. And if you and Lev ever want to come and talk with me together about all these issues, I'm here."

We stood, and he hugged me.

"Any time," he said. "Come by any time."

"Thank you, Rabbi."

I walked all the way home from the temple, about an hour and a half, and during that walk, I came the closest I ever had to wanting a baby. I imagined that once I converted, Lev and I would have a girl, and name her Frieda, and that our Frieda would grow up hearing about her namesake, a woman who had loved Lev like family, and who had strived to bring people together and to make the world better. Our Frieda would learn that the first Frieda invited a wide circle of friends, Jewish and Gentile, to her home every Friday for a Shabbat potluck, and that she had invented a game for the occasion called Highlights and Lowlights, in which everyone offered the best and worst moments of their week. The only rules were, no interrupting, always end on a highlight, and the Shabbat dinner itself doesn't count. I'd found Highlights and Lowlights two-thirds corny, one-third delightful when I'd participated, but walking home from the temple, I was ready to take on Frieda's trademark Shabbat tradition for the rest of my life. Halfway home, I entered a pharmacy, where I bought a bottle of folic acid pills. You were supposed to take them before getting knocked up, I'd heard.

It was as though I'd gone for surgery, then walked home high on painkillers. A couple of hours later, as I chopped kale and tomatoes for dinner, the anaesthetic started wearing off, and I realized I was in pain. I hadn't gone to the rabbi's office to be talked into having a baby. Who was he to tell me I wasn't living my life right? If I had a baby, it would be an eating and shitting machine, and then eventually it would turn into a person, possibly a great person, but it wouldn't be Frieda, a re-incarnation of Frieda, or even an homage to Frieda. And I didn't want to hold a potluck in my house once a week. And I certainly didn't want a kid sleeping in my bed for ten years, or even for one year, or at all. The rabbi's poor wife hadn't spent a moment alone, or alone with her husband, in ten years? But then how had they conceived their second and third children? Anyway, he had been talking about what was right for himself, not for me. I needed time alone, time reading and writing and thinking, and I needed long conversations with like-minded adults, and I needed regular sex, the loud kind, to be happy. And come to think of it, the rabbi hadn't said anything comforting or wise about death, Frieda's death, which was what I'd gone there wanting to discuss. Had he really blamed Frieda's death on her parents and her friends? Had he really compared Frieda to his dog?

Over spaghetti with kale salad, I told Lev about my conversation with the rabbi.

"He thinks that you really want children, whether you know it or not," I told him. "He seems to think I'm ruining your life by not doing it, that I should get with the program."

"Did you tell him that we've *agreed* not to have kids?" asked Lev.

"Yes, but he said you agreed just to make me happy, and though you might not even know it yet yourself, you can't be happy without them."

"And you're afraid he might be right?"

"You know I am."

"Well, I know what I want and don't want. You should trust me. And who's he to say he knows what I want better than I do?"

"It's like he feels bad for you—that you're a nice Jewish boy and you accidentally married someone like—like me. Like you're under some weird spell, living an unwholesome life because I'm leading you astray."

"I'm sure he doesn't think *that*," said Lev. "You're being paranoid. You're being too sensitive."

I moved to the sofa and lay down, and Lev turned to face me from his seat at the table. "He thinks raising Jewish children is the whole point of being Jewish," I said. "He thinks there's no point converting unless I'm planning to raise Jewish kids." The conviction that had sent me to the vitamin aisle only hours earlier had completely worn off by now, and I felt deflated, even more depressed than before. "Maybe he's right," I said. "Maybe I *am* ruining your life. But I told you from the beginning. Having children is just not for me. It's so sad, because Frieda wanted children, and to raise them Jewish, and now she won't get to. But I'm not her, and I don't long for that life, and that means I shouldn't do it. The world's already overpopulated, so really the ethical choice for people who want to raise children is adoption, but anyway, the point is, I've never wanted children, not for a second. And the last thing in the world I'd want to be is a bad parent, a mother who resents her kids for getting in the way of her work—" I'd slipped into my script, the explanation I'd offered a million times, to Lev, to myself, to all the people who felt entitled to ask me why my womb remained empty.

"I'm really pissed off with Rabbi Gerry," said Lev. "I'm going to say something to him about this."

"You know," I said. "When I think about it, he was really saying that if one of us has to be unhappy, it should be me. It's unacceptable for you to be unhappy, but if *my* life is ruined, who cares?"

"You're not going to convert, are you?" He was disappointed.

"I'm sorry. I'm *sorry*."

Lev sighed, and I curled up into myself, turning face down so my tears soaked into the couch cushion. I couldn't do it. I couldn't have babies. I couldn't be a proper Jewish wife. I couldn't immerse myself in the mikvah and emerge a real Jew. When I died, my loved ones would not gather and shovel earth into my grave, and no one would sit shiva. What had I been thinking? Now I pictured my family and friends going through the motions, and knew that most of them, Lev and Yael excepted, would find the whole affair inauthentic and foreign. What did it matter to me, anyway? I would be dead.

The next time I saw Rabbi Gerry was Passover. After the service, Lev and I joined the rest of the congregation for an array of kosher-for-Passover snacks. When the rabbi saw us standing near him, he flung open his arms to hug Lev, and accidentally punched me, his fist smacking the bridge of my nose.

I never did convert. And the bottle of folic acid sat in the medicine cabinet for the rest of my marriage, unopened.

☀ I continued along the Seine with my phone in hand. To my surprise, I passed very few people. It looked like there were more people on the other side of the river, and I could see the building my Airbnb host had pointed out, with his club inside. Should I go there? Just to do *something*? Instead of texting Yael or Matteo, I scrolled down and opened my text history with Val. We'd never had real conversations by text, though; we'd spoken on the phone after setting a date in advance. Our last recorded exchange was dated March 4, 2015, not three weeks before she died.

Me: 'Feel like chatting?'

Val: 'Just about to go to bed cuz have an early morning tomorrow... How about tomorrow?'

Me: 'Can't tomorrow. Weekend?'

Me: 'Sleep well!'

Val: 'Thx!'

She had not actually agreed to speak on the weekend. And had we? I didn't think so. No. I knew we hadn't.

I scrolled up to an exchange from a couple of months earlier:

Val: 'Got a minute?'

Me: 'I'm just buying groceries. But I can shop and talk. Sec.'

And then down again:

Val: 'I'm so-so, but whatever, I need to have hope that I can get my life back on track and that this pessimism won't last forever.'

I knew that Val's parents had seen her earlier the day she died, and almost every day leading up to then. I knew they'd done everything in their power to save her from the undertow, and so had her doctors. Just as Danica couldn't have said the right thing at the right time and made all the difference, neither could I, and it was insulting to Val and her family to imagine so.

At the next bridge, I crossed the Seine and headed for the nightclub. Outside the place five minutes later, I looked up at the crush of people on the rooftop. A cloud of tinny triphop dispersed into the night sky, along with, surely, a cloud of perfume and cologne. There was some kind of laser show happening. I turned around and made for the river again, the apartment with the mattress I'd paid for.

Close to half past five I arrive at the Gare d'Austerlitz, which means that I still have several hours to wait. My already sombre mood doesn't improve when I see the indescribable chaos and noise of the station, which is beleaguered by people. All seats in the ordinary coaches and in the sleepers are certainly reserved for at least the next ten days, and it is obvious that I will have to be thankful if I manage to get to Bordeaux at all, camping in the corridor of a car. It may be these facts or the after-effect of my failed trip to Dijon and Chalon, the alarming news about hunting of suspicious individuals, and the weariness of this long day, or simply the fact that the journey, which by now has lasted nearly ten days, is becoming too much for me—but my nerves are breaking down. In the Metro I already had the feeling that people were suspicious of me, and suddenly I am certain that no matter what the cost I must try to avoid this journey to Bordeaux, which fills me with an inexplicable horror.

There is still somebody else whom I can try to get hold of: Olssen, a Frenchman, despite his Scandinavian name. He is a man with many connections and the best personal friend I have in Paris. If so far I did not want to bother him, it is because he works for the government and moreover has certain business relationships with Germans who are also known to me. Although thoroughly convinced that he would help me, I did not want to ask him for services which might compromise him—or even put him in an illegal position. Now I throw all scruples overboard and phone his home from the station. No reply.

With lead in my shoes, I purchase my ticket for Bordeaux. What else can I do? But after that, I phone his house again. I am possessed by the will to have done everything in my power before I allow myself to be dragged to that cursed Bordeaux. This time I receive a reply, the housekeeper tells me that he won't be home before eight o'clock. Thank God, at least he is in town. At eight o'clock, I wait my turn for the telephone box, hear again the housekeeper. Olssen is not yet back. I go back to the trains.

The platforms are still closed. It is a quarter past eight, half past eight. The platforms are still closed. The station hall is now half full of waiting people, at least three times as many people behind me as in front of me. It is oppressively hot, clammy, and sticky. Another ten minutes—and I can't stand it any longer. The people around me must think that I have gone insane to give up my good spot in the waiting masses, but I push out, stumble over piles of luggage and human legs, and run once more to the telephone. When the call goes through, I hear Olssen's voice. I am so befuddled, but at least I am able to explain who I am, and then I hear an enthusiastic welcome. I tell him that I need to speak with him this evening and impose on him for the night. He replies that those are things which should not be discussed over the phone, and that there will be a bed waiting for me. I clamber out of the phone box and feel weak from my reaction and am a hair away from having tears in my eyes. Then I descend to the Metro. I am not able to think much more, but one thing I feel for sure: I am through the blackest low point of my journey.

When I arrive at Olssen's house, my host is waiting for me in the stairwell, grips both my hands, and nearly embraces me, he is so excited by this unexpected meeting. The guest room is ready, and an abundant supper with the pick of the larder and the black market is served. The simple fact of my presence in Paris has been sufficient for him to guess nine tenths of the truth, and unasked for he tells me as a first thing that I am of course on my way to the "unoccupied zone," and that he will help me get there. One of his good friends happens to have to go to Blois tomorrow morning for business. He will take me along and take me by bus from Blois 20 kilometres further south to Montrichard, which is right on the demarcation line. There he has a quite sufficient number of relatives who can take me to the unoccupied territory.

When I explain to Olssen why I hesitated at first to contact him, he is almost outraged that one could ever have misjudged his feelings to such an extent. In the first place he would do anything for a good friend, but moreover: "Mon cher ami, je me fous des boches, et toutes autres considérations sont d'importance secondaire." Olssen, merci!

"Boches," I learn online, or "the Boche," was a pejorative term for German soldiers.

Back at the Airbnb, I couldn't close my sheets all the way, so changed for bed in the dark and lay down exposed to the hallway. My head throbbed with overstimulation.

Who was this Olssen, who'd saved Opa from almost certain death, and where did he live, and did they see each other again? I wished I could thank this Olssen who would do anything for a good friend—or at least thank whatever Olssens lived today. But in this vast Paris, this vast world, how could I even start to look for them?

I looked at my phone again, its screen lit up in the dark, and wrote to Matteo: 'I almost went to a nightclub, but there was a laser show. I just wanted to go to bed, and I thought, what would Matteo do? So now I'm in bed. Goodnight!'

I opened my history with Val again and flicked my thumb to scroll arbitrarily between banal messages.

'Can you talk?'

...

'Happy birthday, my dear!'

...

'Good. You?'

...

'Good. I'm okay.'

...

'Good.'

...

'Good good.'

...

'I have to have hope.'

...

'How about tomorrow?'

For the second time in a week I stroll through Paris in the early morning, now accompanied by Olssen's friend and together we go to that same Gare d'Austerlitz which was so full or horrors for me last night. It appears that we were mistaken and that the train leaves one hour later than we thought, but that has the advantage that we find comfortable seats and I have the opportunity to reclaim the money from my unused ticket to Bordeaux.

On Tuesday, July 28th, 1942, the Nazis murdered ten thousand Jews in the Minsk Belorussia Ghetto.

On the morning of Tuesday, July 28th, 2015, I waited for the grumpy financial analyst to finish in the bathroom, showered, then dressed in the middle of the living room where anyone could see me—I just didn't care enough to do anything about it. And that was it for my very limited experience of Paris. I pulled my blue suitcase to Gare Montparnasse, not the same station Opa left from, not the same route. I couldn't figure out how to purchase the correct tickets from the grey machines set up around the station, and so went to the ticket office, where I sat across from a cheerful young man. He printed out my tickets, explaining that my train would take me to Saint-Pierre-la-Cour, and then I had to catch a second one to Montrichard.

As I bought my ticket, a twentyish Asian-American woman stood at the counter across the room, speaking rapidly at the man before her—"I have to be there, you don't understand"—who kept repeating in the same slow soft French accent that her train had left, but she could purchase a ticket for the next one, which departed late that night. She spoke faster and faster, telling him he didn't understand, it wasn't her fault she'd been late, and her friends were waiting in Lisbon. He repeated that her train had left, but she could purchase a ticket for the next one, which departed late that night. She writhed in dismay, yelled, "This isn't *fair*, sir. This isn't *fair*!"

I got everything wrong—failed to validate my ticket at one of the station's yellow boxes, and then, on the train, shoved my garbage in a little nook that the thick-eyebrowed man beside me indicated was *not* a trash receptacle. I typed on my phone: translate, English to French: *I would like to go to.* My phone told me: *je voudrais aller à.* The man beside me leaned close to my ear, whispered, "San Francisco?"

I giggled and shoved my phone into my bag. And then, as though to make sure he felt all right, I giggled nervously *again*. I thought of the wedding ring in my pocket. A man to protect me from other men, the suggestion of a man: I'm someone's. I felt dismayed and idiotic about my mistakes. The unvalidated ticket, my apple core and cheese wax in the wrong place. These seemed facts about me, rather than facts about the world. I was stupid, ridiculous. Finally I shed the thick-eyebrowed man in Saint-Pierre-la-Cour.

On Tuesday, July 28th, 1942, Jos's train from Gare d'Austerlitz stopped in Blois.

It seems to be my lot to retrace all my former vacation trips. In '33, nine years ago, I also travelled from Paris to Blois which was then my starting point for a hiking tour, the first stage of which was the same Montrichard that now, I hope, will be the gate to freedom.

Meanwhile I somehow missed my connection to Montrichard, just watched it sit there and then leave, without realizing it was my train, and had to wait for the next one.

By about two o'clock we arrive in Montrichard and S. immediately chats up a chap in the café at the terminus whilst I unobtrusively take a seat a bit further down with the luggage.

Finally I arrived under a grey sky at a little train station, just a few benches around the walls and a ticket booth. Montrichard. I didn't see a café; the train station must have changed in the seventy-three years since Opa arrived. My GPS told me I had a bit of a walk ahead of me, down the highway, which was not really a highway, just a road, with a few cars easing by. I pulled my suitcase along the road's shoulder, toward town, umbrella in my other hand. The drizzle thickened as I progressed, and I wanted to check my GPS to see if I'd somehow missed the turn-off, but would have had to stop and give up the shelter of my umbrella. I couldn't have missed the turn-off; I just hadn't reached it yet. Every car that passed, I could practically feel the occupants glance at me, wondering, what is that woman playing at?

A little while later, S. and I stroll through the town which lies quiet and deserted in the hot afternoon, and along the Cher, the river on the northern bank of which Montrichard is situated. Here the Cher forms the border between the two zones in this area, so that I have a free outlook over the unoccupied territory. Along the way, S. explains that I will have to cross the river at night, somewhere further on, but he doesn't know the details yet. The little town is crammed full of German forces and there seem to be elements amongst the population who will report strangers, so one has to be extremely careful. For that reason, we soon return to our café, where I can sit in a little back corner practically unnoticed. S. drifts around all afternoon waiting for final confirmation from our as-yet missing link, and he checks in with me every now and then.

Finally, I turned off the highway onto a narrow, cobblestone street lined with beige and grey buildings. As I stepped around the next corner to see the Cher, the wind picked up and blew a gust of rain into my face. I wiped my eyes on the sleeve of my jean jacket, and could see again. I'd pictured a wide raging beast of a river, the kind we have in Canada, but the Cher was narrow, and gentle even on this windy day, with straight clean edges. On my side, a road ran alongside the water, separated only by a concrete divider. A grassy, treed bank ran along the river's other side.

Slowly the hours creep by whilst I sit with a book in front of me, but unable to concentrate on it. S. shows a concern far exceeding what I may reasonably expect. He has taken a room in a hotel and he is not willing to return to Blois and resume his work before he is certain that I am actually in the free zone. The long-expected message comes at last that everything is okay and that I can go tonight. It seems that quite a group of fugitives will be brought away this night by the smugglers of human bodies—the new profession known as "passeur"—and I can join them. Costs are two thousand francs, an amount for which S. apologizes as it seems high to him, but which I think not unreasonable in view of the value of the services rendered.

My hotel was right on the river; when I checked at the station, the GPS told me I'd turn at the water, walk for two minutes, and voila. I turned at the water and walked for five minutes. Turned around and walked for seven. The hotel sat right across from a stone and concrete bridge, a series of arches. Montrichard Bridge, built in the fifteenth century. The rain was heavier now, and the air thick and damp, no good for wandering around outside. I was relieved to have my own bedroom (no sign of bedbugs), with a bathroom and, best of all, privacy. I stayed up there reading, then went down for dinner, found a table by the window, mere feet from the Cher. On the opposite bank sat some kind of amusement park. I could see tents, and another carousel.

I am sent to another hotel which is guaranteed kraut-free. It appears to be a typical holiday place, boarders with children at fixed tables, an environment in which I am a bit out of place. After dinner I hang around a bit until S. turns up with a friend. At the last minute, we have one for the road, so strong that it nearly knocks me out, and then the three of us stroll through the little town.

Our guide opens a little gate somewhere, and we are on a small plot of land, half courtyard, half neglected garden with a car in a little shed. At half past eleven my passeur will come and fetch me here. If something unexpectedly detains him I must not leave the garden on any account but instead have a snooze in the Chevrolet. S. and his friend will come back here early tomorrow morning regardless and make sure that I have made my getaway. The passeur receives one thousand francs and will bring us to a ford in the Cher. Other passeurs are waiting for us on the opposite bank and I am to ask for Mr. André. I can stay the night in his house and he will get me a taxi tomorrow which will take me to Chateauroux, some 40 or 50 kilometres further into the free zone. From there I can continue my journey by train. An excellent plan!

A whispered farewell, two handshakes and then I am alone in the garden waiting for what is to come.

The blue of the sky slowly pales, a single star becomes visible. Darkness falls. A cat comes noiselessly along the garden path, then sits down a couple of metres away to observe me. Then she suddenly disappears in the unknown night. I am reminded of Goethe, during the battle of Valmy, when he registered and analysed his own feelings in the face of danger. At this moment one would find nothing interesting to observe in my case. I do not feel any fear or impatience, only a kind of amused interest that for once I can take part in a real adventure, and in the background the vague recollection of a half-heard remark, that a good deal of the money paid to the passeurs serves to bribe the German patrols.

Shortly after half past eleven soft footsteps, the garden gate opens, and without a word I follow the figure that appears in the doorway. One behind the other we steal through the deserted street, while I deposit my banknotes in an outstretched hand. Then we come upon a large plot of land with trees and bushes. A confused whispering of many voices; in the semi-darkness—the moon has risen in the meantime—I discern the beginning of a long row of figures camped on the ground and which, though invisible to me, apparently continues deeper into the garden. The guide tells us that he will now go out for a reconnaissance and come and fetch us in an hour's time.

There is a suppressed nervous mood: one hears whispers everywhere, sometimes a half stifled laugh, while time and again quiet is insisted upon; as for me, sleep is my priority. Then the passeur returns, and in a long procession we follow him along the quiet roads which now lie before us clear white in the moonlight. A second passeur is at the end of the procession: eighty people are being led away tonight!

At the front of the column we obediently walk in each other's footsteps, in the grass on the verge to muffle the noise as much as possible, but at the rear they seem to have gone completely insane. They come stamping and scuffling six men abreast over the full width of the road as if this was a demonstration or an excursion. Gestures and whispered orders restore a semblance of order in this mess. Much later I realize that it must have been fear that made these people act so foolishly, fear that made them rush forward like a herd of sheep.

We go west, apparently to a point downstream of Montrichard. When after twenty minutes we stop for a moment in a field, the passeur confirms my question that it will be wise to wear shoes while wading through the water in the dark as the riverbed is rather stony. A little later we go on and come to the Cher; the passeur says that the ford is a few hundred yards further down and asks some of the younger men to form a kind of rearguard to provide help, as

needed, to the women and children who will cross before them.
I step aside and see the whole convoy pass by, including old men and women, families with small children, many loaded with cases, parcels, or rucksacks, silhouettes hurrying along feverishly in the moonlight.

When we approach the ford, the spectacle is really fantastic. Here the Cher flows between sloping wooded banks, a silvery ribbon in the silent peaceful summer night.

When I arrive at the water at the bottom of the slope, I find only about a dozen people left who still have to cross. Amongst others an elderly lady of about sixty with her grown-up daughter and a young woman with a three-year-old boy on her arm. Initially everything goes fine, mother and daughter support each other, whilst the younger woman stays close by my side. When the water gets deeper and the current stronger, I brace diagonally against it. But mother and daughter end up a few metres further down, and the old lady stumbles. The daughter manages to hold her, but she floats in the water, cannot get up again in the current, and starts screaming when she momentarily goes completely under once or twice. I splash toward her whilst the young mother grips me tightly in a sudden attack of fear; the child begins to cry. We manage to put the old lady on her feet, but she is paralysed by the fright and falls again. I ask the other woman to in God's name let me go for a moment so that I can offer better help, but her only reaction is to throw her free arm around me whilst she mutters meaninglessly, "Oh mon gosse, mon pauvre gosse."

With the three women and a child clamped onto me in a strong current nearly a metre deep, I cannot move either backward or forward and I wonder just how long it will take with all this yelling and screaming until a German patrol will open fire, when we get help. A passeur and a young chap who was already safely across come rushing through the river. One looks after the old lady, the other takes the little boy on his arm whilst I support the young mother whom I hear uninterruptedly moaning at my side "Oh mon pauvre petit gosse." When we get ashore I see that all the women are barefooted, which explains at least half our incessant misery. It appears that the old lady is not only thoroughly soaked, but in her shock the poor dear has also let her handbag slip, with all her papers and money.

The next day I happen to hear from the passeurs that a normal crossing is arranged in such a way that first a passeur crosses out of the free zone with a rope indicating the exact ford, where there is no spot deeper than 30–40 centimetres of water. People can then easily cross one by one following the rope. In our case, however, people did not wait the few minutes it takes to establish the connection; instead people immediately rushed like madmen into the water and made the crossing ten or fifteen metres too far downstream, where it is at least twice as deep.

Everyone is in safe, and everywhere little groups of people are standing or sitting together, talking and laughing in great excitement. If I didn't feel any fear beforehand, I now don't feel very relieved either and am somewhat astonished—wrongly, by the way—at their display of emotion.

I ordered salmon on toast, coq au vin, and a glass of red wine. And I toasted Opa. Here was the place it happened. He got out. He went on. And on and on. He would live; he had fifty-nine years still to live.

Cheers to that.

I meet up with Mr. André and then we leave the river, first following little pathways, later along a main road heading east, therefore back upstream. Our convoy, consisting of Belgian reserve officers, escaped French prisoners of war, and Jewish refugees of French, Belgian and Dutch origin, dissolves quickly, and at last there are only about twenty people left. We reach his home after about three-quarters of an hour, and there he takes me aside and secretly lets me in through a window at the back of the house into a little room. The others gather together in a large room where they wait to continue their journey by bus early in the morning. I fall in my bed, it is nearly 3 a.m., and when I get up again at eight o'clock all my fellow refugees are gone, and it appears that our contact has been limited to those few dark hours: "ships that pass in the night."

I pass the day in comfortable idleness. The view from the house is rather curious as I look straight towards Montrichard, not more than three-quarters of a mile away, from which last night we had so much trouble escaping.

I'd lost my beige silk scarf with the little red flowers, but I didn't know when. Before getting out of bed on Wednesday, I glanced around my Montrichard hotel room, and my eyes landed on my grey backpack, which I'd set on the room's little writing desk. The grey backpack, bare. No scarf. How long had it been gone? Since Paris, or the train, or a public toilet? Had it worked itself free and fluttered to some sidewalk somewhere? Naked before my shower, I searched my room half-heartedly, knowing I wouldn't find the scarf.

Outside, it still smelled like rain, but the sun was out, provisionally out, between giant puffs of cloud. I followed the river a long way, until I reached a stone wall separating houses and their private gardens from the public walkway. Turning into town, I made my way to the highway again, which I followed back past the train station, to a big boxy grocery store. There I bought a baguette, a round of Camembert cheese, two tomatoes, a knife, and a bottle of Perrier. Backpack full of picnic, I walked back the way I'd come, all the way past my hotel to Montrichard Bridge.

Halfway across the bridge, I stopped and leaned against the stone balustrade, and looked at the water. Jos had crossed that river, had splashed across, had been caught in the middle, a thirty-three-year-old man with three women and a little boy clinging to him, unable to go on or turn back. I thought of myself, at sixteen, wading into Ottawa's Rideau River, bag on my back, boots slung around my neck, driven on by emotion, driven recklessly on by the danger behind me and the promise of safety somewhere on the other side. A whimsical picture, space-times collapsed into each other, Opa and me struggling in the water together, stuck for a few gasping moments, halfway.

I took the white gold wedding ring from my pocket and held it in my palm, turned it, trying to catch the light, but the sun was halfway behind a cloud now. The ring, this little object I'd bought from an online vendor and had planned to wear every moment for the rest of my life, to show the world that my heart belonged to my husband, to Lev. Had I given Lev my heart? He'd been asking for a long time, I realized, why I went around offering my whole self to this and that friend but not to him. At first, he'd had most of me, but piece by piece I took myself back, until we were attached like train cars, on the same track but detachable, each with our own cargo safe in its container. We said, it's good that we're so independent, together but still our own selves. And that was true. But also, I longed. Though I knew about longing, how it can obscure and even destroy its object. In our vows, Lev and I had promised to accompany each other through "all of life's terrain," but we hadn't; we'd followed our own paths, each refusing to lose our way, and those paths had led us into terrains inhospitable to each other. I'd accused him of wanting me to be someone different, a different kind of wife. And that was true, but I'd wanted him to be someone different, too. He'd wanted me to pull him across some threshold into adulthood, and I'd wanted him to do the same for me, but those worlds we'd wanted to enter were different worlds. None of this was what I thought when I found that he, with the support of the make-or-break woman, had been working himself free. A lot of thoughts had occurred to me then, none of them forgiving.

I reached my arm out over the stone balustrade, and turned my palm down. The white gold band fell without a sound into the Cher.

Anxiety seized me. Had the ring been caught by the current; was it sweeping under the bridge and away; was it sinking to the riverbed; where was it now? And where was my green canvas bag, and where was my silk scarf? And where were the mouldering pages of my old diaries, and where were my *Winnie-the-Pooh* books and the favourite stuffed troll I'd apparently lost on a train when I was three, and where were all the other mementos I'd lost, and which would I lose next? How was I supposed to ward off forgetting without them? Then the anxiety rushed out of me as though from a popped balloon. My shoulders relaxed, and my jaw loosened. I inhaled deeply, as though I'd been holding my breath. My stomach growled; I thought of the food in my bag.

Built into the bridge near its other side stood a small white house, and as I approached, I saw that it was a pub. "Le Passeur" read the sign. Le Passeur—named after the *passeurs* who'd helped Jews and members of the Resistance across the river, who'd helped Opa that night seventy-three years earlier, when he crossed with eighty other people? I tried the door, but it was locked.

One of the strangest stories Oma had told me, shortly after moving from her home into the "home," had started out familiar: she'd accompanied Opa to receive his war medal, which had been presented by Queen Wilhelmina of the Netherlands.

"After Jos received his medal," Oma told me this time, "the queen took me aside and said, 'Mary, it's you who really deserves that medal. You were very brave.'"

"You were brave, Oma," I said. "And I guess women didn't get the kind of recognition men did, right?" More wish fulfilment, and understandable, I thought. "Driving that ambulance," I went on. "The foot in the boot—"

"She said I was brave because during the war I helped Jews escape from unoccupied France."

"You—did?"

"I used to drive across the border in my ambulance. I would hide Jews in the back, and drive them to safety. I had to bring injured soldiers across, or supplies, and while I was doing that I also smuggled in Jews."

Could it be true? I wondered, just for a moment—was it possible she'd just never told me this before?

"I was in terrible danger, you know," Oma continued. "If I'd have been caught, goodness knows what would have happened to me. I was in terrible danger each time I did it. But in wartime, one does what must be done. That's what I said, when the queen told me, you were very brave. I said, I just did what must be done." Oma paused, as though trying hard to find the next line. "The queen took my hands. She said, 'Mary, it's you who ought to have a medal.'"

Oh, I wanted to believe her, and she told the story so convincingly. But no. Oma had never been a doctor or a countess, and did not require a mastectomy, and would not be keeping her breasts in a jar. And she had not smuggled any Jews across any borders. But at least she wished she had.

Though Oma's stories had become increasingly farfetched as she moved toward wordlessness, occasionally they seemed accurate after all. Chloe and I had visited her one day, and she'd asked about our lives, asked about Chloe's latest artists' residency, and about Andrew.

"I miss Opa," Oma us. "Poor Opa. He wasn't very good at being a husband, I'm afraid, but he was an unusual person, charming, kind. He was sick for ten years, and those years were terribly difficult for me, I don't think anyone realized how difficult, terribly lonely. I tried to care for him myself, but then he came to a state where he couldn't shower, couldn't dress, I had people in to help, a nurse, but not every day. And at last I couldn't do it, and he had to live elsewhere, with more help. I visited him. I missed him, I missed the old him, and just having him around. I visited him. They said it was Alzheimer's, but it wasn't, you know. But he knew almost until the end. Me. He knew me, even at the end, I think. I used to go and visit him. Almost every day. And I'd sit on his lap and have a cuddle."

We'd heard all this before, and didn't mind hearing it again. Next came the part where he told her, on his deathbed, that he'd never known how to be a husband.

"Before he died," said Oma, "I went every day. He was asleep by then, all the time, strapped into his bed, and I sat with him. I said to his nurses, if he gets worse, call me; I need to do something, to run an errand. Do you think it's all right for me to leave for a day? I needed to go to Toronto to do some shopping, and I took the bus. On the way back, the bus drove right past the nursing home. Right past. And when I got home, they phoned me, and he'd died."

Chloe and I exchanged a quick glance, neither of us wanting to speak, potentially to startle her out of her lucidity.

Oma went on, "I kept thinking, my bus drove right past the nursing home, right past the bus stop. Maybe I was on the bus, and drove by, and he was still alive. Maybe if I'd left the bus, I could have been with him when he died. I saw the bus stop coming up, and I even thought, maybe I should get off here and see Jos, but I was tired, and I had my shopping with me. I had all my shopping with me, and it had been a long day taking the bus to Toronto, shopping, and taking the bus back. But if I'd left the bus at the bus stop outside the nursing home, I wouldn't have missed him. Even though he was sleeping and didn't know where he was, he would have known I was there. Maybe he wouldn't have known, but I think he would have. I wish I could have been with him."

I strolled along the river on the other side, the free France side. What I'd taken for an amusement park the night before turned out to be a little beach, and I settled in the grass with my food. I felt as though I hadn't eaten properly for days, and the food, so inexpensive, was the most delicious I'd eaten since arriving in France. To the sounds of a family kicking a soccer ball off in the distance, I ate my whole baguette, both tomatoes, and all the cheese.

Josette had said I was looking for secrets. As though life were a children's book, or a house with a hidden attic, or a time machine. But there was no secret, not really. Dad had told me he'd known the first time he saw me, as a newborn, that I had secrets. But I hadn't been born with secrets of course, and forty years later I still didn't have any. Not of my own, and not that I'd unearthed. I still hadn't come any closer to finding the *it* at the bottom of everything. Was that what it meant to be an adult? To stop looking?

The sun came out again, and I lay on the grass, full and cozy, my head resting on my bag. When I woke, I'd rolled off my backpack, and the uneven ground was cold against my face. I put my hand to my cheek as I sat cross legged and felt the sleep marks on my face. The sun was lower now, glowing pink behind a small greyish cloud.

Here I was, right here, on the bank of the river, in the town of Faverolles-sur-Cher, blinking awake over the water at Montrichard. I'd done it. I'd come.

The next day, I'd go on to Lyon, and then back to Amsterdam, and the rest of my trip would just be vacation, museums and a pedicure, markets and big meals. Then back home to Calgary.

✳ In Salman Rushdie's essay "Out of Kansas," he celebrates *The Wizard of Oz* as his childhood favourite too, but criticizes the ending, the whole it-was-just-a-dream cop-out, but especially the conceit that Dorothy really just wants a one-way ticket back to Kansas. No place like home? Rushdie doesn't buy it. Dorothy's Kansas is a dun-coloured shit-hole, and Oz a magical technicolour paradise. In L. Frank Baum's *Oz* novels, Rushdie points out, the magical world is real, and Dorothy goes back again and again, until finally she gets to take Uncle Henry and Auntie Em along, and stay there forever, as a princess no less. For Dorothy, "The imagined world becomes the actual world." The same could be said for Marty McFly, in his better-than-home paradise, his ideal 1985. Even if he'd long at times for that other world, that childhood world he remembered, this new one was, if not better, the world he'd helped create.

"The truth," writes Rushdie, "is that, once we leave our childhood places and start to make up our lives, armed only with what we know and who we are, we come to understand that the real secret of the ruby slippers is not that 'there's no place like home,' but, rather, that there is no longer any such place *as* home—except, of course, for the homes we make, or homes that are made of us, in Oz."

Tonight, I thought, I'll buy another plane ticket, for the fall, to visit Matteo. I shook my head, and grass fell from my hair.

I'd stay there, by the river, for ten more minutes. Opa spent a whole day in a house on this side of the river, somewhere not far from this spot. A different kind of man may have come back here after the war, maybe decades later, may have brought his daughters to this spot, and told the story of his crossing. He may have remembered, every July 28th. A very different kind of man indeed may have named his daughter Cher after the river he crossed. But this was not the story Opa had made of his life; I was making my own story, and I'd come here not for him, but for myself, after all.

Jos had wanted to get further from the demarcation line before interacting with strangers; some elements, he wrote, might force him back across the border to be arrested, despite that being technically illegal. After sundown on the 29th then, he would walk twenty-one miles to the town of Loches, a route he'd travelled years earlier, on a vacation; there, in the morning, he'd catch a train to Lyon.

After two months in Lyon, during which he wrote a thirty-page account of his escape, Jos would enlist in the army, and travel through Portugal and Spain before serving mostly in England, as a translator. He would meet Betty, and they would marry, and shortly before the birth of their first daughter, a driver would take him into Delft, where he'd be hailed as the city's liberator. By the time his wife and daughter followed, he'd know, thanks to a letter, that his mother had been arrested for leaving her place of residence, and had died in Sobibór. Jos would receive the award of MBE (Member of the Most Excellent Order of the British Empire) "for gallant and distinguished services," and Queen Wilhelmina of the Netherlands would tell him he was very brave. He and Mary would live in Delft and soon have another baby, then move on to Jakarta, to Amsterdam, to London, and to Barrie, and he would celebrate Christmas every year, never mentioning that his mother was arrested by the ss on December 25th. He would celebrate his eightieth birthday with his wife, daughters, sons-in-law, and grandchildren in a revolving restaurant at the top of Toronto's CN Tower, and would live another sixteen years before dying in a nursing home with or without Oma by his side, and would never tell anyone about the journal he'd written in both Dutch and English.

Jos had a long dinner with his hosts in Faverolles-sur-Cher and started out after eleven, hiked through the night, with only the moon and the stars to light his way. The walk took him through a plain and a valley, villages and forest, and on every shooting star, he wished that "the future, for my kin in Holland and also for myself, will look rose coloured enough." He grew tired carrying his suitcase and his coat, and his feet ached. In the wee hours of morning, a cyclist passed, and Jos lay flat in the ditch, afraid the night rider might be a patrolling gendarme. His ancestry still marked him as a fugitive; his papers were still fake; his safety was provisional at best, but he had made it this far. He stood up and brushed himself off, just had to keep on until morning.

ACKNOWLEDGEMENTS

Thank you to everyone at University of Alberta Press, especially to Peter Midgley for supporting this book.

I received funding for this project from the Alberta Foundation for the Arts, and I wrote the first draft while writer in residence at the University of New Brunswick.

From conception to completion, this book has changed quite drastically more than once, and several close readers were instrumental in helping it change for the better: Aritha van Herk, Kat Main, Samantha Warwick, Deborah Willis, Tonya Davidson, and Chloe Lewis. Kimmy Beach's insightful editing facilitated the final, vital revisions and touch-ups.

My book and I benefitted from the generosity of many informers, inspirers, and supporters, and I am especially grateful to Hazel Mousley, Josette Rutgers van der Loeff, Hermien Dijkstra, Giuseppe Iaria, Nikki Sheppy, Angela Waldie, Christian Bök, Sydney Schwartz, Sydney Sharpe, Deborah Sword, Rona Altrows, Sarah Steele, Brian Singh, and Maha Zimmo. Nomi Claire Lazar has been constant, inspiriting, and inquiring. My parents have always encouraged my writing, and for that I am truly grateful.

As I wrote and revised, I spent many hours in the fine company of the NSWGFTIAVI writers who haunt the Kensington Pub "hot tub"—Natalie Simpson, Marc Lynch, Colin Martin, Weyman Chan, Ian Kinney, Jani Krulc, Emily Ursuliak, et al.

Aaron Giovannone has been an incisive critic and editor, and the world's dreamiest co-conspirator.

Some scenes in this book are composites of real incidents, some characters in this book are composites of real people, and in many cases I have taken steps to protect people's identities. This is my own story, filtered through my memory and my interpretations. I have quoted and paraphrased real emails and text messages; thank you to the authors: you know who you are.

The excerpts from my grandfather Josua van Embden's journal are essentially as he wrote them; however, in a few small instances (of words and short phrases), Aritha van Herk, Dymphny Dronyk, and Peter Midgley suggested more precise English translations from the original Dutch than Jos's own. I have sometimes compressed entries, as well. Punctuation and spelling have been adjusted occasionally for clarity.

WORKS CITED

Audiat, Pierre. *Paris pendant la guerre, juin 1940–août 1945*. Paris: Hachette, 1946.

de Botton, Alain. *The Art of Travel*. London: Penguin, 2014.

Goldstein, Rebecca. *Betraying Spinoza: The Renegade Jew Who Gave Us Modernity*. New York: Schocken Books, 2006.

Greenberg, Blu. *How to Run a Traditional Jewish Household*. New York: Simon & Schuster, 1985.

Rosbottom, Ronald C. *When Paris Went Dark: The City of Light Under German Occupation, 1940–1944*. Boston: Little, Brown and Company, 2014.

Roth, Philip. *The Ghost Writer*. New York: Vintage Books, 1979.

Rushdie, Salman. "Out of Kansas." *The New Yorker*, May 11, 1992. https://www.newyorker.com/magazine/1992/05/11/out-of-kansas.

Steiner, George. *Language and Silence: Essays on Language, Literature, and the Inhuman*. 1967. New Haven, CT: Yale University Press, 1998.

Styron, William. *Sophie's Choice*. 1979. New York: Vintage Books, 1992.

Other Titles from University of Alberta Press

Shy
An Anthology

NAOMI K. LEWIS & RONA ALTROWS, *Editors*

Shyness needs no cure, claim the authors of thoughtful, raw, and humorous essays and poems.

Robert Kroetsch Series

small things left behind

ELLA ZELTSERMAN

Lyric-narrative poetry of a Russian-Jewish refugee's flight to Canada during the Cold War.

Robert Kroetsch Series

What You Take with You
Wildfire, Family and the Road Home

THERESE GREENWOOD

Personal account of fleeing a Canadian wildfire that devastated a community and garnered international attention.

Wayfarer Series

More information at uap.ualberta.ca